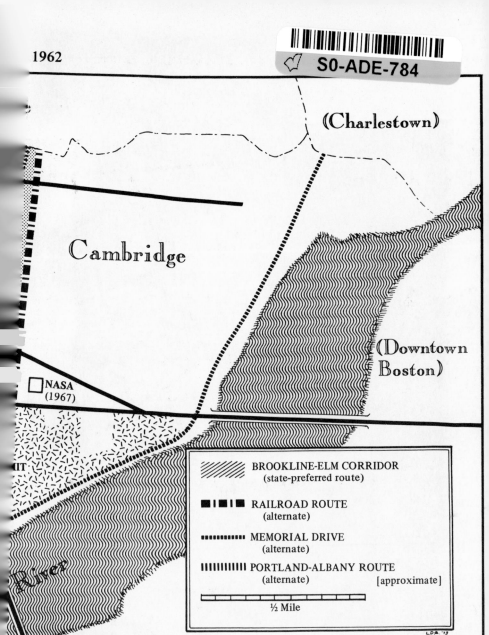

1962

(Charlestown)

Cambridge

NASA
(1967)

(Downtown
Boston)

IIT

River

BROOKLINE-ELM CORRIDOR
(state-preferred route)

RAILROAD ROUTE
(alternate)

MEMORIAL DRIVE
(alternate)

PORTLAND-ALBANY ROUTE
(alternate) [approximate]

½ Mile

LDA '13

301.592
F33d

89469

THE
DECEIVED
MAJORITY

THE
DECEIVED
MAJORITY

POLITICS AND PROTEST IN MIDDLE AMERICA

GORDON FELLMAN
in association with
BARBARA BRANDT

TRANSACTION BOOKS
Rutgers University, New Brunswick, New Jersey
Distributed by E.P. Dutton and Company

Copyright © 1973
Gordon Fellman

Transaction Books
Rutgers University
New Brunswick, New Jersey 08903

Library of Congress Catalog Card Number: 72-82197
ISBN: 0-87855-043-7

Printed in the United States of America

TO ALL PEOPLE WHO ARE TRYING
TO INCREASE THEIR CONTROL OVER THEIR OWN LIVES
AND
TO THOSE WHO HAVE STOPPED TRYING.

The feeling of being able to have some effect on people, to get them to listen, provide some of the things we need, do some of the things we want, receive some of the love and help we want to give— this feeling of social competence is a substantial foundation stone of self-respect and security.

—*Robert W. White,*
Ego and Reality in Psychoanalytic Theory

The elite cannot be truly thought of as men who are merely "doing their duty"... they are the ones who determine their duty, as well as the duties of other men.

—*C. Wright Mills,* The Power Elite

CONTENTS

INTRODUCTION

SOCIAL CLASS AND CONTEMPORARY
AMERICAN CRISES

In the past decade, American society has "discovered" crises in relations between whites and blacks, between older and younger generations, between men and women, and between America and a growing number of other nations. We have "discovered" crises in housing, education, prison conditions, drug use, employment, taxation procedures, welfare, population growth, the power of corporations, foreign policy, highway development, automobile design, treatment of the environment and the edibility of some processed foods. And we have "discovered" crises in leadership and followership, crises in confidence in all levels of government, and crises even in the purposes and directions of our society.

Traditionally, we cope with such problems by isolating a single issue and applying short-term remedies to the ailment we define. Drug therapy programs abound today, as public housing projects did a few years earlier. Police put down one prison riot and authorities at another prison try to ease restrictions there a little. Money goes to experimental education programs here, to better auto engine design somewhere else, and to increased social security benefits in another place, in the good old American hope that spending money on a problem will solve it or at least help ease it.

Our society resists, for the most part, though, trying to find broad conditions underlying this myriad of problems, probably for fear that if we learn of major difficulties suffusing all our problems, we might have to consider making fundamental changes in the society. Since people in authority who try to respond to crisis have it in their interest to keep things more or less as they are, it is reasonable to find them applying limited solutions and not looking for basic difficulties that might require more than a special fund of a few million dollars, or an intensive treatment program for a specific problem. But the rest of us can, and must, look further.

I began the research reported in this book about eight years ago.* I wanted to discover something about the nature of protest and, in this particular case, whether a given urban highway plan could be stopped. Only gradually and painfully, as I went along, did I realize that behind the seemingly simple issue of whether some Middle Americans whose homes were threatened by a proposed highway could stop that highway or help relocate it—lay the social class issue in American society, the power of corporations, and the relationship of business to government.

What began as a problem of learning how some people of little power and wealth might or might not be able to affect a plan that directly touched their lives became a problem of freedom in general—the freedom of anyone to have a major say in matters that affect his or her own life. If freedom means opportunity and choice, then it is folly to consider a highway location decision as a kind of issue different from the pleasure one has in work, the freedom from subserviently defined roles for blacks and other "nonwhite" minorities,

---

* Throughout the discussion, "I" refers to Fellman, and "we" to Fellman and Brandt.

narrowly defined roles for women, constricted curricula for students and so on.

I mean this book to be a case study in oppression, unnecessary repression. And I mean it to focus specifically on social class oppression, which has somehow almost been lost in the growth of liberation movements for Third World peoples and for blacks, Chicanos, Puerto Ricans, women, students, homosexuals and others in American society. We have yet to see the rise of political movements for poor people as a class (including the poor of all color and ethnic groups), for working people, and for Middle Americans in general. I hope this book will help define the need and dimensions of such a liberation movement or movements, which would crosscut the others and intricately involve them all.

POINT OF VIEW

We cannot be impartial, only intellectually honest.
Impartiality is a dream, honesty a duty.

—*Gaetano Salvemini*

During the school year 1963-1964, I became interested in an anti-highway protest movement near where I lived in Cambridge, Massachusetts. I wanted to learn something of how and why some protest movements on a specific issue work and others do not. I defined the problem at the outset as one of understanding how certain neighborhoods would be affected by a proposed highway and how and why a protest movement would take the course it did. Over a period of time, I found that to study this problem meant to ignore the benefits of the highway—the Inner Belt—such as convenience for commuters and the business, political and other communities that would profit, directly and indirectly, from its construction. The case for such benefits is well made and understood by highway planners and their supporters and will not be repeated here. The social costs and complexities of road-building are less widely studied and comprehended.

In the summer of 1965 I began observing the Brookline-Elm Street area, the Cambridge corridor of the planned eight-lane expressway. I talked with householders and storekeepers about what was happening, how they perceived the problem and what they expected would occur.

At the end of that summer, I learned that a Cambridge architect was calling together several people in various professions to see if they might be able to devise some way of minimizing the number of homes to be taken for the Inner Belt in Cambridge. Although initially I had an activist interest in the issue, it soon became clear that I had little of political or technical value to contribute to the group. My decision, then, was to concentrate on my research interests in the Inner Belt controversy rather than to take a major activist role. At the same time I was able to follow at close range the ideas, philosophies and work of a group that was eventually to play a significant part in the efforts to protest the Cambridge designation for the Inner Belt.

An inevitable value position shapes this work. My own values relevant to this study are formed in part by a lower-middle-class background, which taught me the extremely limited sense of power, the pride and dignity, the aspirations and the frustrations of people in modest positions in our society. As a sociologist, now by class position on the lower fringe of the upper-middle class (more by prestige of occupation than by income or power), I have come to believe that effectiveness in matters affecting one's life, from day-to-day housekeeping decisions to issues of community planning and even beyond (e.g., environmental, foreign, national economic and political policy) can and should be stronger throughout parts of our society traditionally deprived of effectiveness in all but the most immediate, limited areas of life. Trying to promote this effectiveness is a desirable goal for anyone interested in coming nearer to a democratic society.

This value led me to focus my study on the people in the neighborhoods to be affected by the proposed highway. The study ought not, I caution, be discounted because of this value stance. A viewpoint with a growing number of adherents holds that value-free sociology is impossible.[1] What passes as "objective" is commonly either sociology of trivialities or sociology with hidden values difficult to detect. The responsible investigator must make clear to himself and his audience where his predispositions lie; once an investigator has made his values known to both himself and his readers, a really "objective" study is much more possible.

METHOD OF INVESTIGATION

In sociology, there are generally two ways of learning how people feel about something in their lives. The *survey method,* in its numerous variations, means devising a questionnaire and interviewing people with it. Answers to questions are tallied, and conclusions drawn up from the totals and their correlations with each other. The *field work method,* by contrast, means qualitative study of as much of the field situation as possible—by open-ended systematic recording of interviews, casual conversations, community meetings, other daily or special events, miscellaneous happenings, etc., in the area of investigation.

I used both methods in this study. I decided to concentrate on field work, in the belief that prolonged and direct exposure to the complexities and subtleties of a social issue is the most useful, honest and fullest way to try to understand it. As I used it, the field work method meant my col-

leagues and I immersed ourselves as observers and sometimes as participants in the milieu and lives of people we
wanted to understand. It meant keeping ourselves open to
observations and insights that could not be anticipated. It
meant trying to see lives, problems and interests of other
people from *their* point of view as fully as possible.[2]

A survey can not take into account the perspective and
the unique circumstances of a population unless the investigators acquaint themselves thoroughly with them, the place
and the problem beforehand. For one does not know even
what questions to ask people without developing a feel for
them and their situation.

For two reasons I decided to supplement the field work
with a survey of 10 percent of the population that would be
affected by the highway. It seemed desirable to verify any
field work impressions in a more systematic way, and as I
hoped my data to come to the attention of planners, engineers and government officials, I believed this further veri-
fication would be more convincing to people unfamiliar
with the field work method than would the field study
alone.[3]

I completed preliminary interviews of about 20 residents
and shopkeepers during the summer of 1965, to get the lay
of the land, geographical and sociological. In these interviews I learned that some people believed the Belt, then in
the planning stage for 17 years, would never really be built.
Others expected that it might come, but whether it did or
not was beyond them, that is to say, the decision-making
process was either incomprehensible or inaccessible to their
efforts or wishes to change it, or both. A few welcomed it;
most hoped it would not materialize. That summer also
allowed me time to interview about a dozen local officials
and clergymen, and to examine back issues of the Cambridge weekly *Chronicle and Sun* and other documents, to
learn the history of the Belt plan and of Cambridge responses to it.

From September 1965 through May 1966, I continued informal interviewing and followed at first-hand the birth and growth of the protest movement against the Brookline-Elm alignment of the road. My primary method here, as in much of the above, was sociological field work, which consisted of some interviewing and much observing and note-taking.

The field work observations form the foundation for, and are supplemented by, information gathered in a survey of a random sample of 120 residents—approximately 10 percent of the households that would be displaced by the highway—conducted during the summer of 1967.

Assistants and I gathered field notes on community protest meetings, rallies, meetings of the Cambridge City Council where the Belt topic was discussed, meetings between local people and state officials, and other such occasions before, during and after the 1967 survey.

ACKNOWLEDGEMENTS

Barbara Brandt has been my colleague and assistant in interviewing and in interpreting the data and has been extraordinarily patient and insightful in helping me clarify my thoughts and structure the presentation coherently and logically. We drew on her excellent field notes and interviews, from a two-year period, at least as much as from my own, and from her interpretations and analyses of our material. Particularly hers are the sections on the role of the protest leader, interaction between Middle-American and organization-class people, the critique of the concept of "working-class authoritarianism," and the focus on the relevance of the Inner Belt protest to broader issues of the political development and nature of Middle America. But beyond these contributions, Ms. Brandt's help has been crucial in every part of the book including her preparation of the index. From her early entry into the project, she has understood it thoroughly and worked heroically and with dedication far exceeding what was expected.

During the summer of the survey, Roger Rosenblatt was a great source of wisdom, skill and friendship. My link to the world of the computer, he worked on the questionnaire itself, designed the computer program for it and analyzed the machine results of the survey.

Both Ms. Brandt's and Mr. Rosenblatt's keen grasp of the purpose of the study and its procedures, their enthusiasm, intelligence, energy, insight, and their wonderful élan and the friendship I came to enjoy with each are great treasures which added immeasurably to the pleasure of engaging in work which we all believe to be significant and worthwhile.

Several faculty research grants from Brandeis University, the Federal Work-Study student employment program, and a research grant from the U.S. Department of Housing and Urban Development allowed me to employ people, most of them Brandeis students, in parts of the research project. Carol Tavris, Betsy Shevey, Shirley Young, Susan Fischlowitz, Risa Gabelnick, Joy Strohbeen Wood and Nancy Tucker Whit performed tasks as varied as gathering data from the city directory, helping to construct the questionnaire, interviewing, and interview coding and tabulation. Their work demanded patience, autonomy and intelligence; and I could not have found abler, more congenial associates. In the late stages of preparation of this book, Peter Wortsman checked quotations and references for accuracy. I thank him for his able, careful accomplishment of these tedious, necessary tasks.

Carol Schwartz and Thomas Melone, both formerly of the Office of Urban Technology and Research, Department of Housing and Urban Development, were far more attentive to my project than I expected of busy federal officials. Mr. Melone's close and careful reading of a report which is the basis for this book was most considerate and useful. My gratitude also goes to them and to HUD for sponsoring the third year of my project by way of an Urban Planning Research and Demonstration Contract (Mass. PD-5) awarded by the Department of Housing and Urban Development under the provisions of Section 701 (b) of the Housing Act of 1954, as amended, to Brandeis University.

I am extremely grateful to a number of good friends and colleagues who read my manuscript at various stages of its development, and who offered criticisms and encouragement. They are Victoria E. Bonnell, Nancy Chodorow, Phyllis Ewen, William A. Gamson, Zelda F. Gamson, Herbert Gans, Chester Hartman, Paul Kecskemeti, Miles Morgan, Lisa R. Peattie, Jon Pynoos and George Ross. As is usual in these matters, I followed some of their suggestions and let others go. I thank them deeply for the time and care they took in advising me.

ISSUES

SOCIAL CLASS DISCRIMINATION IN AMERICAN SOCIETY

, The problem of social class discrimination in American society is as important as the problems of racism and sexism but more elusive. It bears features similar to racism and sexism. Indeed, it seems entirely appropriate to use the term *classism* to describe discrimination by members of one social class against members of another.*

Americans are accustomed to thinking of "opportunity" as available to all, even though most acknowledge that few black Americans have had the same chance as whites to realize their opportunities. But while efforts grow to make the American dream come true for blacks, other groups are beginning to call attention to their own bitter experiences, and to question whether equal opportunity really exists for them. Puerto Rican-Americans, Mexican-Americans, American Indians and women are among the groups starting to recognize that many of the difficulties they face daily stem not from individual inferiority or incompetence, but from the fact that they belong to groups in some major ways unfairly treated in our society.

---

* The term *classism* has been used effectively by the Schoolboys of Barbiana, in *Letter to a Teacher,* a remarkable social-class analysis of rural education in Italy, written by eight adolescent boys there (Schoolboys of Barbiana, *Letter to a Teacher* [New York, Vintage, 1971]).

We add to such groups, social classes. (We recognize, but will not explore here, the yet-to-be-understood connections among such forms of oppression as racism, sexism and classism.) Like many social scientists, we see American society as composed of various "classes"—groups that differ from each other in power, wealth, education, occupation, and general values and life style. According to our analysis, some of these classes operate at unfair advantage over others, and some, conversely, are faced with severely limited opportunities and unfair disadvantages.

For this book we shall not define class in a way that can be considered universally useful or true for all purposes. Indeed, we do not believe that class can be defined that way at all.

There is a long tradition in American sociology of trying to identify and name social classes. Investigators puzzle over the relationship of class indicators like occupation, income, education and style of life with one another. And some even try to measure such factors precisely and combine them into elaborate statistical devices. Such efforts are barely interesting and surely beside any reasonable point. People do differ from each other in terms of occupation, education and so forth; and particular occupations, levels of education and levels of income usually go together.

But concern with accurate descriptions of *status*—the chief issue in many American stratification studies—distracts attention from examining and understanding the relationship of *power* to *life chances*. We believe that the important issue is not the delineation of prestige differences, but the identification of significant human problems and the discovery of useful ways to speak of the relationship of people in different parts of society to their problems and the perpetuation, modification or exploration of them.

"Social class" is a useful way to organize certain information about social reality so as to see who affects whom, how and with what results. It will become clear in this study that the political problems of the protesting people we study here are problems of power—how to gain it and how to exercise it. By power, we mean the capacity to make or otherwise sway decisions that affect one's life. Our focus on the power dimension of social class, and our definition of power as the fundamental dimension for purposes of our study, allow us to identify four social classes in America.

The Rich-and-Powerful Class

Members of the "rich-and-powerful class" are those who hold key positions of influence and power in this society—on the national, regional and (sometimes) local levels.[1] They include leaders of industry and government and the very wealthy—owners, large stockholders and top executives of large corporations and banks; old moneyed members of the American "aristocracy"; and high government (including military) officials. Some of these people were born into wealth and power; some may have married or worked their way up into this status. Family ties and traditions are strong among them. Wealth, power and position are consolidated by marriage with others of the same class, and are perpetuated through the generations, even though there is always some movement upward into and downward from this class.

The rich and powerful control all major institutional activities within the nation (and many outside it), by overlapping and interlocking memberships on boards of directors and as trustees and overseers of virtually all organizations of size and consequence.

The members of the rich-and-powerful class do not always engage directly in the actual work of running institutions. Rather, those lines of work fall into two broad categories: executives, managers, lawyers, financiers and so forth, who design and facilitate the institutional programs, and large cadres of employees who carry out the details of the actual work.

The Organization Class

Members of the "organization class" are the agents of the rich-and-powerful and are more visible than the latter. Politicians are more visible than their financial backers; industrial managers are more visible than the major stockholders behind them; college administrators are more visible than boards of trustees; and so on.

The organization class is the group usually called "upper-middle class." By using the name organization class, we emphasize the degree of control its members have over others; by virtue of their institutional positions they set and administer policies in most organizations—business, governmental, professional, educational, religious, recreational, cultural and civic.* (Institutions class would be a sociologically more accurate term, but it tends to remind one of hospitals and prisons more than of educational, industrial and other institutions.) These are the professionals and business and government executives who have fairly high incomes, often advanced degrees and noticeable prestige in their communities. They include the bureaucrats, managers, academics, doctors, lawyers, ministers, and other professionals and intellectuals who frequently participate in a wide variety of formal organizations and activities, who often concern themselves with public affairs, and who have access to some degree of power and influence, both through and outside their occupational positions.

---

* It is unclear to what extent typical organization class people feel personal control in their work or feel themselves executors of others' wills. This is the place to note, but not to investigate, organization-class alienation from work.

Organization-class people run schools and universities and design their curricula, but do not determine how they shall be financed or whether their supposed objectivity in various ways promotes the interests of some groups in our society over others. They are the officers in armies and in corporations, but do not determine the major policy thrusts of those organizations. They conduct research for business, the military and government, but do not decide which problems are worth researching and which are not. They design highways and bridges and organize work forces to build them, but do not decide that money shall be spent there rather than on mass transportation. They manage money for the rich and powerful and invest some of their own, but do not decide what products companies shall make or with whom they will merge. These are typical kinds of organization-class work, indicating limits of and on it.

Extended family ties are less important among organization-class people than in the working class and lower middle class. Even nuclear family ties between parents and adult children are usually rather weak. Its members place great emphasis on individual social and geographic mobility and on occupational and educational advancement.

This is the class that apparently enjoys thinking of its work as technical, expert, objective, detached. We wish to suggest as strongly as we can that, on the contrary, the organization class is the active, overt agent of classism in America. If Mills, Domhoff, Lundberg and others are correct in defining a ruling power elite, then it is surely time to understand that this elite is served mightily, and at handsome recompense, by people who may be oblivious to their active role in maintaining a class-structured and classist society.

Although our class designations are, of course, imprecise, we reject the more common use of "upper class," "upper-middle class" and so on, because those terms are completely devoid of behavioral content. By being solely comparative, they focus on status, neutralize and bypass differing power and life-chances issues associated with them and, further, insidiously imply objective superiority-inferiority relationships among classes.

Middle America

Members of the organization class supervise the work of large numbers of people who are ordinarily called by sociologists the "working class" and the "lower-middle class." We combine these groups here into one now commonly called "Middle America." Middle Americans are neither at or near the levels of great wealth and power or the levels of those who administer it, nor are they poverty-stricken and powerless. This class is described more fully in the following pages.

The Poor-and-Powerless Class

A "poor-and-powerless class" completes the class picture we draw here. It includes the very poor; the poverty-stricken and almost totally powerless; the poorly paid, partly employed or chronically unemployed people on very small pensions, Social Security benefits, welfare or no income at all. Nonwhites and residents of the rural areas of our nation are disproportionately represented in this group.

The primary concern of members of this class is the intensely personal one of simply getting by. They live from day to day, with very little power over the direction of their own lives, let alone those of other people. Family ties are often weak, organizational affiliations usually nonexistent. Much has been written about the condition of the poor in recent years, although little has been done to change it. We believe the difficulties of Middle America, as we present them here, apply also, and even more so, to the poor-and-powerless class.[2]

To summarize our class scheme, we see four classes: at the extremes

—the rich-and-powerful class: those who make the biggest decisions and benefit most from them

—the poor-and-powerless class: those who make only the smallest decisions and who benefit little from anything

The other two groups are those who keep "the system" going:

—the organization class: those who organize and direct the work of the system within the framework set by the rich-and-powerful class

—the Middle Americans: those who take orders, who function within the framework set by the executives and professionals of the organization class

This book is about freedom and how it is unnecessarily limited in America. All people are subject to some limitations on their desires. Some freedom has to be limited to continue society at all. Taxes, traffic regulations, codes of law forbidding attack by one person upon another, etc., are necessary. But many limits on freedom are not necessary for social order; rather, they serve the interests of some groups at the expense of others. When some people's capacities for judgment and decision are systematically limited by others for their own gain, we can speak of oppression. In racism, people of one "color" group limit the freedom of, or oppress, members of another group unnecessarily. In sexism, people of one sex group limit the freedom of, or oppress, those of the other group unnecessarily. In classism, people of one level of economic and political position limit the freedom of, or oppress, people at one or more other levels unnecessarily.

We attempt here to demonstrate how, in one case study, Middle Americans are oppressed by members of the organization class and, indirectly, by the rich and powerful people who employ them. It is, in other words, a study in classism, to the fullest extent that we can examine the specific case and draw general implications from it. We need now to look in greater detail at Middle America.

PROBLEMS OF MIDDLE AMERICA

Middle Americans often describe themselves as "the little people," "the average," "the middle class," "the Silent Majority," "the guy in the middle—not too rich, and not too poor." Middle Americans control some major aspects of their home and family life but have little power outside that sphere (and surely often have less control even here than do members of the rich-and-powerful and organization classes).

Middle America includes a large proportion of Americans who seem disturbed by the many forces of change around them, and who are not at all certain which changes operate in their interests and which against them. Members of this class are troubled by rising taxes, prices and unemployment; challenges to authority over political issues; challenges to the conventionally accepted American patterns of consumption and aspiration; and charges by dissenting groups that America is not all we were taught as schoolchildren it is supposed to be, or could become.

In 1969 and 1970, both *Time* and *Newsweek* magazines devoted issues to this group.[3] The *Newsweek* article, based on a Gallup survey, includes in Middle America the "middle-income group—the blue- and white-collar families. . . ."[4] *Time* estimates that the total number of Middle Americans approaches 100 million, including the 40 million blue-collar workers, service employees and farm workers; many of the nation's 20 million elderly citizens; and a substantial portion of the 36 million white-collar workers.[5] Both magazines stress that membership in Middle America is based on a common life style and set of values. *Newsweek* summarizes the typical Middle American:

> He wears white starched shirts, suits with baggy pants, work shirts with his name in red on the breast pocket, white ankle-high cotton socks. Toothpicks. Lunch in a paper sack. Off-duty bourbon and 7-Up.

> She wears wire-stiff bouffants, girdles, at-the-knee print dresses. She saves Green Stamps, is active in the Girl Scouts and PTA. A Bible adorns her coffee table and there's an American flag decal on the family car. She lives for "the kids."

> They live in a box-like suburban tract house or just ahead of the urban-renewal wreckers in a gritty, decayed inner-city neighborhood.

> Vacation is visiting relatives, or staying home and painting the house. . . . A treat is dinner at the Burger King, or a movie. Family fun is a Sunday drive, a backyard hamburger barbecue, or watching TV.[6]

"Above all," says *Time,* "Middle America is a state of mind, a morality, a construct of values and prejudices and a complex of fears"—fears of "crime in the streets," the "breakdown of law and order," confusion and anger at black militants, peace marchers and student protestors; at rising prices, rising taxes, shrinking incomes, drugs and ever more visible sex; at a war in which they bore the brunt while upper-middle-class college students avoided military service and academic "liberals" questioned the morality of fighting. "The American dream that they were living was no longer the dream as advertised," *Time* observes. "'This,' they [Middle Americans] will say with an air of embarrassment that such a truth need be stated at all, 'is the greatest country in the world. Why are people trying to tear it down?'"[7]

In terms of values and life style, Middle America would appear to cut across wealth and power lines to some notable extent. But we wish to refine and limit *Time*'s and *Newsweek*'s definitions. Indeed, by focusing essentially on values and life style, the media obfuscate the dimension of Middle-American experience that we consider the most telling of all—the nearly total powerlessness except for immediate home and family issues. (Even the small merchant, Middle American by nearly everyone's standards, either has his prices and marketing styles forced upon him by powerful competitors from other classes, or operates in a casual, traditional style that more and more commonly simply puts him out of business.)

We estimate the size of Middle America at half our population. It includes the families of blue-collar and service workers, or what is traditionally referred to as the "working class"; low- and medium-salaried white-collared employees (such as clerical and sales people) and owners of very small (one-person or small family) businesses (what is traditionally called the "lower middle class"); and modestly salaried professionals like public school teachers, social workers, engineers and various types of technicians, and managers of medium-sized businesses (all members of what might be called the upper edge of the lower-middle class).*
We estimate the income of such people, as of 1967, very ap-

---

* Many people who carry out the plans and orders of organization-class members probably identify more readily with the organization they work for than do, say, migrant farm workers or workers in a factory identify with their employers, and thus might prefer to consider themselves members of the organization class. These include secretaries and other office workers, teachers, engineering draftsmen, nurses and numerous others who work for decision-makers. But our emphasis is on those who make decisions, in contrast to all others; thus we label Middle Americans many people who probably prefer to think of themselves as having the same interests as members of the organization class.

proximately at between $3,000 and $10,000.*

The personal concerns of people in this class are frequently oriented toward the future—either toward self-advancement or the education and advancement of their children. Family ties often play a central role in their lives; and although formal organizations are not very important to them, some Middle Americans belong to social or civic groups, such as the American Legion, a union, a church organization or the PTA.

We use the designation "Middle America" to refer to the nature of political power and income of the people about whom we are writing, but we include secondarily the values, life style, status and education levels that commonly accompany the wealth and power limits of Middle Americans.

POLITICS OF MIDDLE AMERICA

In recent years, "oppressed group" has been virtually synonymous with "minority group." We somehow have been led to assume that the majority is well off and more or less content. But now there appears to be a growing awareness of widespread dissatisfaction among Middle Americans, and they themselves are beginning to bring this dis-

---

* There is no decisive way to define class limits in objective terms like income figures, since power, life style and related considerations are so crucial to the issues we raise. We offer this estimated range in a *very* approximate way, fully realizing that skilled craftsmen from Middle America may make as much as $15,000 or $20,000 a year, while organization-class teachers with advanced academic degrees may fall below the $10,000 income level. As of 1967, 53.2 percent of the nation's families earned between $3,000 and $10,000 (with 12.5 percent making under $3,000 and 34.4 percent over $10,000); we call $3,000 to $10,000 the range including most Middle Americans in 1967, and estimate that the range will be closer to $6,000 to $13,000 by 1973.

content to public attention.

> Middle America is united in its discontent—and, increasing-
> ly, sees itself as an oppressed majority. "I think the middle
> class is getting the short end of the stick on everything," says
> a computer technician from Brooklyn. "The welfare people get
> out of taxes, and so do the rich," says a construction foreman
> in Baltimore. "The middle-class family is just forgotten."[8]

In one respect, this growing discontent among Middle
Americans is another example of the questioning and protest emerging as a dominant form of political expression in
America today. But Middle America's protest does not at
present take the same forms, nor deal with the same issues,
as the headline-grabbing protest that challenges the authority and priorities of the establishment. While Middle Americans are aware that something has gone wrong with the
American dream, they are apt to blame "dissenters" and
"protestors," "liberals" and "eggheads," rather than
questioning the country's established institutions and the
way they operate. This seems puzzling. Since the antiestab-
lishmentarians decry corruption; a war that has killed tens
of thousands needlessly; inequalitarian draft policies; governmental hypocrisy, etc., how can it be that Middle Americans, who are deeply affected by all these issues, refuse to
join the protestors?

We believe there are three reasons that Middle Americans neither identify with nor support "antiestablishment"
protest.

First, the widely publicized protests by liberal and radical
students and adults seldom deal with issues that appear
germane to the central problems of the lives of Middle
America. Loyal to the verities of the American tradition,
Middle America sees some organization-class adults and
many youths question and even mock those verities. Under
attack are patriotism, clean-shaven faces, biweekly trimmed
heads of hair, escalating consumption, unquestioned deference to institutional authority, obeisance to rigid notions of

a benevolent God and equally rigid notions of a communist threat. The naturalness of war, hard work, "mastery" over nature, male superiority, unlimited technological innovation, manifest destiny of the United States over all other peoples and the absolute truth of Christianity, the nuclear family, female virginity at marriage and exclusive heterosexuality—all are more and more questioned. It is not overstating the case to say that in our period, some critics, most of organization-class backgrounds, are doubting all norms and values of our society.

Middle America, by contrast, worries about unemployment, declining purchasing power and increasing taxes; it wonders why its tax monies should be routed to the poor, and whether it carries proportionately more of the tax burden than the organization class and the rich; it has begun to discover that its own opportunities and municipal services do not match those of the organization-class suburbanites, and it wonders what is going on. Although mounting national dissatisfaction with the war in Vietnam began to reach large numbers of Middle Americans by 1971, until then they were (and most continued to be) perplexed by demands that they sacrifice their men in Indochina, while dissenters at home seemed to support the enemy and offered praise for young men who resisted military service. In similar ways, most "liberal" and student protest movements seem irrelevant, if not overtly harmful, to Middle-American concerns.

Second, when the issues under question are as far ranging as those mentioned, it is inevitable that a population surrounded by so much uncertainty will feel confused about causes and effects, symptoms and messengers, prophets and tyrants. Dissidents who attack "progress" and bare inconsistencies and failures in American society place themselves in vulnerable positions: the bearer of bad tidings is universally resented; in some places and times he has been killed. Thus, many Americans are likely to express anger at the critics of society, rather than looking seriously at the issues critically examined.

If the dissidents are unjustly condemned by Middle Americans, they have in many ways asked for it. Usually insensitive if not fully blind to the lives and concerns of Middle Americans, the dissidents—mostly from the organization class—barely conceal their discomfort with, "superiority" over and scorn for the majority of their fellow citizens. Middle Americans' envy and hostility about the privileges of organization-class youths form one of many bases of conflict between the two groups, conflict whose nature and meaning seem little recognized by members of either class.

Third, the people in power find that they can best deflect citizen interest from the real issues onto the messengers of woe, and thereby gain importance (or at least save their own political skins). George Wallace of Alabama and Louise Day Hicks of Boston are recent examples of politicians who gained support from many Middle Americans by deflecting attention from real life conditions onto groups trying to change conditions, and accusing these groups, such as students, blacks and professors, of damaging the lives of the majority. By appearing to speak to Middle Americans' situation and recognizing them as the previously ignored "little people," such politicians movingly express solidarity with them without ever defining or speaking to real solutions for problems like housing, jobs, the quality of education, etc. Similarly, President Nixon and Vice-President Agnew, who directed much of their 1968 presidential and 1970 congressional campaign rhetoric to "the forgotten Americans" (and who originally named them "the Silent Majority"), have made it clear they now hope to convince Middle America that Democratic "radical-liberals" and leftist students, faculty and hippies are responsible for disruption of the social order and for causing havoc and uncertainty.

In the 1972 presidential campaign, the Nixon-Agnew effort to brand McGovern as radical, unrealistic, irresponsible, too responsive to hippies and so on, suggests to us a successful turning of public attention from the real issues McGovern and Shriver tried to make central to the campaign. The war in Vietnam, taxes, military spending, a guaranteed income and other issues were barely addressed by the Republicans at all.

Leaders like Nixon and Agnew have encouraged Middle Americans to move beyond their traditionally passive behavior and vent their frustrations against our society's critics. By doing so, they act essentially like Wallace and Hicks. And, like spokesmen for many corporations and professional associations, whose interests so clearly lie in directing attention away from their role in creating and sustaining war, unemployment, housing shortages, inadequate medical care, etc., Nixon and Agnew encourage Middle Americans to confuse challenges to authority with the substantive issues that constitute the challenges (for example, even the growing segment of Middle Americans unhappy about the Vietnam war has seemed always reluctant to confront the authority responsible for it).

But once Middle America gets the feel of directing its anger against others, it may be able to turn to its real problems. In other words, the scapegoating of critics could backfire against the authorities that encourage it. Surrounded by protesting blacks, American Indians, Mexican-Americans, Puerto Ricans, students, organization-class women and so on, aggrieved members of Middle America may slowly come to wonder, may ache slightly with the possibility that condemning all dissenters may mean missing out on something fundamental that is going on. Blacks' achievements in gaining minimum quotas in many employment situations and schools and in forcing greater attention to their problems appears already to have stimulated aggressive interest group activities on the part of other minority groups, such as Mexican-Americans, Italians, Poles and Jews. By raising issues of human respectability, suffering and potential, the rhetoric and politics of minority protest bring to the consciousness of more and more Americans the possibility that their lives, too, could be changed for the better.

It seems that Middle America is opening up to the possibility of major political protest; leadership of it and direction seem very much up for grabs. It is difficult to predict the forms that such protest might take. Middle Americans could come to see that the problems they experience are not caused by dissidents or accident or poor leaders, but are inherent in institutions that operate, we believe, far more for the interests of the organization class and the rich-and-powerful class than for those of Middle America and the poor-and-powerless class. They can try to gain political strength in such a way as to change the institutions so that they work in the interests of all people. Or Middle America can continually be deluded by unscrupulous leaders into placing the blame for its troubles on antiestablishment protestors, personal inadequacy or on individual rogues to be turned out of office every two or four years.

This book examines the current political situation of Middle America in order to comprehend its structure and dynamics, through detailed analysis of a single historical event: a recent protest against a highway planned to cut through a series of Middle American neighborhoods. Mostly from the poorer end of the Middle America class continuum, the people living there illuminate in stark terms several crucial political and life-style issues that we believe are common throughout this class.

Since members of the organization class were responsible for the specific highway plan in the first place, and played leading roles in responding to the protestors (in some cases as opponents and in some cases as allies), we emphasize

in addition to the lives and politics of the neighborhood people, the roles played by the organization class in our case
study.

2

MIDDLE - AMERICAN LIFE STYLES: THE MEANING OF NEIGHBORHOOD

They [the government highway planners] say, "People will go to suburbia," but everyone doesn't want to go to suburbia. *I* don't.

—*woman from Brookline Street in her late fifties*

I'm going to stay right here if I have to shoot them .... I'm going to stay where I am, I mean that.

—*man on Brookline-Elm*

Moving—it does something to you—I can't say. It's like losing a member of the family.

—*80-year-old woman, homeowner on Brookline Street**

"SLUMS" AND SOCIAL CLASS DIFFERENCES

Cambridge, Massachusetts, is one of the many cities in the United States that are homes for a number of colleges and universities. The city and its surrounding areas house Harvard, MIT and several smaller schools. In addition to its academic institutions, Cambridge has a large industrial base. Some cities of similar size are neighbors, and the

---

* The quotations that will be used to illustrate various points in the text came from interviews with or observations of Brookline-Elm residents. Unless otherwise specified, the speakers are members of Middle America, and almost always have a high school education or less.

metropolis of Boston, considerably larger and more varied, borders it on one side. Most Cambridge residents are poor and Middle Americans—many of them factory workers and technicians. University and other professionals, and students, also find this city particularly attractive, and live there in large numbers.

The area where the state made plans to build a major highway we call "Brookline-Elm," after the names of two streets defining the route through the city. The proposed route down Brookline and Elm Streets is not a natural pathway but cuts through at least a dozen areas that could be considered coherent neighborhoods. The homes range from large, old, stately edifices through medium-sized bungalows and triple-decker frame or asbestos-covered units to small apartment buildings of frame or brick construction. In condition they vary from extremely fresh and clean to shoddy and decrepit. There are many yards on the route, most with gardens and shrubbery, some with nothing but dirt. There are a few small parks and playgrounds; but children usually play (and neighbors sometimes congregate) around houses, stoops, porches, backyards and sidewalks. Along some parts of the route, noise and dirt mark small-scale industrial operations: a printing shop, machine shops, a welding shop. Singly or in clusters, little grocery stores and cafes dot the area.

Brookline-Elm is the kind of crowded, tree-sparse, frame and asbestos-shingled area that many organization-class people unthinkingly label a slum. In it one sees a bungalow painted light bright blue and trimmed abundantly with loud dark blue; many little statues people the front lawn; and a fence clearly announces the separation of this house from its neighbors. Another lawn sports a scalloped old tire, painted white and laid flat, with geraniums sprouting from the center. Asbestos siding in imitation brick and stone covers old clapboard on one- and three-story homes. Laundry flaps from clothes lines on back porches and backyard posts and trees; not all Brookline-Elm people own automatic dryers. There is litter on some sidewalks and streets, and in some parts, kerosene smells linger long past winter. One would not guess that in some of the houses with poorly kept exteriors, the interiors are immaculate and fairly expensively furnished. Lace doilies protect the arms and backs of overstuffed chairs and couches in rooms decorated with souvenir plates and figurines from fairs and carnivals and trips to far-off places, crocheted tablecloths and framed samplers appealing for God's blessing on this home. Walls and rooms are usually crowded; patterned wallpaper and linoleum "art squares" are common. Such scenes are unknown to the suburbanite, except perhaps those who have "risen from," "escaped from," or otherwise departed from the working and lower-middle classes.

As Herbert Gans has pointed out, wealthier people frequently do not differentiate between a slum and a low-rent district,[1] or if they do, they often view the life style of the low-rent district as a half-culture at best, one easily transportable from one asbestos-shingle or clapboard-sided three-decker to another with little loss. When this study began in the 1960's, the Brookline-Elm area was considered of little consequence by many organization-class people. "Why don't they tear it down?" one colleague at Harvard remarked.

In the early days of my field work in Brookline-Elm, I found I was frequently depressed.

> One of my early thoughts in walking down (Elm) street was, maybe it wouldn't be such a bad idea to tear it down. Besides the litter, and the pall cast by a thickly grey day, there is an indefinable smell along parts of this street, made up of about 3 percent garbage odors, 20 percent leftover fragrance of last winter's space heating operation, and about 10 percent must and mildew. The rest is unaccounted for.

Two weeks later I noted:

walked up and down Brookline (Street) with curious mixture of feelings. The first five blocks or so from the river north are pleasant, feel like my childhood neighborhoods. Beyond is upper-lower class sort of dwelling area, and unattractive factories and businesses.... I feel uncomfortable here. (Probably one feels "right" with areas like those of his own experience or wealthier ones to which he aspires in fact or fantasy, present or past, and uncomfortable with all "below.") I felt depressed, not for the first time in this work. Musty and dirty and garbagey smells bothered me, as did litter in yards and on sidewalks.*

Esthetic taste is not the only difference. Middle-American life style also differs significantly from organization-class life style in the kinds of social relationships people like and in attitudes toward work, politics and social mobility.

The organization-class American usually assumes that members of "lower" classes share or envy his achievements and hopes for geographic, economic and social mobility. While many Middle Americans do aspire to organization-class status, even sociologists have only recently discovered that some Middle Americans are satisfied with the way they live and have little desire to "move upward." (Such conditions obviously vary with age, time of immigration and realistic income expectations. Many Middle Americans have probably once hoped for upward mobility, found the possibility blocked, and simply adapted to their position as best they could.) In general, the part of Middle America represented by Brookline-Elm is characterized by a way of life centered around a geographically stable, closely knit

---

* It is likely that the antisepsis of organization-class life prepares its members to be offended by the smells of poorer-class life. Deodorizers for every part of the body and every room of the house together with what might be called "reodorizers" that, once the real smell is extinguished, replace it with the aroma of pine, roses or lime—condition the organization-class citizen to take offense at olfactory experiences not his own, just as readily as at sights like asbestos siding, clotheslines and cars in the side yard.

family (including relatives beyond the immediate family),
nearby friends, and sometimes also around an ethnic group
or a local church. By comparison, the organization-class
pattern is more career-oriented, less locally based.*

Different views of neighborhood and attachments to it
also distinguish urban Middle Americans from organization-class members. Planning professionals with responsibility for "the broad view" are frequently surprised and
angered at the extreme emotion and the occasional violent
reactions of neighborhood people to plans for demolishing
their neighborhoods. A common first impulse—whether
one is a decision-maker or a seemingly unbiased observer
from the sidelines—is to view highly charged opposition to
a government plan as old-fashioned sentimentality or the
selfish response of a handful of uninformed people. In either
case, this view assumes that the people in question will unfortunately have to make a personal sacrifice for the social
good.

We believe the charge of being self-centered or uninformed is applicable to both sides in such conflicts. Organization-class professionals usually appear to make policy
decisions affecting others on the bases of their own organization-class values and life style; that is, they regularly ignore or are oblivious to the different desires, conditions,
interests and behavior of the people affected by their decisions. For example, in 1958, Boston's West End—a predominantly working-class area housing approximately
7,500 people—was demolished for "urban renewal" (con-

---

* Not all members of the Middle-America class, of course, treasure
their class life style. Some, particularly those with white-collar occupations and higher education, aspire to organization-class life. Blue-collar
families are more likely to show the traditional family-based nonmobile
patterns than are the other segments of Middle America. Some writers,
such as Herbert Gans, distinguish between "working-class" life style
and "middle-class" life style on this basis (see Chapter 11 of Gans' *The
Urban Villagers*).

struction of a luxury high-rise development). In a detailed case study of the West End just before demolition, Herbert Gans demonstrated that what appeared to a "slum" to the planners and politicians responsible for its demolition was, in social fact, a healthy, well-kept, vital area where life was pleasant and meaningful to its low- and low-middle-income inhabitants.[2]

This all suggests that the nature and worth of neighborhoods should be determined not by supposedly "objective" other-class outsiders, but primarily through the eyes and values of the people who live there. The Brookline-Elm area in Cambridge appears to many outsiders as a slum. To most people who live there, it is not.

THE RESIDENTS: MOSTLY WORKING-CLASS MIDDLE AMERICANS

Well, there's ordinary people—good people . . . nice quiet people . . . plain, common people . . . all kinds—Jewish, Lithuanian, Portuguese, Italians, colored, every kind . . . most people are friendly. Most get along . . . average, hard-working, nice, friendly. . . . You know—medium class . . . just average working people.

*—comments by Brookline-Elm residents
about their neighbors*

Brookline-Elm is located between Harvard and the Massachusetts Institute of Technology—the two large, influential universities in Cambridge—so it is not surprising that an increasing number of students from these and several other nearby schools have been settling in the area's old, inexpensive apartments. Students represented about 7.5 percent of the population of Brookline-Elm in 1967, according to our study*; that figure has probably grown since then. Many residents bitterly describe how some landlords raise rents, thereby driving out older tenants, and then modernize the apartments and charge exorbitant rents that only several students living together can afford.†

Besides students, a small number of other academic and professional people—about 10 percent of the population—also live in Brookline-Elm. Another 5 percent are owners or managers of small and medium-sized businesses. Six percent are clerical and sales people and 54 percent are blue-collar workers. About 25 percent are poor or nearly so—supported by welfare, pensions or social security benefits.

Most residents, then, are members of working-class families. The husband may be employed at a nearby candy factory, book bindery, electronics plant, or he may drive a truck (almost half the men work at unskilled or semiskilled occupations, and another sixth are skilled workers). The wife is usually at home, but in one-fourth of the families she works full-time, at a factory, as a sales clerk, or as a nurse or nurse's aide. Many of the men put in overtime or take more than one job.

More than half our sample are not high school graduates. Another 20 percent have high school diplomas, and 15 percent (including the students) report some college experience.

---

*   All figures are from our random sample survey of 120 residents made during the summer of 1967. Our study contradicts many of the claims of the State Department of Public Works Relocation Study conducted during the same period (see Chapter 3, note 11).

†   This practice is one of the causes of a current housing crisis in Cambridge. There is almost no turnover in low-income housing, and rents in this city rose 36.9 percent between 1966 and 1969, while the national increase for that period was 11 percent. Demands that Harvard redress housing shortages and inflated costs caused in part by university and student expansion into the poorer areas of Cambridge, such as Brookline-Elm, formed one of the main issues in the Harvard student strike of April 1969.

The residents' annual incomes are typically lower than the national average. In 1967, 85 percent of the sample reported combined family incomes below $7,500, and the average family income in the neighborhood was between $3,000 and $5,000.* For 1967, median family income in American metropolitan areas was $8,673[3] and the median family income for all households in the United States in 1967 was $7,974.[4] In general, the Brookline-Elm population, while not impoverished, lives on the periphery of the affluent society which surrounds it.

Brookline-Elm is located in a section of the city where many immigrants to America first settled. Almost one-third of the residents on the route are themselves immigrants, and another one-fourth are the children of immigrants. Their ethnic backgrounds vary so much that a visitor to the neighborhood feels himself in a condensed version of Manhattan. Twenty-two percent are white "old Americans" (third generation or more in the United States); 15 percent are black, either of North American, Latin American or Caribbean descent; 13 percent are Portuguese, 12 percent Canadian, 11 percent Irish, 8 percent Italian, and the remaining 21 percent are of other European, Middle Eastern, or Latin American origin.

These various ethnic groups live in clusters along Brookline-Elm. One section is part of a Portuguese neighborhood, where the residents still speak their native language and center their social life around ethnic clubs and churches. Another area houses a Lithuanian group of similar be-

---

* Income data are always suspect. We learned from a number of respondents, for example, that they had overreported their incomes to interviewers from the state Department of Public Works. Perhaps they thought it would affect compensation favorably; perhaps pride was involved. (Apparently because they felt antagonistic toward DPW interviewers, our respondents told us they dissembled on a number of questions. Ideally, yet another set of interviewers should learn what they thought *our* purpose was, and how that perception might have affected their answers to our questions.)

havior. Several black families live near a black Protestant church just next to the proposed route, and Puerto Rican families have begun to settle along Brookline-Elm. Irish, Italians, other black families and other whites are scattered all along the route.

Cambridge has a history of infrequent conflict among minorities, and several of our respondents referred proudly to the high degree of racial and ethnic integration in their neighborhoods. Our research uncovered virtually no inter-group hostilities.

The area is also highly mixed in terms of family composition, with large proportions of married couples with young children, older couples, blood relatives living together, and single adults, both young and old, living alone.

About half the residents are Roman Catholics, slightly over one-third are Protestant, and the remainder are Greek Orthodox, Jewish, or claim other religions or none at all.

THE MEANING OF A NEIGHBORHOOD
TO ITS INHABITANTS

Objective and Subjective Considerations

Planning agencies have long ignored the subjective experiences of the people they would displace by their plans. The people of Brookline-Elm who may be displaced by the Inner Belt worry not only about the inconveniences of moving and the problem of finding a new dwelling at comparable cost. Feelings about friends, neighbors, nearby relatives and the neighborhood in general—that is, their social ties to the neighborhood—are as much a concern of the people's lives as the economics of renting, owning and relocating. Social ties can be measured by objective criteria such as length of time in the area, use of local facilities and institutions, and informal social relationships, and by subjective criteria such as residents' feelings about their area and their lives there.

Almost half our sample have lived on or near Brookline-Elm for more than 12 years, and over a third have lived in the area over 20 years. At the same time, a fairly large proportion of residents have moved here only recently. Thirty-five percent have lived in this area for four years or less; 25 percent, two years or less. Comparison with length of residence figures for all urban Massachusetts given in the 1960 census reveals no greater transiency in the Brookline-Elm population than in other urban areas of the state. In fact, in comparison to the state as a whole, as of 1967 Brookline-Elm had a greater proportion of residents who have lived in the same house for more than ten years.[5]

Two Groups: The Nonmobile and the Mobile

Two distinct groups live along Brookline-Elm: a majority who are socially and emotionally tied to the area, and a minority who are upwardly mobile in their economic and social aspirations, and thus less strongly tied to where they live now. The first group is composed mainly of married couples with adult children, older widows, widowers and divorcees, and people living in three-generational households.* The more mobile group—people who view the area as a temporary home—are mainly unmarried adults, young couples and students. These short-term residents are on the move upward or outward—to the suburbs or a "better" part of Cambridge, or to California where there is the possibility of better-paying electronics work, to "the country," or to another university after student or junior faculty status has ended. Couples with young children are

---

* All correlations are significant at the .05 level of confidence or better.

found in both the stable and mobile groups, in about equal proportions.

The area means one thing to the rooted majority (the long-term residents plus that part of the more recent arrivals who want to remain there), and something else to the transient minority.

THE NONMOBILE MAJORITY

The Neighborhood as Familiar Object and Community

People living in Brookline-Elm express three kinds of attachments to it. For one, the place itself is valuable to the person who has become accustomed to its sights and events. The simple love of neighborhood, or at least feelings of belonging to an area through familiarity, is a concept foreign to many mobile organization-class people whose careers force them to form tenuous ties to any particular spot. That some people might prefer residential stability to upward mobility, or may retreat into the former after failing at the latter, is rarely perceived by the upwardly mobile group.

Second, the neighborhood may be the preferred place for spending time away from work. Nearly all our respondents—82 percent—say they spend most of their leisure time in the neighborhood; two-thirds spend it in their own homes.* Unlike organization-class urbanites and suburbanites, whose automobiles and values allow a geographically diverse social life, only half our sampled number of residents own cars.

---

* Leonard Reissman writes that in his leisure time the working-class person "tends to limit his social interaction more to his immediate family, in contrast to the higher class person who more willingly ranges outside of the family, outside of his own neighborhood, and at times outside of his own community" (Leonard Reissman, "Class, Leisure, and Social Participation," *American Sociological Review,* Vol. 19, February 1954, p. 76).

Third, the long-term resident grows into and becomes part of the neighborhood. Along with his relatives and neighbors he develops informal sharing arrangements—if one neighbor is sick, for example, others may come over and help; adults often keep an eye on each other's children at play. In such ways a long-settled neighborhood shows aspects of a community.

Many Brookline-Elm people speak with fierce attachment to their neighborhoods for these reasons.

A lady from a similar neighborhood in adjacent Somerville says at a meeting of the highway protest group that even if she won the Irish Sweepstakes and had a million dollars, she would not move from her home. "You know why?" she asks. "Because I sleep in the same bedroom where I was born."

A man speaks of his Brookline Street neighborhood in tones approaching love. Three of his children go to Blessed Sacrament School and one to the Morse (public) School, both within about three blocks of his home. He is proud that many prominent people live in the neighborhood—a former city councillor and a present one, a man who owns several garages in Cambridge and has a son in a state agency, and a fireman next door. In a gentle, happy, warm way he breaks out into a grin as a little neighbor girl walks by, and he calls out "Hi, Rhonda," to her. For a nickel, his children use a public outdoor swimming pool near the Morse School. His church is two blocks away, and a public library branch is near. Saying that his neighborhood "has everything," he points out that his family buys food at a supermarket three blocks away and clothing, children's shoes and "things like that" in Central Square, half a mile from his house.

An old lady being interviewed one Sunday afternoon in early fall as she sits on the doorstep of her Elm Street three-decker with a friend from next door continually waves to men driving by who yell "Hello!" back to her and her friend; constantly makes observations to her friend like "That's Manuela's new baby," as a young woman walks by wheeling a baby carriage; answers some of the interview questions with gossip about what's going on in the neighborhood; and often explains to the

interviewer, "Everyone thinks. . ." and "Around here everyone says. . . ."

Several respondents mention classic examples of community
involvement, such as the case of the arthritic woman on Elm
Street whose neighbors do her shopping, and the time after a
hurricane when all the neighbors on Hamilton Street helped
pump out each other's cellars.

Ties to local facilities are striking. Twenty-two percent
of the residents we interviewed report moving to Brookline-
Elm because it was near their jobs. Slightly more than half
work in Cambridge. Many who work outside the city have
jobs in adjacent towns and cities.

The Brookline-Elm people are not typical American
commuters since one-quarter of the sample walks to work,
and 35 percent take public transportation. These percent-
ages are double those for all urban areas in Massachusetts.[6]

About one-third of the respondents have school-age
children; and in general parents are pleased with the local
public and parochial schools. Sixty-one percent say they
would object if their children had to change schools, and
only 11 percent would welcome a change. Those with school-
age children were asked what they like and dislike about
their local schools. Only 11 percent had any complaints.

Most respondents claim religious identification; about
two-thirds attend churches, most locally. Over one-third of
the sample belongs to either Blessed Sacrament or St.
Mary's, the two large nonethnic Roman Catholic parishes
in the area. Others are members of small Portuguese and
Lithuanian Roman Catholic parishes, or of the local black
or white churches of various Protestant denominations.
Thirty-six percent say they attend church weekly, 21 percent attend at least once a month, and the remainder are
evenly divided between attendance less than once a month,
and never. Rates of church attendance appear to be about the
same as the national average, according to several national

samples.[7] However, over 80 percent of the respondents never take part in church activities (fellowships, sodalities and so forth) other than services. This reflects the general working-class pattern of rare participation in formal organizations.

Another index of the Brookline-Elm people's ties to their neighborhood, or the importance it has to them, is the extent to which they use local commercial and professional facilities. Seventy-three percent of our respondents buy food at neighborhood stores or in nearby Central Square (usually within walking distance), 50 percent purchase appliances and clothing near at hand, and 88 percent use local facilities for drug, laundry and shoe repair needs. Forty-four percent are patients of doctors and dentists within walking distance of their homes.*

Family and Friends

More than the organization class, Middle America, particularly its working-class segment, lives a family-centered social life: "family" means "extended family"—sisters, brothers, in-laws, grandparents, uncles, cousins, aunts. Drawing on his detailed study of working-class residents of Boston's now demolished West End, and on an analysis of many other studies of working-class groups, Herbert Gans summarizes:

> The working-class subculture is distinguished by the dominant role of the family circle. Its way of life is based on social relationships amidst relatives .... the outside world is to be used for the benefit of this circle .... work is primarily a means of obtaining income to maintain life amidst a considerable degree of poverty, and, thereafter, a means of maximizing the pleasures of life within the family circle. The work itself may be skilled or unskilled; it can take place in the factory or in the office—the type of collar is not important .... identification

---

* "Walking distance" is defined by each respondent.

with work, work success and job advancement—while not absolutely rejected—are of secondary priority to the life that goes on within the family circle.[8]

While they do not usually live in the same household, extended family members get together with each other often enough to make the extended family the meaningful unit of social experience. In a study of about 800 white people in Greensboro, North Carolina, Bert Adams points out that while relatives outside the immediate family are extremely important to blue-collar men, they are even more important to their wives.* An excellent book on working-class women, by Lee Rainwater and associates, describes in detail their family-based life style:

> Working class wives are family-type people and relatives are the people they like best. . . . [If a working class wife] . . . went visiting during the week, it was usually with a mother or sister or in-law. Also, in a large number of working class households, "getting the whole family together every weekend" is labeled "automatic." (The whole family refers to the extended family:

---

* Adams discovered that relatives beyond the immediate family were more important to blue-collar workers than to upwardly-mobile white-collar workers, stable white-collar workers and the downwardly mobile. The former group consider relatives "a very important part of their lives. In addition, these are the only respondents who are likely to spend, and to desire to spend, their leisure with kin rather than non-kin" (Bert N. Adams, *Kinship in an Urban Setting* [Chicago, Markham, 1968], p. 31). In all four of Adams' categories, relatives are even more important to women than to men.

Adams points out that while mobile middle-class people may consider kin obligation "barbaric and anachronistic," to most working-class people "selective obligation to kin is the one method the family uses to adapt to industrialism and the urban environment" (Adams, *Kinship,* p. 5). And he notes that working-class people are less likely to be geographically mobile in their search for job opportunities, which means that *"working-class kin networks are* generally *less scattered* geographically, and are therefore *available for more frequent interaction"* (Adams, *Kinship,* p. 4).

parents, married sisters and brothers, aunts and uncles and the grandparents.) In fact, whenever working class women mention doing anything wit. ..ver people (going on a picnic, shopping, getting together for dinner, or celebrating a holiday) the other people are relatives more often than not. [The middle-class woman] talks about being out in the world of other people and places more often than do working class women, and relatives enter her recital far less often.[9]

Family relationships are, indeed, important among Brookline-Elm people: 33 percent of our sample visits one or more relatives outside the immediate family almost every day, and 51 percent spend time with relatives at least once a week. Most striking is the physical proximity of these relations: 60 percent of our sample have relatives in Cambridge, and 46 percent—*almost half*—have kin within what they consider walking distance. (Twenty-three percent of our sample have relatives outside the immediate family on the same block or in the same dwelling.) It is not unusual to find a woman whose widowed mother lives next door, whose married daughter lives two blocks away, and whose son lives near enough to stop each morning to see his mother on the way to work. In contrast to the mobile, isolated nuclear family common in the organization class, for the working-class people of Brookline-Elm—and for many Middle Americans—the neighborhood itself provides the most important experiences of their nonwork lives.

In the same vein, 87 percent report having friends in Cambridge, and about 60 percent report friends with whom they get together at least once a week within walking distance of their own homes. Over one-quarter contact nearby friends every day; 61 percent report getting together with nearby friends at least once a week.

Most of our respondents report not knowing their neighbors well. Their spontaneous comments, however, reveal that while frequent or intimate socializing is *not* highly prized, they clearly value their neighbors:

"[I know my neighbors] fairly well," says a 40-year-old woman from the Brookline Street area. "We don't go into each other's houses, but spend time talking while we garden, and of course in emergencies."

"[The neighborhood is friendly] without prying into your affairs. They're ready to help you when needed; people don't go into others' houses, but talk outside," says a 45-year-old woman from the Elm Street area.

The Home

In a study in Kansas City, Havighurst and Feigenbaum discovered two distinct leisure styles: "community-centered" and "home-centered." Most of their working-class respondents displayed the home-centered style, which seems to characterize very well the pattern followed by many Brookline-Elm residents, as observed in our field work.

Leisure activities are engaged in jointly by the members of the family for the majority of the home-centered, whether it be a church outing, a fishing trip, or watching television. Sex-differentiated activities, such as sewing and embroidering for the women and carpentry and "fixing around the house" for the men, still allow for conversation and interaction between spouses. Friendship and sociability are cultivated by visits from neighbors rather than through any membership other than in the church or perhaps a fraternal organization. . . travel may be quite circumscribed; one (working-class respondent) spoke of "taking a trolley trip to see the city."[10]

Since Middle Americans seldom attain status in work or in community affairs, the home and their control over the home environment are major sources of feelings of pride and self-worth. The personal investment in homes among Brookline-Elm people is revealed by phrases used by many interviewees, such as, "My blood and tears are in this house," or "My body and soul. . . ." referring to the often extensive do-it-yourself repairs and remodeling that both owners and renters have made. A number of the homeowners spend most of their free time working on their property, both inside and out, and will proudly show the visitor "before and after" photographs.

Working-class Brookline-Elm people often lavish more attention and care on the interiors of their homes than on exteriors. In 73 percent of the homes in our sample, the interior was rated "good" or "excellent" by interviewers, and in 82 percent of the homes the interior was rated at least as good as, if not better than, the exterior (not counting cases where the exterior was rated "poor").* It is common to find absentee landlords letting the outside of their property run down while the tenants maintain the interiors of their apartments more carefully.

Seemingly endless projects of painting, wallpapering, adding new paneling, kitchen cabinets, bathrooms or spare rooms, reshingling the outside of the house, and so forth, occupy much free time. A quarter of the residents have spent over $1 thousand on repairs and remodeling from the time they moved in. (Fifteen percent of the sample estimate they have spent over $5 thousand.) Almost half report doing all repairs and remodeling themselves, or with the help of friends and kin. Most residents report doing personally at least small-scale tasks such as painting, but about a quarter of the residents, all tenants, say they have spent nothing on repairs, and spend ten hours or less a year in repairing or remodeling their apartments. For some this may reflect uncertainty as to the length of their stay in the neighborhood; others probably would not put money into repairs or remodeling in any rented dwelling.

The widespread do-it-yourself repairs, combined with the generally increasing prosperity since the late 1940s, when

---

* The condition of the homes and of housekeeping was rated by interviewers as "excellent" (in perfect repair, with some concern for taste and attractiveness), "good" (clean, neat, well-kept), "fair" (not entirely well-kept, needing some minor repairs or cleaning) and "poor" (in disrepair, very dirty and/or disorderly).

the road was initially discussed, accounts for a general up-grading of Brookline-Elm properties in the last 20 years, a fact about which many residents are proud. But the threat of the road, especially since 1962, now discourages many homeowners and tenants from maintaining or improving their property. Uncertainty over whether the road will actually be built affects neighborhood upkeep and residents' morale and is frequently the subject of passionate discussion. For example, one woman says:

> At least if they would let us know, one way or the other. A lot of people are not keeping up their places because there's no point in putting money into your house if you're going to have to move. That goes on for a long time, then the houses *are* run down.

More than half the residents we interviewed claimed that they or their landlords had stopped making repairs on their homes in anticipation of displacement by the Belt. Several people said they were unable to obtain bank loans even when they were willing to gamble on home improvements. The woman quoted above, who bought her home two years earlier, says that her husband, working alone, put in a new furnace and is now completing a new bathroom costing over $1 thousand; they would like to cover their asbestos siding with aluminum, but are waiting to see if they will be "thrown out." Another woman says that her neighbors do not know whether to go ahead and fix a roof or blacktop a backyard.*

---

* Frequently, when a government agency designates an area for razing, either for a highway or urban renewal project, the designation has the effect of condemning the area to substandard status even if it was not already substandard. Uncertainty over whether or not to maintain property, inability to obtain home improvement funds, the increase in a poorer transient population as more well-to-do elements flee, the sight of vacant homes and boarded-up stores—all of which are increasingly seen in the Brookline-Elm area—hurry the area's decline, lowering the morale of the remaining residents and in a sense making the government's original designation a self-fulfilling prophecy.

In 1967 rents averaged $90 to $100 overall for Cambridge[11]; but in Brookline-Elm, average rent was $73, and the most frequent rent was about $55. Three-quarters of the tenants reported paying rents of $80 a month or less. Half the tenants regarded their rent as "below average"; only 20 percent considered it "above average." In view of the almost universal tendency of tenants to complain about high rents, this is a most unusual finding.

Homeowners make up 21 percent—about one-fifth of the residents. Most own their own homes fully and paid less than $8,000 for their property when they bought it years ago. Together, their labor and the market have raised property values since then. A number of homeowners, whose in-

---

Another example of this frequent phenomenon occured in a poor area of New York City: "In 1952, the city had unwittingly cursed the area by designating several blocks of tenements for public housing. The promise was never fulfilled, although the commitment was renewed year after year. Landlords sold out or let their buildings run down. Meanwhile, during the decade from 1952 to 1962, many younger Italian, Negro and Puerto Rican families, who had begun to earn more money, moved out of the neighborhood in search of better homes. With them went much of the hope for future leadership. . . . " (Norman C. Eddy, "The Unfolding Drama of Metro North," in Hans B. C. Spiegel, *Citizen Participation in Urban Development*, Vol. II—*Cases and Programs* [Washington, D.C., NTL Institute for Applied Behavioral Science, 1969], pp. 35-46; reprinted by special permission of author and publisher, from *Renewal*, January 1967, pp. 6-11).

In several instances during the past 15 years property owners in areas designated for urban renewal have sued city or state agencies on the grounds that their properties had declined in value between the time of designation of the area for demolition and the subsequent evaluation of the property for compensation purposes. In all but one case, the courts ruled that the owner had suffered *damnum absque injuria*, or in other words, that the owner had indeed suffered damage (loss of value) but that legally the government agency was not required to compensate him for his loss (see *Report of the Committee on Condemnation and Condemnation Procedures*, 1959, Section on Municipal Law, American Bar Association; and Donald W. Glaves, "Date of Valuation of Eminent Domain: Irreverence for Unconstitutional Practice," *University of Chicago Law Review*, Vol. 30, No. 2, Winter 1963, pp. 341 ff. 11).

come depends in part or totally on rents, realistically fear loss of income if their homes are destroyed.

The Threat of Moving

Eighty-two percent of the people interviewed say that they would move to the same neighborhood if they had it to do all over again. The majority feel that their location is conveniently close to public transportation, churches and shopping. About two-thirds feel that their neighborhood is safe and friendly, and over half say that their neighbors and the city do a fairly good job of keeping the streets clean. But many residents find that neighborhood recreation facilities for children and teenagers are inadequate, and just over half are not sure whether the area is a good place for children. Perhaps the best example of typical attitudes toward home and neighborhood in the Brookline-Elm area is this statement from a middle-aged ex-machinist who now owns both a home and a small tool repair business on Brookline Street:

> I'm very happy here. It's a noisy place, it's not the cleanest place, but my family—we live nice. We've adjusted to the neighborhood, we know the people, we do our shopping here, we seem to be in the center of anything we need . . . . We like the area, and I'd like to spend the rest of my life right here.

Despite skyrocketing rents, the area is still one of the cheapest in Cambridge; and the residents' financial status is reflected in almost 40 percent saying they moved here because of the low cost. (Just over 20 percent cited "nearness to work" as a reason for moving to the area, and just under 20 percent each gave "nearness to relatives" and "previously lived here" as reasons.)

For the 50 percent who do not own cars, relocation would likely be a major blow to convenience and social life. Many Brookline-Elm people rely on the readily accessible public transportation for travel to work and other destinations, and women in families with no car are usually restricted to the local neighborhood during the day, as are women in families with one car, since the car is most likely out with the husband.

Many residents fear that moving will mean a decline in status. A young female homeowner who lived several years of her married life in a housing project and fears having to move back if the highway comes through, explains:

> Look, people are afraid they are not going to get enough money for their houses. . . . Sure, you can get a fair price for the house, maybe, but not for the improvements. People have put a lot of time and money into improvements. . . . If they could get enough money to make a new start and better themselves, they wouldn't mind quite so much.

Some residents—particularly homeowners, the elderly and long-term inhabitants—compare their situation to the large-scale uprooting of Boston's West End in the late 1950s. They have heard of residents forcibly uprooted from their homes and familiar surroundings who, it is said, subsequently "died of loneliness."[12] One older woman compared the impending highway dislocation with the closing of a local industrial plant after it had provided many years of employment to residents, including her husband. She said that grown men came to her house and cried, and several men actually died as a result of the closing. Some Brookline-Elm residents have spoken of their impending relocation as if anticipating their own death.

In the Boston metropolitan area, vacant housing is so scarce that relocation to existing housing is out of the question for virtually all Brookline-Elm residents. And new replacement housing cannot satisfy most potential displacees. One middle-aged homeowner, when asked what he thought of a plan to build high-rise apartments over the highway, replied (as most brookline-Elm residents, we believe, would reply):

They can build them [replacement high-rises] but are they gonna be the same as they are now? I don't believe it. [How do you mean?] In the happiness of living. Will they have their own yard, and be able to go out and plant flowers in the garden? And have the rooms? These are older houses with large rooms that are comfortable—we like them—and I don't think you're gonna live at the rent you're living now.

The state Department of Public Works considered relocation plans such as 14-story high-rise apartments over the highway, and "joint development," or urban renewal that would provide new housing and other facilities next to as well as over the road. These possibilities appear unreasonable on many grounds:

1. Several years would lapse between moving from one's old house to the new one; people can hardly be asked to make a two-to-three-year "temporary" move like this.

2. Even if housing were "phased," that is, built piecemeal in such a way that any family would make one move only, and that to a place near its old one, any renting family would wind up in smaller quarters, with fewer rooms, at higher rents than it now pays; even if condominium ownership were possible for present owners, it is unlikely that they could afford the prices of such new units.

3. A similar experiment in at least one other city (the George Washington Bridge Apartments in New York City) suggests that noise and air pollution in the apartments over the highway are grave problems interfering with satisfying living.

4. Most people like those along Brookline-Elm consider high-rise apartment living peculiar and undesirable and associate it with public housing, which has very low status in their eyes. They know that management and facilities in publicly owned high-rise buildings for people of modest means tend to be of poor quality.

5. Relocation plans at best relocate nuclear families; to our knowledge the social fact that many people live in extended kinship networks is unfamiliar to most planners and all relocation officials, or at least is not considered in their plans.

In view of all the economic, social and emotional ties to their current homes and neighborhood, and the great costs anticipated with moving, it is not surprising that 63 percent of the sample interviewed in the summer of 1967 could be described as "confused," "upset" or "distraught" at the prospect of forced moving. That they reported that 89 percent of their neighbors had these feelings may be due partly to the probability that even those respondents who were themselves eager to move perceived that the majority of their neighbors were not. In addition, some members of our sample may have been reluctant to admit their own critical or painful feelings (such as fear that they would be unable to find a new desirable living situation), but may have more readily attributed such feelings to others in a similar situation.*

THE MOBILE MINORITY

I don't like it [the neighborhood]. . . . It's not suited to me. I like the suburbs.

—*young father, tenant on Elm Street*

---

* A number of psychological and sociological researchers have suggested that people may project their own embarrassing or discomforting feelings onto others nearby. For arguments for and against the validity of projective methods for measuring attitudes, see Donald T. Campbell, "The Indirect Assessment of Social Attitudes," *Psychological Bulletin*, Vol. 47, 1950, pp. 15-38; Eleanor E. and Nathan Maccoby, "The Interview: A Tool of Social Science," in Gardner Lindzey (ed.), *Handbook of Social Psychology* (Cambridge, Mass., Addison-Wesley, 1954), pp. 449-487; and Claire Selltiz, Marie Jahoda, Morton Deutsch, and Stuart W. Cook, *Research Methods in Social Relations* (New York, Henry Holt, 1959), p. 290.

> I have mixed feelings about this place. I like it here. I
> know everyone. I've lived here all my life, know all my
> neighbors. But I know it's a slum. My children would love for
> me to get out of here.
>
> *—elderly woman, homeowner on Elm Street*

About one-fourth of the residents would like to leave Brookline-Elm. Their dislike for the area often springs not from objective circumstances so much as the symbolic meaning of such neighborhoods. Rejection of working-class Middle-American identity usually means embracing the common organization-class goal of a suburban household away from parents and other relatives. Not surprisingly, the people drawn to that goal include the young, the mobile and those with few children. This group of willing movers includes more than half the single adults in the area, and the majority of young families with one to three children.

Many who want to leave their present homes in the Brookline-Elm area seek a neighborhood that is a "good place for raising the kids" or has "an improved cultural atmosphere," both very likely euphemisms for a more socially desirable neighborhood. Economic considerations and desire to be near family and/or people in the same ethnic groups brought many current residents into the area. For some of those who desire to leave these have ceased to be motivating forces.

But social mobility is not the only reason that people want to move out. Some of the respondents explained that they were upset by the uncertain prospect of the Belt looming over their heads for so long; rather than live in uncertainty any longer, they preferred to get out now, even if they liked the neighborhood otherwise. Others wanted to move closer to their families or to an area where they had previously lived. Still others indicated they wanted to move to a "better" neighborhood—i.e., the suburbs—but were aware that their finances prohibited such a move. The desire of these respondents for a "better" neighborhood, then, does not necessarily alleviate their distress at the possibility of being forced under current circumstances to move from their present neighborhood.

THE "SURVIVORS"

There is a large group of people whose lives are ordinarily ignored by highway and renewal planners—the "survivors." These are the people on adjoining streets and blocks whose friends and relatives have had to move away, or whose work places, businesses, churches and other community facilities have been destroyed by construction of the road. A survey of 50 individuals living adjacent to the Brookline-Elm route indicates social characteristics and life styles almost identical with those of the 120-person sample living on the route.

In Cambridge, nearby businesses and community facilities such as churches would also lose large portions of their clientele or congregation if the road is built, and access would be difficult for many of the rest because of the physical barrier that a limited-access highway creates between two sections of a neighborhood.

Another result of the construction of massive expressways in cities is racial or social-class segmentation of the city. Frequently, as in Washington, D.C., highways are built on the informal boundary line between wealthier areas and poor—often black—neighborhoods, thereby turning what was formerly a potentially passable social barrier into an impenetrable concrete wall. In Cambridge, the Inner Belt would serve to separate university and Middle-American residential areas.

A majority of Brookline-Elm residents hope to remain in their homes and neighborhoods. Ties to nearby people and places are too strong to break without great pain and inconvenience. Valued ways of life often cannot be reconstructed elsewhere.

For years now, residents have been living with the threat of a major highway that would force them out against their will. One might expect that they would act to preserve their way of life. But effective political action may be bewildering, frightening, incomprehensible, even impossible. Middle-American attitudes toward political action in matters like the Inner Belt case are not simple. The residents may want, for example, to stop the Belt but do not believe in their political power to do so. Their political experiences have been severely limited by a variety of constraints throughout their lives. The ethnic and age heterogeneity of the area offer no "natural" base of organization. And Brookline-Elm people appear to hold attitudes toward "the system" such that a peculiar set of contradictions seems to prevent most of them from developing any conviction that they can act effectively at all. We develop these issues in Parts II and III.

THE INNER BELT
CONTROVERSY

OVERVIEW

One can sympathize with families or businesses displaced, but progress often extracts a high price. Too often, veiled from public view, much of the trouble springs from powerful political pressures.

—*editorial in the* Boston Globe,
July 31, 1963, urging completion of the Belt plan

When we studied the Brookline-Elm area in the mid-1960s, a highway plan had hung over the residents' heads for nearly 20 years. By 1971, a person born during 1948, the year the plan originated, would be 23 years old and still not know whether an expressway would remove 1,300 or so households from Brookline-Elm.

The Massachusetts state highway department (the Department of Public Works, or DPW) issued a Boston-area master highway plan in 1948. One of its components was an Inner Belt (Interstate Route 695), an eight-lane ring joining Boston and the adjacent cities of Cambridge, Somerville and Brookline, and connecting six radial highways entering the Boston area from surrounding suburbs. Although several possible routes were suggested, no specific Cambridge location for the Belt was chosen.

The Inner Belt was to cost $125 million, but the state did not have funds to pay for it. In 1956, an innovative Federal-Aid Highway Act was passed that would allow the Belt to be constructed as part of the National System of Interstate and Defense Highways, with Washington paying 90 percent of the construction cost. This provided the financial basis for proceeding with the proposed Inner Belt. Two years later the Cambridge Planning Board recommended a route down Brookline and Elm Streets in the eastern part of the city.

The DPW held a major public hearing in Cambridge in 1960 on the design for the Cambridge and Somerville parts of the road. An audience of 2,500 people heard state and city legislators and local clergymen question the need for the road and decry the predicted massive disruption of residents, physical and social division, and the esthetic damage the road would do to the city. The audience also expressed a good deal of antagonism to the road plan.

In 1962 the DPW issued a comprehensive report on the Boston area expressway system. It reviewed a number of possible Belt locations in Cambridge, and recommended the Brookline-Elm alignment, which would displace 1,300 to 1,500 families (3,000 to 5,000 people) or about 5 percent of the city's population.*

The proposed highway system was enthusiastically supported during most of its long history by many prominent

---

* The figure of 1,300 to 1,500 families or 5,000 people—about 5 to 6 percent of the population of Cambridge—was publicized for years in the local paper, at anti-Belt meetings, and by politicians opposing the Brookline-Elm route. It probably derives from the 1962 Master Plan (*Inner Belt and Expressway System,* Boston Metropolitan Area, 1962, prepared for the Massachusetts Department of Public Works by Hayden, Harding & Buchanan, Inc., and Charles A. Maguire & Associates, Boston, Massachusetts), which estimates that the Brookline-Elm route will displace 1,541 households (*ibid.,* Table B-1).

A survey made in 1966 by independent planners associated with the Cambridge Committee on the Inner Belt, a group opposing the route, individuals and institutions: the Greater Boston Chamber of Commerce; two Boston newspapers, the *Globe* and the *Herald-Traveler;* the Department of Public Works; John A. Volpe (whom we shall shortly see held no less than five key posts throughout the Belt controversy); and, up until 1970, Francis Sargent (following partially in Volpe's footsteps, as DPW commissioner and later as governor). Opponents of the Belt System, or of particular segments of it, included the Massachusetts Turnpike Authority (a rival organization to the DPW during the late 1950s and early 1960s, later won over), and at one time or another, the governments of Boston, Cambridge, Somerville and Brookline.

Although there was always support in Cambridge for the Brookline-Elm route, a number of prominent residents, including the mayor, Thomas McNamara, opposed the Brookline-Elm alignment as early as 1958. The Cambridge City Council opposed not only the Brookline-Elm route designation, but "any and all" highways planned through Cambridge.

From the beginning, alternative locations for the Cambridge arc of the route were considered, but each was discarded by the DPW, always for technical reasons such as traffic flow. Beginning with 1966, several million dollars worth of restudies of the Cambridge Belt location were financed and conducted on local, state and federal levels. In 1970, the Governor of Massachusetts declared a mora-

came up with a figure of 1,300 to 1,500 families, or about 5,000 residents. A survey made in 1967 by the State Department of Public Works (see footnote 11, below) estimated that 1,314 families with a total population of 3,149 members would be displaced by the route, as would about 3,500 workers, one-third of them Polaroid employees. The discrepancies in figures may be attributed in part to the different stances of those doing the calculating, which invariably play a role in influencing allegedly "objective" research; they may also be attributed to a decrease in population following the recommendation of the Brookline-Elm area for potential demolition.

torium on nearly all planned highways in the metropolitan
Boston area, and the Inner Belt was one of those affected.
Another restudy on the matter was ordered and, as a re-
sult of it, Governor Sargent announced a final end to the
Inner Belt plan in December of 1971.

The decision whether to build the Belt was delayed for so
many years because of complicated political conflict involving a wide range of actors and political actions.

Although the highway controversy has a national level
of significance, it takes its dramatic form locally, over
specific highway locations and designs. Social-class analysis can enable us to understand the political stances and
actions of supporters and opponents of the highway plans.
In general, road plans are actively supported by members of
the two highest classes we have discussed. Government
road-planning agencies and business supporters of road
plans, like Chambers of Commerce, newspapers and construction companies, are headed and staffed by members of
the two highest classes. Occasionally, members of these
classes oppose a specific road location that would damage
their neighborhoods or other areas and institutions important to them, like universities, museums, historical areas
and parks. In the majority of cases, opposed urban road locations end up running through neighborhoods populated
by Middle Americans or the poor.*

The Inner Belt circumstance is a typical case of working-
class Middle Americans, ill-organized and unaccustomed to
political battle, facing the strength of highway planners and
their   organization-class   and   rich-and-powerful-class
sponsors and supporters. This seems like a straightforward
enough example of "class conflict" but the matter is sig-

---

* "It has been primarily the poor, the near-poor, and lower-middle
class whose houses have been demolished (for highway programs),"
summarizes *Building the American City*, Report of the National Commission on Urban Problems (Washington, D.C., December 1968), p. 82.

nificantly complicated here, as in many current highway controversies, by the assistance and leadership of a group of organization-class people sympathetic to the Middle Americans' cause and active in their advocacy of it.*

A sketch of major actors in the Inner Belt controversy and their actions will help make our analysis clear.

THE ACTORS

Government

The State Highway Builders. The Massachusetts DPW, the state road-building agency, has had the Inner Belt plan "on the books" since 1948. Its primary goal throughout the long controversy was to complete the Inner Belt system as quickly and with as little trouble as possible. Although a recent bureaucratic reorganization may change matters, until now the DPW has never been mandated to consider larger-scale transportation problems such as the comparative costs and benefits of mass transportation versus highways, but has simply built and maintained the state's roads.

The Federal Highway Agency. The Bureau of Public Roads (BPR) has been part of the U.S. Department of Transportation since 1967. Prior to this time, it also dealt solely with road-building, and had no connection with larger transportation issues. The Inner Belt would be part of the gargantuan National System of Interstate and Defense Highways administered by the BPR. Under Federal-

---

* Kenneth R. Geiser, Jr., *Urban Transportation Decision Making:* I— Political Processes of Urban Freeway Controversies (Cambridge, Mass., Urban Systems Laboratory, 1970), p. 384. Geiser notes that organization-class outsiders consistently involve themselves on the side of Middle-American displacees in such controversies.

Aid Highway Acts since 1956, the Federal Government pays 90 percent of the construction cost. Each state pays the remaining 10 percent and must initiate proposals to the federal government for the mileage and location of highways the state would like to build. The BPR usually approves all state-submitted proposals automatically. Lowell Bridwell, BPR head during 1967 and 1968, took the unusual step in the Inner Belt case of responding to local pressures by ordering restudies of the route designation.

State Officials. From 1953 to 1956 John Volpe served as commissioner of the Massachusetts Department of Public Works; during his tenure part of the 1948 Master Plan was built. In 1956, with the passage of a Federal-Aid Highway Act that provided for the 41,000 mile National System of Interstate and Defense Highways, Volpe was appointed by President Eisenhower as the first Federal Highway Administrator, in charge of the Interstate program. In 1958, upon his return to Boston, he served as president of the Greater Boston Chamber of Commerce. During his term with the Chamber in 1958 and 1959, he issued many statements urging completion of the Master Highway Plan, including the Inner Belt, as soon as possible, in order to lead Boston to "a grand new era" of economic development. As governor of Massachusetts from 1961 to 1962 and from 1965 to 1968 Volpe supported DPW recommendations for the Cambridge Inner Belt location. And from 1968 to early 1973, Volpe headed the Federal Department of Transportation (DOT), appointed to that position by President Nixon.*

Francis Sargent, trained as a conservationist, served as Massachusetts State Commissioner of Natural Resources

---

* Starting out as a manual laborer, Volpe founded a construction company which specializes in industrial and public buildings. It eventually reached the ranks of the 100 largest construction firms in the nation, and in 1968 added the new headquarters of the Department of Transportation in Washington, D.C., to its list of buildings constructed.

from 1956 to 1959. In 1963 he was appointed associate commissioner of the DPW, and in 1965 elevated to head of that organization, in which capacity he too urged completion of the Inner Belt. Successful as Governor Volpe's running mate in 1966, he became governor of Massachusetts in 1969, following Volpe's appointment to DOT. Responding to extensive organized pressure to kill the Belt plan, Sargent announced its demise at the end of 1971.

Elected City Officials. The Cambridge City Council not only consistently opposed the Brookline-Elm location for the Belt, it repeatedly declared itself opposed to any expressways through Cambridge.

City Planning Officials. In 1958, the Cambridge Planning Board, in conjunction with two private consulting firms, recommended a route down Brookline and Elm Streets, reasoning that it would benefit commercial and industrial firms nearby and would eliminate what the planning board considered substandard residential areas. For many years thereafter, the head of the planning board—in harsh opposition to most other city officials and employees —actively favored an Inner Belt through Cambridge, as an aid to the city's economic development; he found the Brookline-Elm route satisfactory. He resigned from his job in late 1968.

State Representatives. Several state legislators whose constituency includes Brookline-Elm took stands—some of them accompanied by actions—opposing the Belt, or specifically the Brookline-Elm route. In 1960, for example, former Cambridge Mayor Thomas McNamara, then a city councillor, joined with State Representative John Toomey in sponsoring an anti-Belt petition to be forwarded to Massachusetts senators and representatives in Washington, to the Bureau of Public Roads and to newly elected Governor Volpe.

Federal Representatives. U.S. Congressman Thomas P. O'Neill, a Democrat who represents Cambridge, Somerville, Brookline and parts of Boston, has publicly opposed the Inner Belt since 1965. U.S. senators from Massachusetts took no stand on the issue until the summer of 1967, when senators Edward Kennedy and Edward Brooke received Cambridge protestors in Washington and added their prestige to the cause by issuing public statements that urged restudy of the Brookline-Elm route.

Private Institutions and Citizens Groups

Newspapers and Business Interests. Two major newspapers (the *Boston Globe* and the *Boston Herald-Traveler*) and the Greater Boston Chamber of Commerce actively supported the Inner Belt plan for many years, through editorial stands and political pressures, respectively. Such institutions were not directly affected by the Cambridge Inner Belt fight. They probably supported the road because they are aligned with the interests of the rich-and-powerful-class membership whom a completed highway system would benefit, through construction profits, increased access of suburbanites to downtown Boston and so forth.*

Powerful Local Institutions. Two of the largest, most powerful institutions in Cambridge are Harvard University and the Massachusetts Institute of Technology. Although neither pays taxes to the city, each annually contributes a sizable financial gift to Cambridge; brings untold amounts of business to merchants and landlords; is responsible for the presence of local consulting, engineering, publishing and other businesses; buys large amounts of property and builds

---

* Some of this support later changed to opposition on the part of the newspapers, with the growing effectiveness of local protest and the mounting national pressures for "balanced transportation," reduced pollution, and minimal disturbance of stable urban neighborhoods. The local paper, the *Cambridge Chronicle,* has always opposed plans for an Inner Belt through Cambridge, particularly the Brookline-Elm route.

upon it; and in numerous other ways plays a major role in shaping Cambridge.*

Were it to follow the Brookline-Elm route, the Inner Belt would be located between the two universities and would affect the future of both. The Belt would run less than a mile from MIT. If located any nearer to that institution, at least one MIT structure would have to be razed; and MIT would need to build over or around the road in its expansion operations. The border of Harvard is currently a mile the other way from the projected Belt. Although there is no indication that Harvard expansion plans extend to Brookline or Elm Streets, the university is clearly interested in the overall development of the city. †

Neither institution has ever officially favored construction of the Belt or any particular route. But they were not inactive in the issue. State Representative John Toomey of Cambridge, testifying at a state hearing on the Belt in the early 1960s,

> revealed that in 1959, at a private session at . . . the MIT Faculty building, he had conferred with President Nathan M. Pusey

---

* See Chapter 5, discussion of "Mislocated Enemy."

† A 1968 Harvard report on the university and the city expressed the conflict between the institution's definition of its own interests and its awareness of the not-always-complementary interests of its neighbors:

> No institution of [the] size of [Harvard University] . . . can be neutral about its environment. If it should act vigorously to secure land, erect buildings, and shape events, it will impose, however laudable its intentions, its preferences on others who may not share them. If it should be passive and let events take their course, it will implicitly choose a certain kind of environment—one, perhaps, in which all Cambridge slowly becomes like Harvard and M.I.T. . . . Perhaps that is the environment we wish to have, or we should have, but we cannot pretend that we may remain neutral on the issue.

> If a false sense of neutrality were ever possible, it is no longer so in an era of intense community and neighborhood self-awareness . . . the citizens of our urban environment expect the university to act as a responsible and enlightened landlord, employer and neighbor. Little more than legitimate concern for its own self-interest will lead the university to reflect seriously and act positively on the obligations of its urban citizenship

From the "Preliminary Report of the Committee on the University and the City" (Harvard University, December 1968), p. 7.

of Harvard and MIT President Julius M. Stratton. "The purpose [of this meeting] was," he said, "to stop me from opposing the inner belt highway on Brookline and Elm Streets. . . . Dr. Stratton told me they would never build it [the highway] on the railroad [an alternate route closer to MIT] because they [MIT] had enough power to stop it."[1]

Toomey accused the two universities of caring more about their own growth than about the nonuniversity parts of the city. Although Harvard has apparently kept out of the Belt controversy since then, MIT has continually and vocally opposed any and all proposed routes that would border its current campus—that is, all routes except Brookline-Elm.[2]

Powerful local industries consistently and strongly opposed running the Belt through their property.

Local "Good Government" Groups. Two Cambridge civic groups, the League of Women Voters and the Cambridge Civic Association—both consisting mainly of members of old Cambridge elite families and organization-class people from the other side of town—originally favored the Brookline-Elm route, as conducive to urban renewal of a "rundown" section of the city.*

Volunteer Professionals. In September 1965, a dozen or so Boston and Cambridge professionals in city planning and related fields, some of them on the faculties of nearby uni-

---

* During the early sixties, members of the rich-and-powerful and organization classes, through their civic and other organizations, opposed parts of the Belt system outside Cambridge. In the Fenway area—a parklike section of Boston located near several colleges and the Museum of Fine Arts—protest by the museum and educational institutions succeeded in having that portion of the road redesigned, to be depressed below ground and covered over with fountains and malls. Boston University gained the support of Senator Edward Kennedy and Governor Volpe in its effort to have a portion of the Inner Belt put into a tunnel, as the original plan to put one section of the road on a bridge would have destroyed one of the university's buildings. After these and similar design modifications were won by influential groups, and the other three cities—Boston, Somerville and Brookline—through which the Belt would travel had finally accepted the DPW plans, Cambridge was the sole official opponent of the road.

versities, voluntarily met to consider ways to reduce the number of homes the Cambridge Inner Belt would take. As it had been announced that the Brookline-Elm route would displace around 1,500 families, or about 5 percent of the city's population, they were unanimous in their desire to lower that figure. They called themselves the Cambridge Committee on the Inner Belt (CCIB), and decided to publicize their existence by running a series of articles in the Cambridge weekly newspaper, to define the problem of the road, describe the affected areas of the city and suggest alternative locations for the Belt.

These professionals were the only actors in the Inner Belt drama who had no clear class self-interest to pursue. Although the motives for each varied, of course, and included idiosyncratic considerations, what united them all and what initially brought them together was a common dissatisfaction with the narrowness of the work for which they were trained. An engineer, an architect and city planner, an urban anthropologist, an architect, a lawyer, a city planner, a systems analyst and a sociologist, all found themselves employed in positions that fundamentally promoted the interests of the organization and rich-and-powerful classes. Independently, all wished to use their skills and perspectives for the good of other classes as well, specifically those we define here as Middle Americans and the poor and powerless.

The members of the CCIB shared a common politics too. All believed that our society often works counter to the interests of the Middle-American and poor-and-powerless classes, despite rhetoric about "the common good," "liberty and justice for all," "the greatest good for the greatest number," "community responsibility" and so forth. All believed that the overconcentration of power and money in the rich-and-powerful and organization classes was in itself not conducive to the development of real equality and democracy and that that overconcentration was typically used, with rhetorical masks such as those just mentioned, to violate the rights and dignity of people in the Middle-American and the poor-and-powerless classes. All were committed to using their professional educations and positions to help promote movement in America toward greater equality and freedom.

This group eventually reorganized into Urban Planning Aid, Inc. (UPA), a nonprofit organization identified with the "advocacy planning" movement, composed of professionals offering free services to middle- and low-income groups who seek help in fighting organization-class plans that displease them and in furthering their own interests in seeking good housing, schools and community facilities.

As a member of this group from the start, I was impressed with the high degree of commitment of these varied professionals who had volunteered at no pay to do work which they believed important and just. All had been educated to expect handsome recompense for their services but willingly declined possibilities of high-paying consultantships to devote time, energy and talent to advocacy planning.*

Neighborhood Protest Groups. In mid-October 1965, the volunteer planners of CCIB were contacted by a number of local opponents to the Brookline-Elm route who were organizing one section of the area into a small group called Neighbors United; also concerned were members of the Riverside Neighborhood Association (a community group in a contiguous area), and members of the Neighborhood Four Association elsewhere on the Belt route. These groups became the nucleus of a neighborhood anti-Belt group later named "United Effort to Save our Cities," or SOC.

---

* Given their training, professional experiences and various personal motives, it would be naive to interpret UPA founders' behavior as purely altruistic. The complex satisfactions, attention, challenges, ambitions, etc., involved in this kind of work are worth a study in themselves. Although we cannot examine those matters fully, we touch on some aspects of them in a general way in Chapter 8.

Unorganized Brookline-Elm Residents. Many people whose homes and ways of life were at stake opposed the road in principle, but few thought it would be possible to do anything about it. As we shall see later, some engaged in one or another kind of protest activity, but most did not. While no formal referendum was ever taken, it was clear from the start that the voluntary professionals correctly perceived that the majority of Brookline-Elm people wanted to remain in their homes and neighborhoods, acted on behalf of those interests, and had the support of the majority.

THE ACTIONS

Veto Power

The Cambridge City Council relied for four years on a legal right to veto any proposed location for the highway in the city.

In early 1961, State Representative John Toomey of the Brookline-Elm area added an amendment onto a highway appropriations bill that was then passed into law, which allowed nine communities, including Cambridge, Boston, Brookline and Somerville, to veto plans for any highway passing through them. On June 6, 1961, the Cambridge City Council voted to veto plans for any highway that would pass through their area. This was followed by several legislative attempts to abolish the veto power of communities over highways. In 1963, the Massachusetts legislature reduced the absolute veto to a provisional one, and provided for creation of a three-person arbitration board charged with finding a location satisfactory both to a vetoing community and to the DPW. Mayor John Collins of Boston approved locations recommended by the DPW for parts of the Belt in his city, while Endicott Peabody, then governor, threatened to kill the whole highway program unless the veto amendment was rescinded. Attempts were made to repeal, but the veto, now in arbitration form, remained.

In 1965, Federal Highway Administrator Rex Whitton wrote to DPW Commissioner Francis Sargent (a new appointee of Governor Volpe, who had just retaken office after a two-year hiatus) that the continued fact of the veto power cast doubt upon the likelihood of accomplishing the highway system Massachusetts desired; the state might lose the 90 percent federal financing. Whitton also pointed out that the veto power was at odds with federal regulations requiring state departments of public works to designate highway routes. Finally, in August 1965, largely as a result of pressure from Sargent, the legislature withdrew the veto power in any form from dissenting Massachusetts communities. Thus ended the guarantee Cambridge had relied upon for protecting itself from the Inner Belt.

Alternate Route Proposals

When the Master Highway Plan was first presented in rough form in 1948, possibilities other than the Brookline-Elm location were mentioned for Cambridge. But all alternative routes were subsequently rejected by the Cambridge Planning Board in 1957; River Street-Lee Street (about half of which is a "higher class" area than Brookline-Elm) because, according to the planning board, it would not solve Cambridge's traffic problem; a route along some rarely used railroad tracks because it would allegedly require demolition of several industries and several MIT buildings; and Memorial Drive (a parkway running for miles along the Charles River and past Harvard, residential and industrial areas, and MIT) because construction there would require expensive building over the river, and in addition would destroy forever the last vestige of park-like atmosphere along the Drive [and] would cut off from public enjoyment the delightful vista of the [Charles River] basin as it mirrors the Boston skyline.[3]

In 1960, the planning board again favored the Brookline-Elm alignment on the grounds that it would benefit commercial and industrial firms in the eastern part of the city and would tie in with plans for "urban renewal" of what the board considered substandard residential areas along both sides of the proposed route.[4] Further, the board claimed this route was best for traffic patterns and would cause the least damage to the city.

Local city officials and the few state officials who represented Cambridge strongly opposed this plan and for years after urged reconsideration of either the railroad or Memorial Drive alternates, or pushed for no roads in Cambridge at all.

As mentioned earlier, civic groups such as the Cambridge Civic Association and the League of Woman Voters supported the Brookline-Elm route because it would tie in with "urban renewal" plans in the city.

In October 1964, then State DPW Commissioner James D. Fitzgerald remarked publicly that officials of the National Aeronautics and Space Administration (NASA), soon to locate a major installation in Cambridge, wanted the Belt to be constructed, but objected to the railroad route, which would be closer to NASA property than would Brookline-Elm. (Ironically, the NASA construction meant the removal of most of the East Cambridge industrial area that the Belt was once planned to service. Even more ironically, the NASA facility itself was shut down in early 1970, either due to federal budget cutbacks or possibly for other, partisan political reasons. The NASA facility, which MIT very much wanted located next to it, was replaced by other federal government operations, some of them in transportation.)* Fitzgerald also mentioned that General James McCormick, corporation vice president of the Massachusetts Institute of Technology, objected to the Memorial Drive alternative route.†

In November 1965, the CCIB—which was concerned with reducing the number of homes that would be taken by the Belt—presented the Cambridge City Council with several alternative locations for the Belt. (The CCIB favored an alignment down Portland and Albany Streets, three to four blocks east of Brookline-Elm. The Portland-Albany alternative would take one small MIT building, about 110 homes and 2,500 jobs. By comparison, the Brookline-Elm route would take more than ten times as many homes, about the same number of jobs and no part of MIT.) The city council defended its now long-standing opposition to all possible Belt routes through Cambridge, while the CCIB tried to convince the council that if a Belt could not be stopped, it would be wise to press for the least damaging alternative to Brookline-Elm.

During November and December 1965, CCIB people convinced the two "good government" groups, the Cambridge Civic Association and the League of Women Voters, to reverse their earlier endorsements of the Brookline-Elm route. CCIB also obtained the formal endorsement of their

---

* More ironically still, one justification for the Brookline-Elm location was its proximity to areas planned for urban renewal. Citizen protest in the mid-1960s led to the end of most urban renewal plans in Cambridge.

† MIT has consistently opposed every proposed route but Brookline-Elm. It has denounced the Memorial Drive alternate route, which fronts its southern border (see reported statement of MIT President Julius Stratton, *Cambridge Chronicle*, February 15, 1962; and reported statement of MIT Corporation Vice President James McCormick, *Cambridge Chronicle*, October 29, 1964), and the route along the old Grand Junction railroad tracks, which fronts its northern border and would take at least one of its buildings (see statement by Dr. James R. Killian, Jr., MIT Corporation Chairman, *Boston Globe*, February 22, 1966). It also opposed the Portland-Albany alternative (see below).

Portland-Albany alternate route from U.S. Representative O'Neill, and from the pastors of the two large Catholic churches in the Brookline-Elm area. One priest from each parish—Fr. McManus of St. Mary's and Msgr. McDevitt of Blessed Sacrament—now became active leaders of the recently organized neighborhood movement.

Preliminary to making a decision on alternate routes, a public hearing on the Belt was called by the Cambridge City Council for Sunday evening, February 20, 1966. The city councillor chairing the meeting of about 600 people opened it with the statement that the city had best have a favored route in mind, in case it became impossible to stop the road altogether. Two members of Barton-Aschman Associates, Chicago consultants hired by the council to devise an alternate route to Brookline-Elm, presented their firm's version of the railroad route, with the comment that they were instructed—by whom was not specified—to present a feasible location other than Brookline-Elm, and they had decided not to take the needs and interests of MIT into account. Hence, the alternate they designed would take the MIT instrumentation lab, its cyclotron, power plant, hydrodynamics lab and other buildings.

Now, as earlier, a number of local industries objected to any Belt route that would violate their interests. On October 29, 1965, for example, the Simplex Wire and Cable Company, a large Cambridge employer located on the east side of Brookline Street, issued a report denying rumors that they were planning to move from the city and urging that, if the Brookline-Elm corridor were chosen, the road should not go on their side of Brookline Street. (In 1969 Simplex announced it was moving after all and that MIT had first option on the property.) At the February 20, 1966, hearing, representatives of two other large local factories, the NECCO candy company and Boston Woven Hose, objected that the Barton-Aschman railroad route would take part or all of their plant operations, forcing them to move from Cambridge.

Edward Hanify, counsel for MIT, then presented that institution's case.* Acknowledging that the Belt route problem admitted of "no happy solution," Hanify asked that MIT "be accorded the same respect in defending its interest as we accord to all." He quoted newspaper and magazine articles pointing to MIT's role in New England's economic renaissance (MIT has played a key role in the growth of the electronics industries in the metropolitan Boston area), cited its employment, payroll and budget figures and suggested that many other cities, envious of this major New England educational and technological institution, would be pleased at the disruption of its facilities and hopeful of coaxing MIT to relocate. MIT, Hanify explained, devoted its resources fundamentally to preserving homes and jobs and alleviating suffering.

> "Moreover," he said, "we all know that we live in times of mortal peril, always on the brink of devastation by those Communist powers that seek to crush us by moving ahead of us in scientific techniques. These nations seek the perfection of intricate devices, weaponry, missiles and air power. In this way they confidently expect that they will gain the mastery of space, the domination of the tides and the conquest of the atmosphere. The laboratories and research facilities which this so-called recommended route will destroy or cripple constitute a primary scientific arsenal of democracy in this grueling struggle to maintain the balance of scientific power in the service of free man."[5]

The MIT instrumentation lab that the railroad route would take works on, among other projects, guidance systems for the Apollo moon landing and Polaris submarine projects.

---

* Earlier that day, MIT Corporation President James Killian claimed at a press conference that the proposed alternative Belt location along the railroad tracks would take 17 MIT buildings and cost the Institute "at least $80,000,000" (see the *Boston Herald*, February 21, 1966).

If there is a communist attack someday, Hanify suggested, Polaris missiles may save far more American homes and lives than would be taken by a hundred Belt routes. The high voltage research lab at MIT, which he said would also be taken by the Belt, includes research affecting thousands of cancer victims. Hanify detailed the functions of 15 other buildings the road would take and suggested that the continuation of Western civilization itself might well depend on not interfering with any of these MIT facilities. He included in his listing a number of buildings the Barton-Aschman route would not take, apparently summing all the buildings all of several railroad routes proposed over the years would have taken. No mention was made of the Portland-Albany route, which would have taken a small instrumentation laboratory, reportedly to be relocated anyway, and no other MIT buildings.

One citizen in the audience, who announced himself as a lobbyist only for himself, said he wished the fellow who was going to take his house would come now and give him the money for it. "I'd hate to think I was standing in the way of all those companies and the security of the United States. I guess MIT can't build a new building; the guy must have lost the plans. . . ." Various councillors and others spoke their piece and urged people to write their views to federal senators and representatives.

Four days later the city council held another meeting on the Inner Belt, at which representatives of local industries clashed with residents' spokesmen. A representative of the large Polaroid Corporation complained that the Portland-Albany route would take four Polaroid buildings. (As the Portland-Albany route in question took no Polaroid buildings, he may have confused it, naively or deliberately, with an earlier pre-CCIB version of that route.) Msgr. Donovan, of the Church of St. Mary's of the Annunciation, located next to the Belt route, called MIT's recent statements "exaggerated and insincere" and predicted "violence and

chaos" in Cambridge were the DPW to select the Brookline-Elm route. Msgr. McDevitt of the Blessed Sacrament
Church, also adjacent to the Brookline-Elm route, invoked
the rights of people to stay in their homes, the impossibility
of adequate financial compensation for homes, and the
duty of the city council to help avoid selection of this route.
He complained of procedures that took economic costs of
moving industries and other institutions into account
while ignoring human costs.

SOC Meetings and Demonstrations

The effort to gain consideration of alternate route locations was spurred on the one hand by the CCIB professionals backed by prestigious organizations and individuals
whose support they had won, and on the other hand by
meetings and demonstrations sponsored by the neighborhood protest group known as Save Our Cities (SOC). The
advocate planners worked continually with city and state
officials, out of the public eye, while the neighborhood
people publicly met to discuss their plight and learn the
current status of the controversy. CCIB also met regularly
with the SOC executive committee, offering suggestions
and advice; and periodically it reported to SOC public
meetings on the state of the Belt issue.

On October 27, 1965, CCIB joined with several anti-
highway neighborhood groups in cosponsoring a public
meeting on the Belt, the first of many. These citizen protest
and information meetings, held in school auditoriums and
church halls once or twice every month, were chaired by a
combination of CCIB planners, local priests and neighborhood leaders.

Observations of around 30 such events held between
October 27, 1965, and May 2, 1968, reveal a pattern. Attendance varied between 20 and 200, but the average and

usual number of people at each gathering was approximately 70. About ten or 15 of these were regularly interested outsiders not directly affected by the Brookline-Elm route; such outsiders included students there to observe or help; members of anti-highway or civic groups in Brookline, Boston, Somerville or other parts of Cambridge; people living on other possible Belt routes through the city; and occasionally a state representative and a city councillor or two. There was a hard core of 20 or 30 regular attenders, mostly middle-aged homeowners who lived on the route.

The proceedings of each meeting followed a pattern. CCIB planners gave detailed technical discussions or reported on the latest negotiations with the DPW over alternate route proposals; neighborhood leaders delivered heated exhortations to citizen action ranging from letterwriting to civil disobedience (but primarily the former); priests offered political analysis and encouragement flavored with religious moods and allusions; and members of the audience cheered their supporters and damned Belt proponents.

While it is significant to note what regularly happened at these protest meetings, what did *not* happen should also be noted. The protest was limited to stopping the Inner Belt through Cambridge. We recall few or no references at any of these meetings to the fact that the Cambridge Belt is part of a regional system. And although the Cambridge group made a few contacts in 1966 and 1967 with groups protesting segments of the road in Somerville, Brookline and the Roxbury section of Boston, the focus of the protest was not changed until 1969, when the Greater Boston Committee on the Transportation Crisis was formed (see below). SOC did not, for example, consider opposing the whole concept of the Inner Belt and radials. From time to time a Cambridge neighborhood leader might mention that "we favor mass transit instead of highways," but there was never any exploration of what such a goal entailed, or how it might be implemented.

The Brookline-Elm people attending these meetings had entrusted their case to the volunteer professionals. They had no sense of themselves as a class or even as an area-wide interest group. As is typical in our society, people whose own homes were not threatened did not join in common cause with neighbors and relatives in distress. Indeed, it will be argued in a later chapter that Middle Americans are educated in such a way as to discourage group consciousness and group action, even on their own behalf, let alone on the behalf of neighbors and fellow workers.

We shall discuss later the possibility that CCIB might have worked directly on organizing the Brookline-Elm people to be more active politically rather than more or less limiting CCIB activity to informing their clients. As their work, education and community experiences did not prepare Brookline-Elm people for the kind of political work demanded, the CCIB task would have been formidable. And the CCIB people took several years to question seriously the wisdom of their approach of professionally representing clients' interests, rather than helping them learn how to do their own work in defense of their own interests (see Chapter 5).

Some direct action resulted from the SOC meetings. Usually following CCIB recommendations, an occasional resolution in support of an alternate route or a proposal for restudy was forwarded to the city council or the local newspaper.

Several rallies and marches also marked SOC anti-Belt activities. Between 500 and 600 people attended a major Beat-the-Belt rally on April 3, 1966, at St. Mary's gym. On September 9, just two months before state elections, another large rally was held to generate enthusiasm for a coming protest march. In early October, the Cambridge City Council allotted SOC $1,500 for publicity and other expenses associated with the event.

The long-anticipated mass march, announced from

church pulpits, at SOC meetings and in the Cambridge *Chronicle-Sun,* was held Saturday morning, October 15, 1966. There was an unusual, perhaps unique, aspect to the event: a city council had hired buses to take people to a protest against a state agency and the governor.

At the Boston Common, adjacent to the Massachusetts State House (the state capitol building), 500 to 600 people, about two-thirds of them Brookline-Elm people, including a large number of children, and one-third or so organization-class supporters and students, gathered at a bandstand. The St. Mary's High School marching band, in full dress, played "Downtown." The program began with a speech by Fr. McManus of St. Mary's Church, emphasizing that the people assembled were engaging in a "democratic proceeding" in an "orderly and proper way" (as if he were exhorting and instructing them at the same time). After a loud baritone, accompanied by an accordion player, sang "The Star Spangled Banner," Msgr. McDevitt of Blessed Sacrament invoked God's blessing and declared that God intended that people live as they wish to. A priest from neighboring Somerville and the mayor of Cambridge spoke briefly. They were followed by the minister of a black Episcopal church near the Belt area, who decried how callous people in power must be if they want to disrupt the lives of people in well-integrated neighborhoods like those of Brookline-Elm Streets. "Cambridge would be," he said, "reduced to a monolithic, middle- and upper-income city." A local resident named and thanked all those who had worked on the rally; then a liberal Protestant minister from a church in Harvard Square offered the benediction.

The program having ended, the next move was a one-block march to the State House. A number of Brookline-Elm residents, most of whom had never taken part in such a demonstration before, were admitting to each other how embarrassed they felt demonstrating and wondered if they would see themselves on TV. At the State House, which was locked (it was Saturday), marchers filled the space below the steps where Cambridge dignitaries were posing with their anti-Belt signs. The crowd seemed to feel that now they were there, something should happen, but people stood for minutes and nothing occurred. One girl, who looked like a student, tried to start a chant, "Beat the Belt," but after two tries she gave up because nobody joined her. Then, as people looked around at each other, waiting, Governor Volpe's name was heard and the chant swelled spontaneously: "We want Volpe! We want Volpe!" The children were most enthusiastic, but almost everyone seemed to be chanting. Instructions came down immediately from the clergymen and officials standing on the State House steps: "Quiet down. We've been fine until now. Let's keep it that way." People stopped as quickly as they had started. A few residents murmured, "Now what?" Then one of the leaders made an announcement about returning to the buses and the people filed back down the street to their waiting vehicles and rode home.

This demonstration was undoubtedly a new experience for most of the participants, judging from their comments during it and their response to later interviews. Many of them, however, both children and adults, had apparently put a great deal of effort into making the signs they carried. A number of posters were quite detailed, well drawn and strikingly original. Aside from the standard "Beat the Belt" and "Cambridge Is a City, not a Highway" slogans, there were also signs reading "Beat the Belt or Cambridge Will Melt," "Beat the Belt, Baby," "Save My Nana's Home," and "We Support Our Boys in Vietnam—Save Their Homes." On one small dog was a sign: "Bite the Belt."

Studies, Restudies and More Restudies

It is impossible to assess the influence of the advocate planners and their prestigious supporters compared with that of the neighborhood people in their meetings and rallies. Neither group would have been successful without the simultaneous activities of the other, but the volunteer professionals probably had more direct impact on the planning process than did the residents.

The state's final decision on the Cambridge Belt route was to be made some time in March 1966 (seven months before the demonstration at the State House). At the Cambridge City Council meeting of February 28, a SOC leader announced that 2,000 people, including 50 prominent individuals and organizations, had signed a petition endorsing the CCIB's alternative along Portland-Albany Streets. Councillor Thomas Mahoney, an MIT history professor, delivered a blistering attack on the Inner Belt, damning it as an "excrescence on our community" and urging development of rapid transit systems instead. He raised the highway beautification and air pollution issues, and related a World War I anecdote of a German commander asking King Albert for permission to cross Belgium in order to invade France. King Albert replied, "Belgium is a country, not a highway."

By the end of the evening, the city council decided that, rather than take a stand in favor of any route, it would again go on record opposing all roads through Cambridge. Plans were announced to transmit the council's opposition to the Inner Belt to Federal Highway Administrator Rex M. Whitton; Somerville, Boston and Brookline were asked to join Cambridge in these efforts. From Councillor Mahoney's talk came one of the two slogans the anti-Belt people have since used widely: "Cambridge Is a City, Not a Highway." (The other is "Beat the Belt.")

By early March, six MIT Planning faculty members had endorsed the Portland-Albany alternative route,* and

---

* In this and other such actions university faculty were acting as independent professionals and in no way represented institutions. Neighbor-

CCIB stepped up its letter campaign, conveying this endorsement to Volpe, Whitton and DPW Commissioner Francis Sargent.

Congressman O'Neill arranged a meeting in Washington for March 8, 1966, at which members of the Cambridge City Council attempted to convince Whitton to restudy the Belt issue. Exactly a week later, on March 15, DPW Commissioner Sargent announced his agency's final decision: the Cambridge part of the Belt would be located along Brookline and Elm Streets.* On a radio program the following Sunday, Governor Volpe defended this choice, saying that "motorists are people too." But the very next day, March 21, Congressman O'Neill informed Cambridge officials that as a result of Cambridge pressure, Whitton had agreed to sponsor a restudy of the entire Belt issue, to take from eight months to a year. This delayed the Belt. Final plans for this restudy, however, were not made.

On September 5, 1966, Governor Volpe, running for re-election in two months, told a SOC delegation that he would ask Washington to stop all work on plans for the Brookline-Elm route and would instead conduct "a full study of alternate routes." Since the outcome of the restudy was to be announced after the election, a number of residents at the SOC meeting where Volpe's promise was announced mumbled that his move was only aimed at getting votes, and that the restudy would point to the same old conclusion: Brookline and Elm Streets. But the SOC lead-

---

hood people, however, sometimes took these faculty stands for the policies of the universities with which they were affiliated.

* One of the reasons for this choice, Sargent explained later in a television interview, was that the Portland-Albany route would take three times as many jobs as the Brookline-Elm route. No data anywhere supported this; the available information indicated that about equal numbers of jobs would be taken by each route, with the Portland-Albany route displacing about one-tenth the number of residents as the Brookline-Elm route.

ers, priests and local politicians continued to express their hope that Volpe was sincere.

Four days after the October 15 State House rally, anti-Belt forces from the professional world held a well-attended press conference, at which Harvard City Planning Department Chairman William Nash and MIT City Planning Professor Kevin Lynch (both of whom had supported the anti-Belt movement) presented a report criticizing the conception and design of the Master Highway Plan.* The report was also backed by about a dozen other eminent city planning professionals, and by Lewis Mumford, scholar of urban history and affairs, then at Harvard. On October 25, in response to the Cambridge rally and the planners' press conference, Governor Volpe officially announced that he was withdrawing the Brookline-Elm route from Washington, in preparation for a restudy of the best route for the Inner Belt in Cambridge.

During this same period, Fr. McManus of St. Mary's, one of the SOC leaders, had attempted to obtain an appointment for SOC representatives to meet with MIT Corporation Chairman James R. Killian, Jr., and was told that Killian was "not available." On November 7, a young housewife who was prominent in the SOC leadership† sat on the floor outside Killian's office at MIT for about an hour along with two other mothers and ten children, making and munching on peanut butter sandwiches. They were promptly given the desired appointment.

---

* CCIB members had by now reconstituted themselves as Urban Planning Aid, Inc. (UPA), a nonprofit "advocacy planning" group offering "counter planning services" to low-income groups and communities in the greater Boston area. UPA began working with community groups that wanted to develop housing plans, or alter official plans of various sorts, and it continued its work with SOC; the report Nash and Lynch presented at the press conference was prepared by UPA.

† A month earlier she had initiated anti-Belt picketing by several neighborhood people and MIT students during the inauguration of the new MIT president, Howard Johnson.

Shortly thereafter, six SOC members met with the corporation chairman. He told them he believed the Inner Belt was necessary, but should not be placed near enough to MIT to harm it. He assured the residents that he was concerned that the people of Brookline and Elm Streets be relocated adequately.

On May 3, 1967, a public advertisement initiated by Urban Planning Aid (UPA, formerly CCIB) members and signed by 528 professors from Harvard and MIT appeared in the *Boston Globe*. The signers opposed the Brookline-Elm route and urged restudy of the Cambridge Belt issue. Included among them were such notables as Daniel P. Moynihan, later special assistant to President Nixon on Urban Affairs; economist John Kenneth Galbraith; Pulitzer Prize novelist Bernard Malamud; Abram Chayes, former legal adviser to the State Department; and George Kistiakowsky, former scientific adviser to President Eisenhower. Moynihan personally delivered a copy of this advertisement to the new Federal Highway Administrator, Lowell Bridwell.

On May 4, with Volpe's restudy results to be made public in less than two weeks, SOC announced that a residents' trip to Washington was being organized, for the purpose of asking U.S. Senators Kennedy and Brooke to assure "balanced transportation planning" for the Cambridge area. Then Volpe's restudy, comparing the Brookline-Elm and Portland-Albany routes, was made public. Using figures on displacement given them by the DPW, Lochner Associates, the consultants commissioned to do the study, said that the Portland-Albany alignment, "beyond the fact that it achieves fewer residential takings, is detrimental to the city of Cambridge in every other aspect of urban existance (sic)." Lochner noted that eight "major companies" and MIT would either be put out of business or would be harmfully affected by the Portland-Albany route and that "all of these firms and MIT have written to the Department (of

Public Works) voicing their opposition to this alignment."
Lochner concluded that beyond a doubt Brookline-Elm was
the preferable Belt route through Cambridge.[6]

According to the *Boston Globe,* the Greater Boston
Chamber of Commerce promptly "applauded" this decision, but "grim" Cambridge officials said that they
would go to the Bureau of Public Roads in Washington to
ask for a halt to Inner Belt plans through their city.[7]

On May 24, 1967, approximately 100 Cambridge and
Somerville residents, including 25 children, met in Congressmen O'Neill's office with Senator Edward Kennedy
and his newly elected colleague, Senator Edward Brooke.
Priests, social workers, city officials, volunteer planners
and threatened residents spoke out against the social harm
the Belt would cause and urged restudy of alternate routes,
while the children sang an anti-Belt song written for the
occasion. The two senators declared that they believed in
"people before roads." Kennedy added that this small
group before him represented "hundreds of thousands" in
the nation caught in the "(highway) program-people conflict," and Brooke promised to see that alternate routes
were adequately studied.[8] The group also spoke to Federal
Highway Administrator Bridwell. A UPA spokesman for
the group told Bridwell that the DPW figures on which
Lochner had based their Brookline-Elm decision were
"80 to 90 percent off." Bridwell admitted there were discrepancies between figures supplied by Cambridge and by
the state, and said he would have his own staff check on the
discrepancies.[9]

The following month O'Neill again arranged a conference in Washington between eight city councilmen and
Bridwell; the Cambridge officials reaffirmed their opposition to a road through Cambridge and urged restudy of
alternate routes to find one that would do least damage.
O'Neill had also talked with Speaker of the House McCor-
mack (from Massachusetts), and Vice President Humph-

rey, who then spoke with Department of Transportation Secretary Alan Boyd.[10] These contacts seemed to influence subsequent action.

Also in June 1967, two UPA planners representing Cambridge obtained appointments through Senator Kennedy's office with both Bridwell and DOT Secretary Boyd. They presented the two federal officials with a detailed critique of the Lochner study, which they claimed was beset with inconsistencies.

Late that summer Bridwell made an unprecedented move; he sent word to the Cambridge City Council that he would like to visit Cambridge in order to discuss the Belt situation with them. He arrived on September 13. After seeing both the Brookline-Elm and Portland-Albany areas, Bridwell admitted that he believed some of the information he had been given by the DPW on the Portland-Albany alternative was incorrect. He ordered a restudy of the entire Inner Belt issue, final details to be negotiated among city, state and federal agencies. Local politicians and residents began congratulating themselves that they had finally had an effect.

Meanwhile, in September 1967, the DPW issued a Relocation Study of the Brookline-Elm route, after interviewing one member of nearly every household on the proposed route. In the preface, the DPW describes the report as "perhaps the most important weapon" in approaching the problem of relocation.

The DPW survey is highly misleading in many ways. It attempts to give the impression, backed by no relevant data, that the Brookline-Elm area is highly run down and contains largely a transient population. It grossly overstates the number of students. It claims to represent

an exhaustive effort to obtain every bit of information possible about those people in the City of Cambridge who will be forced to make extensive personal sacrifice for the benefit of the Interstate Highway program. . . .

but aside from questions on residents' attitudes toward the road, it contains nothing besides standard demographic data on age and sex; relocation preferences; and many tables on number of people per apartment, number of bedrooms per apartment and similar figures. There is no information on residents' length of stay in their houses and area, use of their neighborhood or social ties to it. The report concludes with half a dozen photographs, none of them marked to show where the road would go, and most of them, in fact, pictures of rundown residential or industrial areas several blocks away from the Brookline-Elm route.[11]

Around this time, other prominent figures came out publicly against the road. On October 15, Boston's Cardinal Cushing, who had two years earlier permitted two Cambridge priests to work in SOC, announced opposition to the road and to urban highways in general.*

On November 23, 1967, Mayor Hayes announced the formation of the Mayor's Advisory Committee on the Inner Belt, for the purpose of negotiating the new federally ordered restudy. Some of the committee's members had signed the May 3 public advertisement opposing the Brookline-Elm route. All of them were among the most eminent faculty members of Harvard and MIT. In addition to Lewis Mumford, Daniel Moynihan, William Nash and Kevin Lynch, the committee included Louis Lyons, former curator of Nieman Fellows, Harvard; Charles Miller, Head of the Department of Civil Engineering, MIT; Talcott Parsons, professor of sociology at Harvard and president of the American Academy of Arts and Sciences; deans of several schools at Harvard and MIT; the chief of MIT's psychiatric services. To prepare materials for the advisory committee, the mayor designated a technical committee, its member-

---

* The occasion of the Cardinal's statement was a dinner honoring the 100th anniversary of the Church of St. Mary of the Annunciation, one of the two Cambridge parishes that would be affected by the Brookline-Elm route.

ship consisting of six city planning, engineering and business faculty members of Harvard, MIT and Boston College; a senior staff member of a local consulting firm; and two directors of UPA.

The advisory committee worked out a two-pronged proposal: it urged the Bureau of Public Roads to finance yet another study to determine whether the Belt and radials system is the most efficient solution to greater Boston traffic problems, and, to investigate the possibilities of "joint development" of highway and housing resources, in the manner that the city of Baltimore had recently undertaken to solve transportation and housing problems in a "joint systems approach." Representatives of Cambridge, Somerville, Boston and Brookline began meeting with the DPW to negotiate final terms of this study.

In early 1968, a delegation of supporters of the expressway system, led by the Greater Boston Chamber of Commerce and other business, civic and labor leaders, met with Bridwell, urging him to see to the quick completion of the road plan.

The Growth of Community Opposition to Urban Highways

The first turning point for the anti-highway forces was Bridwell's visit to Cambridge in September 1967. A second turning point occurred shortly after Volpe's departure to Washington in late 1968 to head the Department of Transportation, and the sucession to the Massachusetts governor's office of Lieutenant Governor Francis Sargent. Initiated by representatives of the Cambridge city government and coordinated by UPA, a demonstration was held at the State House on January 25, 1969. Almost 2,000 citizens, calling themselves the Greater Boston Committee on the Transportation Crisis (GBCTC), mostly from Cambridge but representing eight or nine different communities in the Boston area, urged Sargent to cancel all highway plans. In response, Sargent appointed a citizens study group to review the Master Highway Plan and make recommendations. The study group included eminent faculty members from the area's universities and technical consultants.

During 1969, GBCTC (which originated in community groups organized with UPA assistance for dealing with various local problems) worked on gaining support for their stop-the-highways position from a wide range of groups: communities within and outside the core that would be affected by the highways, suburbanites not directly affected, state legislators, statewide civic groups such as Citizens for Participation Politics and Americans for Democratic Action, and professional and scientific groups concerned with the impact of technology on society and particularly with the recently raised environment and pollution issues. In late 1969, the mayors of both Somerville and Boston, aware of growing citizen opposition, and growing national disillusionment with the concept of more highways as a means of solving urban problems, added their voices to the call for a halt to highway plans pending the outcome of the governor's study group. (The *Globe,* the *Herald-Traveler* and the Chamber of Commerce promptly condemned these actions and called for rapid completion of the road plan. But continued citizen communication with the newspapers ultimately convinced both to reverse their editorial policies, and by spring 1970 they had joined the growing ranks of opponents to socially and environmentally harmful urban highways.)

In early 1970 the governor's study group turned in its preliminary report. It urged that most activity connected with completion of the Master Highway Plan be halted pending a review, to include the role of mass transit, of the Boston area's transportation needs. On February 11, 1970, Sargent announced that he was stopping all work on most of the proposed roads, including the entire Inner Belt, and instead would begin the year-long review that his study group had recommended. Sargent revealed at the end of 1971 that as a result of this review the proposed Inner Belt through Cambridge and Somerville was being dropped altogether.

RESPONSE

MIDDLE-AMERICAN POLITICAL BEHAVIOR: ALIENATION AND THE MEANING OF PROTEST

They [the protestors] can fight all they want, but they won't win.
—*young man on Brookline Street*

If the government makes up their mind the road's gonna go through Elm Street, a million people wouldn't stop 'em . . . regardless how many letters you write or anything like that.
—*56-year old man, homeowner on Elm Street*

We don't know nothing [about politics] and don't want to, except for the Belt.
—*old woman on Elm Street*

TWO KINDS OF BEHAVIOR: PROTEST AND NONPROTEST

Our 1967 survey revealed that two-thirds of the Brookline Elm residents had never participated in protest activities, other than signing a petition or two* or posting an anti-Belt sign. Although one-third went to at least one

---

* By an oversight we neglected to ask how many had signed petitions against the Belt. From the large number of petition signers, we presume that more Brookline-Elm people signed petitions than took any other protest step, but what this means is that most residents performed no protest activities throughout the several years of controversy other than signing one or two petitions.

meeting or hearing connected with the Belt issue, only about 10 percent attended protest meetings regularly. Fifteen percent wrote to officials, but only 6 percent participated in demonstrations (mainly the State House rally in October 1966). In view of the vehemence with which three-fourths of the Brookline-Elm people decried the possibility of having to move because of the road, one must wonder why such a small number took an active part in protest actions.

Like most organization-class people, highway planners apparently interpret the fact of little protest to mean that residents living on a proposed route do not mind very much the possibility of moving.* Our data indicate, by crucial contrast, that while Brookline-Elm residents were strongly opposed to moving, most were deterred from protesting by a deep sense that people like themselves are too insignificant to influence governmental decisions such as whether highways should be built or where they might be located.

In their attitudes and behavior toward the Belt, the majority of Brookline-Elm people demonstrated a political style of apathetic noninvolvement. Our interviews and field observations suggest this composite picture of the majority of Brookline-Elm people:

By the summer of 1967, typical Brookline-Elm residents knew that the proposed Belt could displace them and their neighbors, and they opposed it. They knew that alternate routes had been suggested, and thought that another location could be found for the road.

---

* The DPW study on the problems of relocation conducted during the same period as our own study (see Chapter 3, footnote 11), notes that 40 percent of the Brookline-Elm residents were unfavorable toward or opposed to the road. (The DPW attempted to interview one member of each household on the route.) "However," the report continues, "a slightly higher percentage of residents indicates indifference or 'no comment' reactions to the Inner Belt" (*Interstate Rt. 695 Relocation Study*). Our data suggest that most of this latter group were reluctant to express their unfavorable feelings about the Belt.

The average Brookline-Elm resident believed the Belt was favored by "politicians" and "the government," and its principal opponents were the residents themselves. They questioned whether "government" cares about the problems of individuals. Although they claimed to believe that local government could be more responsive to citizens than state or federal government, they simultaneously believed that individuals have little or no say over what goes on in Cambridge. They believed that neither they nor most other citizens influence government decisions in general.

While strongly opposing the Belt, the average residents were neither well informed about the protest nor active in it; they had never attended a meeting of the protest group, did not know the group's name, and were unaware of most activities the group had sponsored, aside from public meetings and the residents' trip to Washington in May 1967. They had no idea who attended protest meetings, who led them or what organizations comprised SOC. They felt that most people do not attempt to oppose unwanted government policies because these issues have already been decided by the powers that be, and nothing further can be done. They believed that ultimately the protest against the Belt would fail.

These typical residents did not participate in the protest movement against the highway. But a significant minority was active. While uncertain whether political work by people like them could be effective, they believed it necessary to try.

These two groups, those who took part in protest activities and those who did not, differed in their objective stake in their homes and neighborhood, and also in several implicit assumptions about the political system and their relationship to it.*

---

* Included in the approximately two-thirds of the Brookline-Elm people who did not participate in protest activities are the people who welcomed the possibility of the road. This is about one-fourth of the sample,

THE NONPROTESTORS

Alienation From the Political System

Alienation from politics works in two ways. Alienated people believe that the political system neither has a commitment to their point of view and life interests nor works in their behalf. They also believe that people cannot influence the political processes that affect them. In this double-edged sense the Brookline-Elm people were by and large estranged from the American political system, and in this respect they are like numerous Middle Americans.

But alienation is more than just beliefs, attitudes and feelings; it is a condition of estrangement both objective and subjective—a condition characterized by not being truly integrated into all aspects of societal life—political, work, educational, etc.

Like the poor, Middle Americans are strangers to the common organization-class experience of initiating innovations and complaints and seeing tangible results of their actions. Indeed, in virtually all institutional areas of life except home, family and friendship, Middle Americans, like the poor, are the objects of the decisions and interests of others and are seldom consulted, let alone actively involved, in establishing or running work, school, church, community and other kinds of organized activities.

These experiences lead them to develop, in the words of James Q. Wilson, a "keen sense of the difference between 'we' and 'they,'" "they" being the outside political forces who make the decisions that affect poor and Middle-Ameri-

---

those who would be glad to leave the area (see Chapter 2, p. 54). When we refer to the non participants from here on, we refer primarily to those who wished to remain in the area. Together with the active protestors, they comprised the three-quarters of the population opposed to the road.

can class people. As Wilson adds, "It is quite natural that 'they' are often regarded with suspicion."[1]

GOVERNMENT VERSUS THE "LITTLE PEOPLE"

The people who are being displaced, no one gives a God-damn for them, understand?—[not] the politicians, Harvard, MIT—[no one] except themselves.
—man in a store on Brookline Street

We're what's called the lower class of people—the kind that can be pushed around. [Who calls you that?] The politicians. We're the little people.
—woman homeowner on Brookline Street

Brookline-Elm people typically described themselves as the "little people. . . of a common class, people that aren't up in politics . . . high school education is the most [we've] got. . . . We work from one payday to the next. . . . The average wage earner, the lowest, the underdog . . . the poor people, not the degree people, an ordinary person."

Brookline-Elm people often spoke with great bitterness about "they" who plan to put the highway through their homes. Residents frequently specified "they"—the proponents of the road—as "the government," "politicians" or, sometimes, "big people."[2] When asked who favors the Belt, almost two-thirds of the residents named some variant of "the government" or "politicians" (including, more specifically, "the state of Massachusetts" and "the DPW"), 12 percent said that no one wants the road, 9 percent said MIT, and 8 percent said "drivers." The government was seen, then, as the main supporter of the unwanted highway.

"It seems the government is not for the people," says one middle-aged man, "and whenever they decide something, it takes a big war to stop them."

Giving his opinion of the protest movement, another middle-aged man praises the October 1966 march because it "let the people above us and the authorities know we're sincere, but it goes in one ear and out the other. I think the [protest] leaders are great, but you can't fight Uncle Sam, you can't fight the federal government."

A third middle-aged man, generalizing his feelings of impotence to other groups in society, apparently sees "they" as a completely unreachable monolith; when asked if he thought there would be a better chance of fighting the Inner Belt if the people in the threatened area were richer or better educated, he replied, "I don't think so. I think that once they want to go through a place, it makes no difference what kind of people [live there]."

Slightly more than half the people interviewed (51.5 percent) suggested that people do not oppose unwanted government actions because "they" decide things and opposition is useless. (Another 17.5 percent attributed political inaction to the fact that people don't like to get involved. Eight percent explained political inaction on the basis of people believing the individual doesn't count, and eight percent said that people are inactive because they do not know what action to take.)

About half of those interviewed believed that no level of government cares about the problems of individuals, such as whether they like where they live, and half the sample felt that individuals have no say at all in governmental decisions affecting them. The conviction of political powerlessness is made even clearer by residents' response to the question of whether they felt they had more or less influence on government decisions in general than most people. Ten percent, probably students and professionals, believed they have more influence than others, and another 10 percent believed themselves less influential than most people. One-third felt they have the same amount of influence as everyone else, but many of these said, "*No one* has any influence." Forty-five percent stated, "I have no influence at all."

By and large, the residents did not view the actions that had been taken against the Belt—the meetings, petitions, demonstrations—as effective. One-third of the sample said outright that these actions have failed; another third said that they didn't know what the results were (probably because the Belt issue had dragged along for so many years and at the time of the survey was still undecided). The one tenth who said that the actions had succeeded were probably referring to the continuing delay of the final Belt decision. One-fourth correctly perceived that since the Belt issue had not been resolved by 1967, a final evaluation of the results of all Belt actions was really still pending.

Eighty-eight percent of the sample predicted that the protest would ultimately lose.* Most of those believed that once "they" have made the decision to build a road, nothing can be done about it; a few gave as their reason the obverse of this, that the "little people" have no power. (The 12 percent who believed the protest would succeed cited as their reason the large number of people who have fought the Belt.)

BROOKLINE-ELM PEOPLE ARE NOT JOINERS AND LEADERS

Brookline-Elm residents' passive stance in politics was not specific to just the highway issue. In fact, passivity before civic, work and other such organizations appears to be the rule.

Middle Americans are not "joiners"; they do not often take part in any formal organization or community activity, except perhaps for membership in a union or a local church.[3] Leonard Reissman observes that "the middle class

---

* The residents' general lack of awareness of other successful protests against proposed urban renewal or highways may also suggest why they were so pessimistic about the protest's chances for success. Only one-fourth of our respondents were able to name some such successful protest, even though one protest against an urban renewal project in a nearby working-class area in Boston (North Harvard Street), which at the time of our survey appeared to have been successful, was given much publicity in the local papers.

(what we have called the organization class) generally tends to dominate the organizational activity, the intellectual life, and the leadership of the community," in contrast to the more home-centered working class.[4] Frances Fox Piven points out that low-income people are too busy with the day-to-day struggle of making a living to have much time or energy left to involve themselves in broader community activities.[5]

Very few members of our sample were involved in local political, community or formal groups of any kind. Less than half the parents of school-age children belonged to the PTA; only 10 percent of the sample were active in local political groups aside from the highway protest, and less than one-fourth belonged to other formal groups or organizations. Only about 5 percent of our sample described themselves as ever holding leadership positions in any organization.

Coping with Alienation

In situations like the Inner Belt problem, Middle Americans appear by and large to be passively resigned to their fate. Few people, however, accept misfortunes of this kind so easily. Arthur J. Vidich and Joseph Bensman suggest a number of possible ways that people handle the dilemma that arises when they need to feel a sense of control over their lives even though they are aware that they have less power than they would like. Methods for living with this contradiction include:
1. The repression of inconvenient facts
2. The falsification of memory and the substitution of goals
3. The surrender of illusions
4. Mutual reinforcement of the public ideology (e.g., ritual acceptance of the rhetoric of democratic participation and control)

5. Avoidance of public statements of disenchantment, and the exclusion of the disenchanted

6. The externalization of the self.[6]

We find that Brookline-Elm people employed all these mechanisms, sometimes in various combinations, to handle their situation. The clearest one is what Vidich and Bensman call "surrender of illusions." Assuming that nothing can be done, many residents fatalistically accepted the Belt plan as another of many injustices that "they" inflict upon the "little people." Such residents perhaps attended a hearing or two to learn if the road was really to go through their homes; maybe they even signed a petition against the road. But typically, they quickly lost hope and stayed quietly at home, waiting for the powerful makers of decisions to tell them what to do next.

Many in this group may have started out believing the rhetoric of democracy and responsive government, taught in school and heard in political speeches, and later learned from experience that it does not apply in their case (see Chapter 5). Some may have surrendered their illusions about democratic participation "before they were born," as it were; they may have been taught from early childhood the attitude expressed by a Boston working-class woman in a similar protest situation. In her words, "We were always taught it was best not to talk out or say anything."[7] Or, as some noninvolved residents of Brookline-Elm said, "I mind my own business," or "I believe in 'live and let live.'"

Some nonparticipating residents took comfort in mocking the efforts of the protestors. For example, one resident, when asked what she would do if she were a SOC leader, scornfully replied, "I certainly wouldn't go around racing to these rallies; I'd go to the politicians; you have to go the the highest." (It should be pointed out that SOC had at this time sponsored both letter-writing campaigns to and personal meetings with relevant politicians such as Volpe.)*

Others practiced forms of self-deception that Vidich and Bensman call "mutual reinforcement of the public ideology" and "avoidance of public statements of disenchantment." For example, in some contexts residents insist that this is the best country in the world, with the best government, the most freedom, and with a political system that is responsive to the wishes of its citizens—despite their contradictory experience in the Inner Belt controversy. They felt bad about this blow to their personal lives, but declared faith in the system which dealt them that blow. This is a complex strategy which we discuss in detail in Chapter 6, in the sections on "Identification with Authority" and "The Role of the Local Protest Leader."

Another form of self-deception in the face of defeat is attempting to avoid the whole issue even while it lives— avoiding the activists because meetings, rallies and parades threaten to arouse the pain of recognizing one's ineffectiveness and its conflict with beliefs about participation in the democratic system.† This strategy involves "repression of inconvenient facts." Concentrating on work, participating in other organized activities, watching television, or whatever (Vidich and Bensman call this "externalization of the

---

* The strategy of conceiving of the protestors themselves as stupid or wrong is not unique to the Cambridge Inner Belt situation. The Boston woman quoted above said of her neighbors, who were battling attempts to "urban renew" their neighborhood into a luxury high-rise complex, "I was too busy to bother with any of that stuff. I'd stand there and laugh at them" (Frances F. Barker, David Greenwald, and Robert Sherman, with Nancy T. Whit, "The North Harvard Street Protest Against a luxury High-Rise Urban Renewal Plan," in Gordon Fellman [ed.], *Implications for Planning Policy of Neighborhood Resistance to Urban Renewal and Highway Proposals* [Springfield, Va., Department of Housing and Urban Development 1970] p. 248).

† At least one respondent broke into tears and wanted to cut the interview short, so painful was it to be reminded of the apparently unavoidable prospect of having to lose her home.

self" and "substitution of goals") can aid this process of repression. Such strategies provide explanations for the large numbers of people who knew few specific details about the protest movement.

These and other kinds of self-deception may be necessary for an individual's self-respect, and may even be successful in seeming to handle the inconsistency of belief and behavior; but they also deflect energy and attention from the issue at hand.

THE PARTICIPANTS: DYNAMICS OF PROTEST

Residents with Most at Stake

Approximately one-third of the Brookline-Elm residents reported some involvement with the protest. Most of these participants, of course, did nothing more than attend one or two meetings, put an anti-Belt sign on their homes or apartments, write a letter or two, or sign a petition over a ten-year period. Perhaps 5 to 10 percent of the residents, judging by attendance at SOC meetings and at the demonstration, were true activists.

Typically participants were better informed about the Belt issue than the nonactivists, had lived longer in the area, owned their own home, knew a number of neighbors fairly well, had friends in the area, and invested much time and money in home repairs and improvements.

The distinction between homeowner and tenant was particularly striking, with homeowners both better informed and more active. *Every* homeowner interviewed knew about the protest meetings, and over half the homeowners had taken part in at least one protest action, compared to less than 30 percent of the tenants. Three observa-

tions may explain why homeowners in the Brookline-Elm
area tended to take a stronger part in the Inner Belt protest:

1. In American society at large, ownership of a home
   means respectability and a valued status; Brookline-
   Elm homeowners may have attempted to implement
   the expectations accompanying this status by acting
   in civically knowledgeable and responsible ways, such
   as showing an interest in the Belt controversy.

2. Homeowners have increased experience in and contact with local government by virtue of their status as
   property owners. They are, therefore, less likely to be
   afraid to "get involved."

3. In view of the emotional and financial stake in the
   home, particularly for Middle Americans, homeowners have the most to lose, and may have participated
   in desperation even though they doubt the efficacy of
   their actions.

Protest Expresses Belief in the System

I thought [the October 1966 march] was ideal. Any protest
is ideal if it does something for [the movement]. The people
are little, but you make a battle. You have a right to make a
scene. You're homeowners, taxpayers.
   —*elderly woman homeowner active with the protest*

Objectively, the neighborhood protestors seemed to be
those with more stake in remaining where they are, Middle
Americans with slightly more resources and perhaps more
experience in political affairs than the majority of their
otherwise very similar neighbors. Field observations suggest that there is an ideological difference as well. In contrast to the majority of Brookline-Elm people, who were inactive due in large part, we concluded, to their feelings of
powerlessness and political alienation, those residents active in the protest were much more likely to refer to the

American democratic ideals of the rights of the governed and the worth of individuals.

"We don't want it here, but I wouldn't want to say put it where someone else lives," says one middle-aged woman.

Another woman objects to the Brookline-Elm route "because I don't want to lose my home. But if it wasn't even me—if it was somebody else—I'd be thinking of all those people [who would be displaced]. I sympathize with everybody."

A young man who has lived in the area only six years, who wants to leave it, and knows very little about the protest, says of other Brookline-Elm residents, "Most are elderly people; their life savings are in their home. It's wrong to take their homes for the road."

Residents sometimes went so far as to compare their predicament with that happens under "communism," what happens "in Russia"—where according to the popular image, the government is all-powerful and the people have no rights.

An old man, a tenant who has never participated, despairs, "I don't know what I'm going to do. I don't see that any kind of protest will do any good. . . . They say this is a free country, but what is it when [this] happens?"

A 45-year-old woman who attended the October 1966 rally complains, "The only thing heartbreaking at the State House was to find Governor Volpe not there. . . . To march up to those iron gates and have them closed in your face—it felt as if you were in Russia."

But the American democratic tratition encouraged and legitimated the protestors.

"This is where you've lived all your life. We have the pursuit of happiness," complains a 35-year-old homeowner active with the movement. "Why should the government put us out of our homes?"

References to the American democratic ideal were frequently made at SOC meetings.

In one speech, a leader announces: "I couldn't believe it was happening in my America. . . . These planners and engineers are for the birds. . . . they don't care about the people who are paying their salaries."

On another occasion, at the SOC meeting just after Federal Highway Administrator Bridwell had come to Cambridge, and held a closed session with Cambridge city officials and representatives of Harvard and MIT on the Belt problem, many residents in the SOC audience criticized the mayor and city councillors to their faces for not insisting on an open session, for not at least inviting neighborhood representatives to the meeting with Bridwell. One woman scolded the mayor angrily, "Why were MIT and Harvard invited? *We're* the ones that live here!"

American democratic traditions, then, played an important role in encouraging and justifying the activists, in the face of apathy and cynicism from their neighbors, and the formidability of their opponent—"the government." But affirmation of the American system, expressed through participation in the protest, played another, perhaps unconscious role for the protestors, as well. We noted that the majority of Brookline-Elm residents, feeling powerless, coped through a variety of avoidance strategies. Many of the activists also shared doubts regarding their power to stop the Brookline-Elm route, considering the nature of the road's supporters.

A 45-year-old homeowner active in SOC, telling who she thinks has the most say over whether the Belt goes through, expresses continual ambivalence: "The people with the money have the most say, in my estimation. But I hope it's also true that *we* have." [If you were the leader of SOC, what would you tell the local people to do?] "I'd tell them to get in contact with these individuals—rich people and the DPW—and play to their sympathy. How would they like it if the bulldozer were coming through *their* homes? But they don't have to worry about that. It'll never happen to *them!"*

Talking about a priest active in SOC, another woman says, "I think he's doing the right thing, but I don't know if it will do any good. They made up their minds. They're not going to take MIT, that's for sure."

Among the Brookline-Elm residents, both participants and nonparticipants in the Belt protest had to reconcile their lack of desire to move with their belief that people like themselves had no power. Most of the nonparticipants simply accepted their feelings of powerlessness and the defeat of their wishes to remain in their homes and neighborhoods. But some residents, notably the active participants, simultaneously practiced a form of self-assurance that Vidich and Bensman call "mutual reinforcement of the public ideology."

By claiming to believe in democratic procedures, as expressed through their participation in the protest, these citizens affirmed the public ideology. Although something may have gone wrong in the Brookline-Elm case, the stability of the society in general was not questioned. The stability of one's own life may be threatened, but the surrounding world is secure. And since one needs to continue living in the world, it is better not to question too much.

Protest Relieves Anxiety

For your own sanity you gotta fight. Gotta try to do as much as possible for your own peace of mind.
                    —*a middle-aged woman homeowner*

The majority of passive road opponents and even some SOC activists doubted the effectiveness of local protest. And yet a small band of opponents continued to support

SOC, pass around petitions, write letters and attend protest meetings, week after week. In the light of such widespread doubt of their political efficacy, we must search for deeper reasons that the activists continued to participate.

Two possible consequences follow when people attempt to handle an unpleasant situation instead of avoiding action altogether. They may behave so as to relieve their anxiety without affecting the objective situation; or they may work to change the objective situation responsible for their anxiety. These two alternatives are not mutually exclusive. Working effectively to change reality may also reduce anxiety, and the actual or possible results may be unclear during much of the course of any political action.*

We saw that the people who were most aware of protest activities and most likely to participate were those with the greatest economic and social stake in their home and neighborhood, those most upset about moving. For many residents active in SOC, joining protest activities may have been a way of relieving anxiety and maintaining self-respect in the face of a painful situation, particularly if they were doubtful of the effectiveness of any political action.

> Giving her opinion of the October 1966 rally, one homeowner active with SOC said, "I don't know if it'll do any good. You can't much lick'em, but you can fight. After they throw us out, we can say at least we fought, we did our best."

We do not mean to imply that SOC had no objective political effect. The organization-class volunteer planners

---

* Robert Merton distinguishes between manifest functions of an activity—the publicly recognized, intended consequences—and latent functions, which are consequences not deliberately intended or recognized by the actor. Political effect is a manifest function of SOC activities (actual effectiveness is another matter): anxiety reduction, we suggest below, is a latent function of that same activity (see Robert Merton, *Social Theory and Social Structure* rev. ed., [Glencoe, Ill.: The Free Press, 1957], Chapter 1, especially p. 51).

and other sympathizers needed the support and encouragement of SOC just as much as SOC needed them. Correctly representing Brookline-Elm residents' wishes and interests, UPA and its organization-class allies developed the counterplans and political strategies, and met with officials in the name of the Brookline-Elm people.

The point we wish to make here is that, for the participants in SOC, a major function of much of their activity—particularly since they so strongly doubt their own effectiveness—was to give participating residents the reassuring *feeling* that they were doing something about the threat of the road.

Protest Meetings as Expressive Ritual

Throughout the several years of its existence, the main activity of SOC was its weekly or biweekly meetings. These meetings tended to be remarkably similar to each other. Someone would suggest that people write letters to newspapers, federal representatives, officials at the Department of Transportation, etc. Someone else would urge that the President of the United States somehow be contacted, for once the case is put before him, surely he will understand.

From the floor of those meetings came varied testimony: someone was born in the home he or she now lives in and would have to be dragged out by the DPW before he or she would move; the only way to defeat the Belt is by more people coming to these meetings; more letters should be written to newspapers or congressmen; more radio talk shows should be called. Such remarks were always followed by enthusiastic applause and spontaneous comments of approval from members of the audience, although a few disgruntled people were occasionally heard to mumble, "If I don't find out anything tonight [i.e., whether or not the Belt is definitely going through] I'm not coming back."

At every meeting, also, neighborhood people angrily damned the various "villains" who wanted to "force the highway down our throats" (namely Volpe, DPW officials and MIT) and enthusiastically praised the small band of elected officials who in their eyes worked ceaselessly to oppose the Belt (one or two of them were regularly present at these meetings). Near election time, meetings elicited emotional speeches from a long string of candidates for various city and state offices, usually about the Belt being "all politics" and about the Brookline-Elm people being "sold down the river" by certain politicians and institutions (who always remained nameless).

The SOC people rarely failed to question why Memorial Drive was not studied or why the road could not go down the old railroad tracks. Such questions were inevitably asked with marked indignation, often accompanied by anger, suggesting a recital of indignities, the naming of which elicited from reciter and audience a shared sense of outrage, a shared definition of being trod upon and ignored.

Organization-class advisers working with the group sometimes answered such queries in statements of clear political feasibility or infeasibility, but political reality is exactly what seemed to offend the questioner. That MIT objects to a proposed route and has the power to fight it was not an acceptable answer because it reflects that basic in-justice: neglect of the interests of the Brookline-Elm popu-lation by those who have power. The questioners wanted an answer acceptable to their definition of justice and injustice. Excluded from the planning process, they could only repeat in a thousand varied ways the cry of the citizen defined by the powerful as insignificant: "You *don't have to* do this to me!"

Most meetings also featured at least one damning or questioning remark about MIT's or Harvard's role in the Belt proceedings. But no effort surfaced for investigating the activities of the universities, or, with rare exceptions, trying to affect them.

The politicians were applauded for their appearances—which happened to coincide with preelection seasons—and were castigated for ignoring the "people" the rest of the year. The city planner of Cambridge, who supported the Brookline-Elm route, was condemned; and a handful of city and state politicians, and, of course, federal Representative Thomas O'Neill, were praised for their constant and energetic opposition to the Belt and their frequent appearances at SOC meetings.

At some meetings there was even a call or two for violent, confrontative action against the authorities; for example:

> At one meeting an SOC neighborhood leader tells the audience, "A year ago the Department of Housing and Urban Development threatened to hold up funds for housing in Washington, D.C., until a highway was built. It was stopped when a black man held up a box of matches and said, 'If you build the highway, we'll burn down Washington!'"
> At this, a woman in the SOC audience mutters to her neighbors, "That's what *we* should do—burn!"

> At another SOC meeting, a young academic tells the group how a recent sit-in by people in Boston's South End section got the Boston renewal agency to halt demolition of houses in the South End. People in the audience are immediately interested. One woman yells out, "Let's have a sit-in!" Another whispers to her neighbor, "They did it; why in hell can't *we*?"

But as in almost every other case, these apparent endorsements of radical action never got beyond the verbal stage.

To the sociologist, there is a ritual character to these assemblies of SOC. The meetings seemed far more useful as a means to release anger and anxiety than as a staging ground for viable political activity. (Sociologists distinguish between *expressive* activity—the purpose of which is to release emotion—and *instrumental* activity—the purpose of which is to have a particular effect on the environment.) Political intentions remained the real, overt purpose of SOC, but the meetings also provided an outlet for anger and anxiety over impending forced relocation from a congenial home and neighborhood. As we have said earlier, many residents responded by turning inward, with a feeling of hopelessness and helplessness. For others, though, taking part in political activity—periodic protest meetings and rallies—brought people of the same predicament together to share their fears and frustrations and gave them the sense that they were doing something constructive about them.

In effect, the near-litany quality of these repeated questions and suggestions at SOC meetings was a duplication of the experience of writing letters, petitioning, picketing and the like. The offended citizens questioned and implored the authority and got little more than a polite "thank you, we'll take it into consideration." In part because their pleas were unheeded by planning and government officials, however good their intentions, they were unable to extend their understanding or participation beyond the elementary questioning stage. The ritualistic incantation of the same questions, meeting after meeting, was a shared reminder of neglect, confusion, bewilderment and impotent frustration.*

BARS TO EFFECTIVE PROTEST

Once a group of people sets a political goal—such as opposing the location of a proposed highway—they must

---

* It should also be noted that activities such as letter-writing, in giving people the feeling that they are accomplishing something, help keep the group together, so that when other actions, such as demonstrations, are planned, there will be a hard core of residents to do the backstage work and give information to their neighbors.

decide whom in the political structure to reach and how best to get their point across. We suggest that the local protest was relatively confused, small scale and ineffective for two reasons. First, most Brookline-Elm people did not know how to act politically. They had no idea whom to reach on an issue like the Inner Belt fight, no idea where to begin. Second, many residents shared the underlying awareness that they could win a political struggle only if they become a match for powerful authorities. But for a variety of reasons, they were unable to follow this point to its logical conclusion in their actions. In the two following chapters, we investigate in depth the political perceptions of the Brookline-Elm people, and their relations with authority.

5

POLITICAL MISPERCEPTIONS AND REALITIES

HOW THE NEIGHBORHOOD PROTESTORS DEFINE AND RELATE TO POWER

You elect these people, and they're supposed to represent
us, so if you have anything you want done, present it to these
people. The only way you can do it is through your
Senator or congressman.
—middle-aged woman not active with SOC

[What have the local protest leaders done?]
They're appealing to the government in Washington and
having private meetings on the Inner Belt. Our congressman
has asked [Federal Highway Administrator] Whitton, Hubert
Humphrey and President Johnson to come to Cambridge
to see the route.
—middle-aged homeowner active with the protest

[What would you do if you were a protest leader?]
I'd go right to Washington. [Where? To whom?] I forget
the name—I think Bob [Senator Robert F.] Kennedy has
something to do with it. [What would you tell your neighbors
to do?] I'd tell them to write letters to Washington.
—young housewife occasionally active with SOC

The Brookline-Elm protest was so weak because most
neighborhood residents did not know how to act politically. They had no idea whom they should reach, no idea

where they might begin. The confusion and bewilderment of most residents about political aspects of the highway issue were reflected in their answers to a question asking for their knowledge of stands taken by 27 relevant individuals and institutions. (Do they know if X supports the Belt, opposes it or has no stand?) Most often recognized were those middle-level individuals and institutions who had been identified regularly—by local newspapers, at protest meetings and in neighborhood folklore—either as villains trying to ram the road down Brookline and Elm Streets, or as staunch opponents of the Belt. Best-known Belt proponents included MIT (position identified correctly by 54 percent of the respondents),* Governor Volpe (48.5 percent) and the Department of Public Works (35 percent). The best-known opponent was the Cambridge City Council (position correctly identified by 44 percent); about one-third knew the opposition of U.S. Congressman O'Neill, Neighbors United, Save Our Cities and Msgr. McDevitt of Blessed Sacrament Church. We call these people and organizations "middle-level" because they were important mainly at the state or city level. Respondents were less able to identify the stands of less prominent local organizations, and most did not recognize the protest's nonclerical leaders (who were known only by the small group of people very active in the fight). The sample was least knowledgeable on stands of remote federal agencies (such as the Department of Transportation) and federal officials (such as Alan Boyd, then Secretary of Transportation).

More telling than whose stands they *did* know is the fact that in 25 out of the 27 cases more than half the respondents had no idea what the stand was. In some instances this lack of knowledge may be attributed to changing or ambiguous

---

* Since MIT opposes all routes but Brookline-Elm, it is logically seen by many residents as supporting the Brookline-Elm route, in deed if not in word; we therefore rated both answers, "supported" and "opposed," as correct in this one case.

positions on the issue, but in most cases it is probably a reflection of the residents' general confusion as to how the political system functions. This confusion takes several forms.

"If Only They Knew. . ."—the Personalization of Politics

Personalization means either seeing political officials as "people like you and me," whose sympathy can be played to; or else seeing particular individuals currently in office as corrupt, so that the solution becomes to "throw the rascals out." Many Brookline-Elm people personalized the political process in both these directions. For example, they often expressed a close emotional or personal identification with highly placed political figures and frequently repeated the hope that some well-known figure (such as President Johnson or Senator Kennedy) would swoop down to save the people once he knew of their plight. "The system" was identified as a hierarchy of specific individuals, and making one's feelings known to them was considered the key to success.

> A 40-year-old man tells the interviewer that the people can do something about the road "if they can impress the people in Washington . . . because as far as I know, President Johnson is in favor of the people. . . . Congressman O'Neill has been trying to appeal to the President [but] it's hard, because he's out of the country now." [Johnson was touring Asia at the time.]

> On a very cold night, people who attended a SOC meeting were urged to write to officials all the way up to the President, telling how residents sat in an unheated building to attend the protest meeting.

> A scrapbook was prepared detailing grievances and editorial support for the protestors. The original was sent to President Johnson, with copies to federal highway officials. On more than one occasion, people at SOC meetings expressed the hope and

conviction that the President would take action to help them once he read the scrapbook.

By personalizing the political process, Brookline-Elm people hoped to move an official. In the words of a middle-aged woman:

> Often times I think if I could get these people who are trying to put the road through, bring them down here, show them my house, have a heart-to-heart talk with them, show them what they're breaking up. . . .

If only the officials knew what they were doing to us, how we feel about having to move, the residents often implied, then they would surely change their decision.

On the other side, there was the tendency to see politicians as corrupt individuals—villains who care nothing about the "little people" of Brookline-Elm. This personalization apparently played a role in the state election of November 1966. The six precincts through which the Brookline-Elm route would go all voted against both Governor Volpe and his running-mate for lieutenant-governor, Francis Sargent, at a rate two or three times as high as in the precincts immediately adjacent.*

The ironic fact is that the Brookline-Elm people continued to appeal to Volpe *et al.* in the same way that they called upon "good politicians" like the President. Apparently, the most important characteristic for being appealed to on the Belt fight was not a person's stand, but his supposed power to stop the road, if only the protestors could convince him how passionately they did not want to move.

---

* See Records of the Cambridge Board of Elections, November 1966. Both Volpe and Sargent, who also served as DPW commissioner, were at the time of the study frequently identified, in neighborhood talk and in the newspapers, as favoring the road.

Defusing Anger

Protestors rarely discussed *forcing* powerful officials
to heed their wishes. Letter writing was the most commonly
recommended method for letting officials know how the
people felt.

At the February 20, 1966, hearing, after professionals from
a traffic engineering firm and other professionals from UPA
differed over the optimum solution to the Belt problem, in
terms most of the audience surely did not follow, after citizens
complained loudly and angrily about the prospect of forced dislocation, after MIT let loose with its elephantine assault on
alternative locations for the Belt, after industrialists and union-
ists had their say on both sides of the issue, three city councillors offered the only form of action discussed during the
entire proceedings: writing letters to federal representatives
and senators.

Four months later, a local priest at a rally drawing a crowd
of 500 to 600 urged people not to panic and sell their homes,
for, he says, the amounts you would receive would hardly be
downpayments on the homes you would be forced to buy.
Write to your representatives and senators, he says. "If they
continue to forget you, you will remember them when they
need you." This is your fight, he tells them, and unless you
fight, you will be walked over and trampled into the dust. Those
who make decisions about highways are not interested in the
fact that many of you will not be able to buy homes and will
have to pay exorbitant rents, and those authorities do not care
about the mental illness that happens as a result of being driven
forth, or about heartaches. Write and pray and do not panic,
are his final words of advice.

A state representative in the audience follows that speech immediately in telling people to write Washington. Then a priest
from another church speaks. He says that the two big parishes
threatened by the Belt have saved the city millions in education [by private financing of their own schools] and that it is
time the city did something for these churches. He wonders
why Memorial Drive has never been mentioned as a serious
possibility for the road and then says that people have got to
make it so hot for the politicians that they will listen. So, he

concludes, write city, state and federal representatives, and don't stop until a favorable decision is announced. Then a federal representative also urges that people write Washington.

And so it goes. Few meetings end without someone running up the letter-writing flag.

Lincoln Steffens wrote: "Liberty to talk, to meet, to write, is a safety valve for feelings which, unexpressed, might cause action."[1] Logically, meeting and talking can be prerequisites to action; but in the case of SOC, no action followed. Letters and meetings can of themselves be action, when the protestors' number is high enough that the political careers of the authorities, or civil order, is threatened by the protest. But authorities need not take seriously a small minority that can convey no threat of follow-up action to its letters or rallies.*

There are three political errors in this widespread counsel to write letters (in addition to a fourth, which is the small likelihood that many listeners actually write): 1) an error of personalization—the political decision-making process is mistakenly reduced to a few officials being assumed in total control of the situation; 2) an error of form—on such matters, letters are unlikely to be really significant political events; and 3) an error we might call "emotional defusing"—the anger often expressed in the letters could be more effectively used in more complex and direct political activity, like neighborhood organizing, forming political alliances with people in other areas and social classes, developing realistic counterplans and so forth. (We recognize, of course, that the kinds of education and work experiences common to Brookline-Elm people do not familiarize them

---

* Protest letters ought not to be confused with letters written to inform legislators of constituents' opinions on a matter. In an area where the legislator genuinely wants guidance, or where his or her behavior might affect popularity among constituents, such letters can be useful indeed. Rather, we address our inquiry here to the point of writing letters to officials urging them to reconsider an action they are contemplating.

with the skills essential to such planning and organizing or
accustom them to dealing as political equals with organization-class people. But those skills are surely there potentially and can be brought to effective levels by imaginative,
dedicated organizers such as Cesar Chavez, for example.)

Mislocated Enemy

There are alternate routes—Memorial Drive, Albany
Street—but they figure they're going to step on the little guy.
MIT is against the Albany Street route. It's just a kick in the
teeth these people around·here don't need.
                                                —young man working on Brookline Street

Just as personalization can mean trying through emotional appeal to reach specific "helpers" in the political
hierarchy rather than organizing to pressure political structures and processes, so can it mean trying to define specific
enemies and venting impotent anger upon them.

Since MIT is highly visible in the neighborhood, locally
it was the best-known institution involved in the highway
issue. Although other institutions (DPW, BPR, the governor and others) were more directly responsible for the road
decision, MIT was an old, familiar neighbor and adversary.
Its involvement allowed its concrete, immediate representation as the enemy.

The fact that MIT was consistently named by so many
neighborhood people as the main force responsible for their
anticipated displacement reinforces two previous observations. First, most Brookline-Elm people are unsure, as we
have seen, of the political aspects of highway construction;
they probably assume that a highway "must" go through
somewhere, and the only point of debate is where it should
be located. Second, MIT is seen by many working-class
Cambridge residents as the exemplification of "they" who

have the power to influence decisions that affect the lives of "little people" like themselves. (It is interesting to note that working-class residents commonly refer to the university as "Technology," in contrast to the academicians, who call it "MIT" or "the Institute.") In general, Cambridge's Middle-American population has a deep and pervasive feeling of hostility toward the two universities, based on general class antagonisms (Harvard and MIT are, after all, major bastions of rich-and-powerful class and organization-class elitism), on the schools' continual expansion into the community, and on the increasing entrance of students into low-rent neighborhoods. This latter factor drives up rents and—in the eyes of the residents—lowers moral values and the desirability of their neighborhoods. Two excerpts from our field notes strikingly depict this attitude toward the universities:

> At the first public meeting on the Belt, in October 1965, a man from the audience delivers a loud passionate statement: "Yah, you wanta know what I think, I think MIT owns this city. . . ." Someone else cries out, "It owns us all, body and soul!" And a third adds, "MIT *and* Harvard!"

> A 58-year-old woman homeowner near Brookline Street, says, "We grew up in Cambridge. As children we were told about Harvard coming this way—first they said it would only go up to [a street about half a mile from Harvard Square], then only up to [another street a little beyond that], then they wanted to go up to Central Square [almost a mile from Harvard Square]—and MIT coming the other way, squeezing us out in the middle." She mentions one street on which she knew all the residents; they all had to move out later because Harvard bought up the property.

Some observers might argue that these feelings toward the two universities are overstated or unfounded.* But the

---

* Yet even a former Cambridge city manager speaks of the two universities in a similar tone. When asked why the railroad and Memorial

opposition of social-class interests is real. And it is important to recognize that these feelings of bitter hostility combined with helplessness before the apparent omnipotence of two prominent local institutions were duplicated in most Brookline-Elm residents' attitudes toward and experiences with governmental forces in favor of the Inner Belt.

ADVOCATE PLANNERS AS MIDDLEMEN

The little people, the city, and the universities have gotten together to fight a common problem. Thank God these people are pushing for us. We little people have gone as far as we can. These people have national prestige and prominence. Together with the city administration . . . we'll be ready to make a reasonable presentation to [Federal Highway Administrator] Bridwell, and hopefully it will be accepted.
—SOC leader, a priest

The group of volunteer planners which started out as the Cambridge Committee on the Inner Belt and later became Urban Planning Aid is a representative case of a recent political innovation: advocacy planning. In a number of cities, including Boston, New York, San Francisco, Oakland and New Orleans, professionals in planning, architecture, engineering, systems analysis, law, social sciences and related fields have combined to form nonprofit firms providing free planning services for urban low-income- and low-middle-income groups. Modeled after free medical clinics and legal aid offices, these advocate planning firms are based on the principle that all citizens are entitled to the

---

Drive routes were scrapped, he replied, "Have you ever heard of MIT? . . . MIT and Harvard decide what they want to do and we [the city] cooperate with them. People think we just say yes to them, but we 'cooperate' with them" [i.e., the city just says yes to them] (cf. Chapter 3, discussion of the roles of the two universities in the Inner Belt history).

professional services they need whether or not they can afford to pay for them at standard market rates. Typically, representatives of one or more neighborhood groups, usually formed in response to a specific planning issue, approach the advocate planners to request help. Planning and political issues inevitably intertwine, and the advocate planners serve their clients in a variety of ways toward the goal defined by the client (e.g., to increase the number of low-rent housing units in a renewal project; to relocate a planned elementary school and make it a "community school" with facilities available for community-wide use evenings and weekends; to oppose the location of a proposed highway). Advocate planners provide counterplanning services (opposition to officially designated plans and proposal of alternatives), as well as initiating plans in response to a community's request.[2]

Although most Brookline-Elm residents believed the highway could be put someplace else, they were in no position to contend with the DPW highway planners on their own terms to push for an alternate route. The world of bureaucracy, technical studies and professional certification is highly intimidating to a factory worker or housewife who may not even have graduated from high school; and, in the eyes of the general public, the cries of a few "uneducated" men and women who do not want to move are hardly equal to the carefully diagrammed and calculated highway plan of a state agency.

Middle American residents of Brookline-Elm display a complex reaction toward college-educated people with whom they must deal. Many stand in awe and envy of them, and some (but not all) consider it extremely important that their own children go to college. On the other hand, many Brookline-Elm residents resent the fact that many college-educated people tend to consider themselves superior to people with less formal education. A 40-year-old woman commented:

Just because you don't have a college degree doesn't mean that you don't have the knowledge. A lot of the people in this area are poor but intelligent. This is what they always do— this is the attitude of the leader—[i.e., the higher status person. They think] that if the people don't have college degrees, they won't know. A lot of people, no matter how poor they are, they have their pride.

In particular, residents frequently referred to their discomfort and inability to communicate with the many professionals who habitually talk at a highly abstract and technical level.

An older woman homeowner active with SOC says about two planning professionals who debated the Belt on a TV show, "I don't make anything out of when I listen to these people. . . . Half the time they're talking over everybody's head anyway. . . . They don't have any feeling."

A middle-aged homeowner talks approvingly of one volunteer professional who regularly reports to SOC meetings on the latest details of restudy negotiations (she contrasts him favorably with other professionals she has had contact with): "He is down to our level of understanding. . . . Our group of people that are not the degree people that he'd ordinarily be talking to. . . . We're people in just an average scale of living and education, and he talks to us like an average person."

At the same time as they respect it, residents tend to view higher education with suspicion and distrust, based partly on their observation that people who go to college are apparently taught to divorce mind from feelings, living experience from book knowledge.*

"They only have knowledge from books," an older man says. "The people coming out of college today aren't well-

---

* Cf. *Newsweek*'s observation that "Middle America" responds favorably to political candidates who express emotionality, "perhaps because they sense that their government has been run recently by soulless technocrats spouting bureaucratic jargon. . ." ("The Troubled American," p. 56).

rounded. That's what the Belt route is—they're just looking at the road, not at what's around it."

A young housewife says there are two kinds of education, and her husband agrees—"Yeah, the way of life and the way of the school."

An older woman active with the movement, who did not finish high school, expresses sharp criticism of higher education. "That's what education does," she says, "they teach you to talk low, not to express your feelings. I think that's oppressive. If you feel a certain way, you should be able to express it. How do they teach you that?" she suddenly asks the interviewer. "Do they tell you that if you get emotional, you can't think clearly?" She tells the graduate student interviewer that she (the student) is getting a broad outlook on life by talking to people here (on Brookline and Elm Streets). "You're learning a lot more than most of them that just stay on campus," the woman comments.

These remarks suggest an important dimension of the communication distance between working-class and "higher" class college-educated people. In a political conflict such as the Inner Belt case, independent organization-class professionals like the planners of UPA, who accept the same assumptions about competence, have similar credentials, and "speak the same language" as government officials and planners, are less likely to be cowed and intimidated by government officials than Middle-American and poor citizens. They also have the technical, legal and procedural skills necessary to gain support and legitimacy for their cause in the eyes of both the government and other organization-class observers and institutions. To put it another way, advocate planners are participants in an organization-class style which conveys in the most tacit way possible that if professionals like them support a movement, then some heed *must* be paid to it even if it is highly distasteful. However rational our bureaucratic society, none of us fails to see as quickly as possible *who* supports a given action; we are not simply content to consider the proposal on its objective merits alone; we take comfort in the usually damned *ad hominem* practice of identifying causes with their sponsors. And none of us is objective enough to separate attention from the "who" of political protest and decision-making and concentrate exclusively on the "what."

The fact that the advocate planners of UPA played such a large role in the Inner Belt fight reveals the existence of a space usually unrecognized in the conventionally conceived planning process—a space which they proceeded to fill partially. That was the need for people who have some idea of what happens on both sides of the planning process, and who are able to transmit the procedures and assumptions of the planners to the subjects of their plans and vice versa. In other words, such political brokers or middlemen would help less politically sophisticated citizens understand that planners are moved not by pleas, but by counterplans backed by power, and would help the public authorities understand the life styles and goals of the people whose lives they intend to affect. As we will see, however, the advocates of UPA fell short of playing the complete role.

ADVOCATE PLANNERS AS
POLITICAL TACTICIANS

The advocate planners originally proposed a technically feasible counterplan—an alternative location for the Cambridge arc of the Inner Belt. They soon realized, however, that reason alone was not enough to change the Belt design. Gradually understanding that government decision-makers respond to pressures from institutions behind-the-scenes, the advocates sought to build a power base to counteract the forces favorable to the Brookline-Elm location. To lend strength to their counterplan, they gained 1) the unanimous support of the Cambridge City Council, 2) the prestige of the 528 MIT and Harvard faculty members who signed an anti-Belt advertisement and of the mayor's Advisory Committee, which was made up of distinguished academics, 3) endorsement by respectable local civic groups such as the Cambridge Civic Association and the League of Women Voters, 4) press conferences publicized in the newspapers and on TV, 5) direct confrontation with officials like Volpe and Sargent, 6) publicized meetings with Brooke, Kennedy and O'Neill, and institutions like the DPW, and 7) the direct backup or implied support of SOC, the Brookline-Elm residents in general, and eventually a much wider anti-highway constituency throughout the Greater Boston area. All these political techniques and supporters indicated the growth of a sizeable public whose wishes could not easily be ignored by those in charge of highway planning.

In other words, the advocate planners moved from a purely technical definition of the problem to a political one. By implication, their evolving politics took into consideration the political nature of institutions.

Power to the Big Institutions

In the American political system, institutions or groups already organized for some specific purpose have a much better chance of affecting events than have unorganized people who suddenly find themselves sharing a common interest. Other institutions and individuals—the DPW, the governor (by virtue of his office), MIT, the Boston Chamber of Commerce, the construction industry, and the automobile and gasoline industries—all are not only already organized, with histories of pushing their interests wherever they are concerned; they are also, by virtue of these considerations, connected politically.*

---

* Throughout this analysis we assume that agencies and institutions may have overlapping personnel such as directors who have informal

Brookline-Elm people are a heterogeneous conglomeration of families and ethnic groupings living side by side but having no reason for organization and activity other than a particular threat to their well-being and ways of life. There are only a few already existing institutions, like labor unions, churches and local government, which might logically represent their interests.

No labor unions came out to oppose the Inner Belt; their constituencies do not coincide with neighborhoods, and there is little tradition in our society of unions involving themselves with issues like highway location.

As for the churches—as we have seen, priests from two large Roman Catholic parishes in the area were active in SOC. But the Roman Catholic hierarchy in Boston did not throw its financial or political weight into the issue aside from one public statement by the cardinal; nor did the clergy or congregations of the score of other churches that Brookline-Elm people attend take much action.

Finally, local government for years took no more concrete action than simply stating its unanimous opposition to any Belt location in Cambridge, a statement which was adequate until its veto power was lost. But the Cambridge City Council took no further action until the volunteer planners of Urban Planning Aid (then called the Cambridge Committee on the Inner Belt) pressured it to engage in technical battle with the state over alternate routes.

Why did the council wait so long to structure its opposition into specific political activity? One possible explanation is political necessity. It will obviously not hurt a councillor

---

dealings which are usually inaccessible to the public or to the sociological investigator. These may take the form of bargaining sessions of the stereotypical smoke-filled-room and cocktails-and-lunch variety, or they may take the form of understood agreements, or even just the tacit awareness that a major interest offended now will be difficult to deal with later, on the current or other grounds. See Chapter 7, the section on pluralism, for a fuller discussion of this issue.

to go on record against a road favored by few, if any, of his constituents. It is another matter to act on that stand, particularly when such action might antagonize another part of one's constituency, such as residents on an alternate route, powerful local institutions or higher levels of government with whom it might be necessary and desirable to remain on good terms. Another explanation could be simply that some councillors, as local politicians with experience and expertise primarily in city affairs, are not especially sophisticated in their understanding of how state and federal levels of government work and how they might be affected. A third explanation could be that the council members, like their constituents, have a sense that they are powerless to alter plans backed by state and federal authorities, that the power discrepancies between state, federal and local government are in fact overwhelming, and that city councillors' inactivity is a reasonable consequence of this perception.

Power to the Advocate Planners

By recognizing the institutional nature of politics, the advocate planners of UPA effectively represented the interests of their clients in the political arena. There is, however, danger when organization-class people enter a battle to assist people of the Middle-American and poor-and-powerless classes. We suggested that two reasons the SOC protest was so weak were that most nonparticipating residents felt themselves inadequate to deal in the world of politics, and that the main role protestors conceived for themselves was as deferential petitioners to specific higher authorities, many of whom were unlikely to involve themselves in the Belt issue anyway.

A danger in advocacy planning is that organization-class spokesmen, rather than attempting to educate their clients

about the structural aspects of political maneuvering—of
the need for mobilizing the support of powerful allies or
organizing themselves into a group that could speak from a
base of power—will take over the battle and wage it on
their own terms. This only reinforces the sense of alienation
that their clients already feel and convinces them that the
world of politics is not their province and that "big people"
must speak for them. To some extent, this situation occurred in the case of the Brookline-Elm people and their
UPA allies.

SOC, the citizens' protest group, stood emphatically for
a "no road" position. At regular meetings and at rallies,
the only proposal that was consistently cheered was any
statement to the effect, "We don't want any highways at
all through Cambridge." The volunteer planners of UPA,
however, assumed for several years that political reality
demanded pursuing the strategy of designing alternate
locations for the road and tried to convince the SOC men
and women and the city council of the wisdom, or as they
argued it, the necessity of this strategy. SOC *leaders* accepted this argument; indeed, it was not uncommon to hear
one and the same community leader speak of wanting "no
road in Cambridge," and then support the Portland-Albany alternative, both in the space of five minutes. But
most people in the audience were generally uncomfortable
with the attempt to push for an alternate route; most
would probably agree with one woman's statement: "We
don't want it here, but I wouldn't want to say, put it where
someone else lives." Even though many residents did not
really care for the idea of an alternate route, most people
who came regularly to SOC meetings accepted the work of
UPA and had a general sense that the volunteer planners
were working in their interests.

For their part, the advocates of UPA believed that it was
"unrealistic" to assume that all Inner Belt plans through
Cambridge could be cancelled, so until the formation of

the Greater Boston Committee on the Transportation Crisis in 1969, UPA suggested only the alternate route strategy to SOC. The no-road option, argued in a UPA analysis of Greater Boston transportation problems, was occasionally mentioned at meetings, but until 1969 UPA did not consider the idea to be of higher priority than the Portland-Albany alternate route.

UPA advocates also did not attempt to educate the Brookline-Elm residents in the political intricacies of highway building. Realizing, however, that government agencies are rarely moved by rational arguments alone, UPA did unite other organization-class supporters (such as the civic groups and faculty of the two universities) who were more friendly to the concept of an alternate route than were the residents themselves.

Thus, while organization-class allies had a key role in helping the Middle American citizens of Brookline and Elm Streets keep away the Inner Belt, they did so by taking over the battle and waging it on their own terms, without actively involving the neighborhood people. Now that the battle appears to be over, the residents of Brookline and Elm Streets themselves surely do not feel differently toward politics. On the contrary, the organization-class allies of the anti-Belt fight may have reinforced the residents' already deeply cynical and bitter feelings that they are politically incompetent and irrelevant, that politics is not for them but is in the realm of the "big people," and that the little people's roles are as observers, petitioners and, frequently, victims.

In fairness to UPA, it should be mentioned that as of this writing, the advocate planning group is moving closer toward the idea that clients may be served better by helping them learn how to handle the political process themselves—when this is possible—than by benevolently trying to solve their problems for them. The difference between these two styles of advocacy, as some see it, is between the model of doctor curing patients and the model of teacher helping another to understand so that he may do for himself.

The advocates of UPA, closer to the doctor model during the Belt struggle, attempted to speak *for* the neighborhood —to educate public opinion in general, and government authorities in particular—with explanations of Middle-American life styles and with logically feasible counter-plans. They appeared at SOC meetings periodically, with detailed diagrams showing where the alternate routes might go; and when negotiations with the DPW on alternate routes began, they regularly reported to SOC gatherings on who attended each session and what was said there. But throughout all this the advocates never took seriously the possibility of educating the working-class people of Brookline-Elm themselves to the national and local politics of highway building, and to what types of action citizens with a full understanding of the structural nature of their problem might take.

We do not mean to criticize the advocate planners too severely for their procedures in the Inner Belt case. The kind of organization and education necessary for residents to take the matter into their own hands is not easily accomplished even by professional community organizers. UPA's members began from different premises and increased their own education considerably in the course of the Inner Belt and other political experiences. They had not originally intended to be organizers and educators, and even if they had, their work would have been much tougher, much slower, and not likely to have contributed so effectively to the actual stopping of the road plan. Indeed, given their backgrounds, expectations and available time, it is not likely they could have succeeded in stopping the Belt by any methods other than those they used. This raises a classic political problem of whether stopping of the road was more important than enabling a group of people to discover how to be politically effective. Obviously, achieving both goals is most desirable, but we are unable to carry our "what might have been" speculation any further.

POWERLESSNESS TO THE PEOPLE

There's a railroad track, but—my good Lord, you can't run [the Belt] near MIT! You see, the *people* don't have the power that *they* [MIT] have. When *they're* threatened—Zap! They put on television programs, radios, lawyers—I mean, this is the end of the world! But when the *people* get put out, well—this is tough. . . . Now if the people could put on those television programs, get the big lawyers, put up the big fuss. . . .
                    —*middle-aged homeowner on Brookline Street*

We believe that politically effective action requires that citizen protestors recognize the structural dimension of political decisions—the role of powerful institutions with various interests in the decision-making process—and then either gain the support of powerful allies of their own, or else turn themselves and others like them into a politically persuasive force.

In an oversimplified way, the cynical beliefs of many residents that "we're just little people, and the big guys always win," reflect their accurate perception of the structural dimension of politics. Brookline-Elm people specify the "big guys"—the individuals and institutions they believe have the power and influence the little people lack:

Higher class—the politicians and people that's got money. . . . Higher education plus wealth—naturally they're going to win. . . . The more educated you are, the more they cater to you . . . . Today you gotta be a crook or a politician or a millionaire or a racketeer to get anywhere. If you just work for a living, you never get too far.

But this political sophistication is most frequently expressed in the griping of nonprotesting residents, who feel so powerless in contrast to "the big guys" that they do not act at all. One middle-aged man, not active with the protest, was asked: If the Brattle Street neighborhood (an upper-class residential area near Harvard Square) were threatened, would the people living there have more success fighting the Inner Belt? He answered realistically and typically:

> Of course! All they [the government] are dealing with [here] are the lowest—the population, the people themselves. They don't have any backing. And the ones with power—the factories—they'll make sure it doesn't touch them.

In contrast to the inactive majority of Brookline-Elm people, with their feelings of powerlessness and political alienation, residents active in the protest were much more likely to express a civic faith that combines belief in the political system as responsive to citizens' movements, with belief in the power of "the people," working together, to affect government policies. At SOC meetings in particular, the neighborhood leaders and the politicians regularly bemoaned the widespread apathy and emphasized that the protest's success was dependent upon participation by masses of residents. As one homeowner, one of SOC's most active members, put it, the people in the neighborhood could stop the Inner Belt "if they unite in unison. If they can get enough people to attend meetings and go to rallies."

But it is naive to believe that in order to win, all that is necessary is for "enough people" to voice their opinions to the "government." The implication still seems to be that the government (seen as an undifferentiated monolith) simply does not know what "the people" want, and once enough people make it known that they don't want the road, the government will change its decision.

Occasionally a protest leader referred to power explicitly. At one SOC meeting, one of the local priests delivered an impassioned speech:

> Why should I be told to get out of my home? Don't we have rights?. . . [We must fight] those who are in authority. . . . If necessary, we can sit in front of the bulldozers. . . . It's you against money, you against power. . . . If the road goes through, we'll hound them as long as they remain in office, because the sanctity of the home comes before any politician, whether he be mayor, governor or even President!

The apparent social-class discrimination aspect of the Inner Belt plan was also referred to by some activists. A 58-year-old woman, active with SOC, said:

> If it was only a matter of they have to put a road through, and this is the route, I wouldn't complain. But to first plan to put it some place else, and then Harvard and MIT don't want it, so they put it down here because they figure we're poor people and can't object—that's why I'm fighting it.

But most protestors did not admit to seeing the Inner Belt fight as a struggle between powerful institutions and powerless, unorganized neighborhood residents. The need to confront power with counterpower was rarely, if ever, openly expressed by SOC members, and did not appear to have influenced their actions, which consisted mainly of "polite" statements of protest to authorities. The reluctance of Brookline-Elm residents, particularly the activists, to conceive of the Inner Belt controversy in terms of social structure or power shaped the nature of their protest and its limited effectiveness.

6

THE PROBLEM OF AUTHORITY

THE REJECTION OF CONFRONTATION POLITICS

> [If you were the leader of SOC, what would you do?]
> The same as the rest of them. Tell them [Washington]
> what you want. After all, you can't demand. . . .
>
> [Do you think the government is right in wanting to put the
> Inner Belt through Brookline and Elm Streets?]
> I'm not going to knock the federal government, but they
> could find other ways of doing it.
>
> [Why do you think people sometimes don't take action
> against things they oppose, like highways through their homes?]
> They go with what the government says.
> > —*conversations with three Brookline-Elm residents*
>
> There will be no Inner Belt through our community.
> > —*Chuck Turner, head of the Black United*
> > *Front, in the Roxbury section of Boston*

Brookline-Elm residents in general limited their political
opposition to the Belt to polite petitioning of responsible
authorities like the governor and the DPW. In contrast,
other traditionally powerless groups have begun in recent
years to press their interests by direct confrontation with
more powerful institutions, including the government it-

self. Most notably, American blacks and college students have discovered—as the labor movement learned three or more decades earlier—that direct action, threats and confrontation, sometimes including violence, may accomplish changes that peaceful petitioning and rational argument cannot. But direct action such as sit-ins, nondisruptive or disruptive demonstrations, and even marches are condemned by many Americans, particularly by political figures who claim to speak for the "silent majority."

The argument for confrontation politics is that the powerful institution being confronted (a business, a university, the government) does not intend to live up to the democratic ideals and values of American society, and must be forced to do so by demonstrators. This has implications for the Inner Belt protest.

The Cambridge Inner Belt issue was sometimes described, by Belt opponents as well as supporters, as one of self-interest versus "the general good." A number of residents who decried the road's personal effect on them nevertheless felt that for the "greater good" they should move without much protest. "We need better transportation in Boston" sounds like a valid reason to require that some people give up their homes. But the unstated questions of which many Brookline-Elm residents are also aware, whether consciously or not, are: Who comprises the "we"? What is "better"? Who defines the "general good"? Many residents believe that "we" refers mainly to rush-hour suburban auto commuters; the proposed road would be of little benefit to people who do not commute long distances to work or do not drive cars. "Better transportation" is not necessarily an eight-lane highway that will bring more traffic downtown; innovative forms of cheap, attractive, convenient public transportation may serve the "general good" far more effectively than superhighways. And a significant proportion of residents believe that the political pressure of other, more powerful private interests was responsible for the choice of this route through their homes. It would seem that the Brookline-Elm people had adequate reason for turning to confrontation tactics.*

Brookline-Elm residents were aware of this possible course of action. The national example of effective confrontation politics is surely familiar to anyone who reads a newspaper or watches TV news. There had been several instances of confrontation politics over similar issues in the Boston area alone. During summer 1967 in Boston's South End (an integrated low-income area), a community group worked for months on reports, rallies, meetings, etc., in an effort to convince the Boston Redevelopment Authority (BRA) to alter an area renewal plan so as to increase the amount of low-income housing to be built. Suddenly and dramatically, a group of residents took over a recently paved parking lot that was to serve as the site of middle-income housing, and on it erected their own "Tent City." Within a few days this action accomplished what months of patient negotiations had not—a BRA guarantee to include more low-income housing in the South End renewal plan.

Another example comes from the "Eviction Day Riots" that occurred in August 1965 in Boston's North Harvard

---

* In an essential sense, the disruption by authorities of the lives of large numbers of peaceful, law-abiding citizens for a highway that will benefit truckers, suburban motorists, and the other economic and political interests that constitute the local and national road-building lobbies (see Chapter 7, on pluralism and lobbying) is disruption, just like the disruptive actions of a small group of anti-highway protestors. The question is actually not, who is being disruptive, but rather, whose disruption is legitimized by established authority and whose disruption opposes it? Southern white opposition to federal plans implementing civil rights measures is also disruptive citizen action. The difference between this and anti-road action, though—and this is crucial—is that the anti-civil rights action seeks to *undermine* a freedom upheld by the society (the right of all citizens, regardless of color, to be treated equally), while the anti-highway action seeks to *maintain* a freedom the society implicitly treasures (the right of people to live peacefully in their homes).

Street section, a white working-class neighborhood slated
for "urban renewal" into a luxury high-rise development.
Residents refused to move from their homes, and succeeded
in halting eviction plans for four years.*

There is even a recent example of potential confrontation
politics over the highway issue. The Inner Belt would run
through Boston, Brookline, Cambridge and Somerville.
For several years, citizens' groups in all four communities
made it clear that they did not want the Belt located where
planners said it must go. But in Boston on July 15, 1969,
a leader of the Black United Front (a coalition of groups in
the predominantly black section of Roxbury, through which
the road would travel) announced, *"There will be no Inner
Belt through our community."*[1] The Black United Front
argued that land already cleared for the road can be better
used for new low-income housing. "We are now planning
how we will use the land to meet our own needs, rather than
the needs of outsiders," the United Front spokesman said.

At least one-fourth of the Brookline-Elm respondents
knew of such instances of successful citizen confrontation.
A number of Brookline-Elm residents, both in and out of
SOC, threatened to lie before or shoot at the bulldozers,
and at several SOC meetings references were made to
blacks' apparent political successes stemming from use of
threats and violent actions; such behavior was usually mentioned in a way that combines admiration, wonder, wistful-
ness and condemnation, and was followed by phrases like,
"Of course *we'd* never do that."

The refusal to engage in confrontation politics was reflected in survey data on Brookline-Elm people's attitudes
towards various kinds of protest tactics. Our respondents

---

* At the time of our interviews, it appeared that some of the North
Harvard Street people would be able to stay in their homes. Although the
high-rise project was eventually abandoned by planning authorities, in
favor of a mixed middle- and low-income development, all of the original
residents' homes were destroyed.

were asked: "What kinds of actions against roads and the like do you think are reasonable? What do you think of —?" Then the interviewer read off the following list: letter-writing and phone calls to officials, going to meetings, using the vote, putting up signs against the road, marches, rallies, sit-ins and demonstrations, civil disobedience (e.g., refusing to move, lying in front of bulldozers), threatening violence, actual violence.

Approximately 30 percent of the respondents felt that almost nothing they could do, aside from perhaps voting or going to meetings, would be of any help against the road. Eighty-two percent said that "the vote" might be a good action*; 79 percent expressed faith in meetings, and 63 percent expressed faith in letters. Posting signs was favored by 55 percent, and more direct, confrontative actions, such as marches, rallies and sit-ins, were mentioned favorably by 55 percent, 47 percent and 46 percent of the sample, respectively.

About one-fourth of the respondents believed that sit-ins might be "harmful to the cause" or "immoral"; 65 percent felt that civil disobedience (e.g., refusing to move, or lying in front of bulldozers) might be harmful or immoral; 82 percent said that the threat of violence was wrong; and 90 percent said that violence was wrong. It is especially significant that several respondents who declared that violence or the threat of violence was wrong then added bitterly, "But it probably would help." These responses suggest that many residents tend to accept enforced dislocation, rather than perform potentially disruptive acts that might succeed in saving their homes.

---

*   Several residents specified that they did not mean voting for officials, but voting on the Belt issue itself, as in a binding referendum.

RELUCTANCE TO ACT AGAINST
THE POLITICAL SYSTEM

A Political Paradox: Respect for Scorned Authorities

[People say that America is a free country. What does this
mean to you—to call a place "a free country"?]
Y ou can have anything you want—and honestly. I can have
a car if I want it, my home—if the state don't want it [for
the Inner Belt]. I think it's a great way of life we have.
—elderly homeowner active with SOC

As we have seen, most Brookline-Elm people believe
that they are not effective politically and that the system
does not work in their interests. This does not mean, however, that they display a single-minded cynicism and dis-
interest toward matters political. The Brookline-Elm people are better able to name their federal representatives
than were a sample of residents of another city.* Most
striking, about 70 percent of our respondents claimed to
vote regularly, the two most common reasons being: "every
individual counts," and "it's an individual's responsibility."

*Although the Brookline-Elm people are deeply cynical
about the political system, they simultaneously speak and
act in such a way as to acknowledge its legitimacy.* There is
a logic to this seeming contradiction, a logic that helps
explain how people who feel angry and helpless before pro-

---

* Of a representative sample of Detroit residents, 13 percent knew only
one senator, another 32 percent knew both, and 18 percent could name
their U.S. congressman (see Daniel Katz and Samuel J. Eldersveld,
"The Impact of Local Party Activity Upon the Electorate," *Public
Opinion Quarterly,* Vol. 25, Spring 1961). On Brookline-Elm, by contrast, 28 percent knew the name of only one senator, 48 percent knew the
names of both (Edward Kennedy and Edward Brooke at the time), and
37 percent could name their U.S. congressman (T.P. O'Neill).

cesses and authorities that hurt them do not rise up against these processes and authorities.

The most obvious reason they do not dare to oppose the system is their fear of losing any political battle. If the government is stronger than they in the ordinary decision-making process, it would certainly be stronger in a showdown of force. (As one woman said, "Violence only leads to violence.") And the emotional pain of losing after open militant confrontation might be anticipated to exceed the pain of acquiescence to unwanted government action. This fear of losing is realistic, of course, but it is enhanced by three social-psychological phenomena of particular importance in Middle American culture: tendency to defer to authority, fear of asserting oneself, and fear of being thought unrespectable.

FEAR OF AUTHORITY

> [Do you know anything about the people who fought urban renewal in Allston (North Harvard Street section of Boston)?]
> No, but I sure would like to know more about them. They seem to have won.[2] I'd like to know what did they have that we don't have? I guess the reason is that they were fighting private interests, whereas we're facing the government [i.e., most people are reluctant to oppose the government].
> —*older woman, homeowner*

Most Americans—and perhaps people in all societies— are taught to stand in awe and respect of those in power. In addition, our political ideology teaches us to accept government decisions as the wisdom of politically neutral bodies. For these two reasons, Americans of any social group would find it hard to oppose government actions, even when they seem unjust.

The Middle Americans of Brookline-Elm are doubly predisposed not to question authority. Asked why he thought many residents in the area did not take action to oppose the road even though they anticipated it would hurt them, a local priest explained:

> A lot of our Catholic people are terribly conservative in a lot of things. . . . We imbue them with respect for law and order—for the laws of the country, the laws of the Church, and the laws of God. Even in our parochial schools maybe there's too much authority exercised; the youngsters don't get a chance to express themselves.

Such attitudes of deference to authority characterize Middle-American-class culture in general.

FEAR OF SELF-ASSERTION

In order to oppose actions initiated by authorities such as the government, one must feel the moral right to act on one's own behalf. And we suggest that most Brookline-Elm people, like Middle Americans in general, cannot conceive of themselves as having this right.

Striking examples of this fear of self-assertion appear in our field notes.

> On a city-hired bus on the way to the October 1966 rally at the Boston Common: The bus had not yet begun its journey to the Common. A lady behind me called out to a man walking outside, about 55, vaguely shabby in dress and appearance, "Hey, Mickey, come on, beat the Belt." Then others recognized Mickey and called to him. The curious thing was not so much that Mickey smiled, uncertainly, and then walked on, probably not clear what this was all about, but that no one really tried to inform him. Even that is not too hard to accept, as that was not the time or place for community organizing, but the women seemed annoyed and frustrated at the windows of the bus being closed. One commented she wished a window were open so they could talk to Mickey. But she did nothing in the way of trying to open a window, nor did her companion, nor did at least four other people who seemed noticeably to wish a window were open. To me, this nearly sums up, as I have seen it, the behavior of these working-class people in the face of obstacles; they assume them to be fixed and beyond their

capability to alter. It apparently did not occur to anyone to open a window.

Consider the Department of Public Works a closed window. During at least 40 minutes on that bus I heard mostly chat on weather, family, etc., or remarks on what a shame it is that the road is planned to come through Brookline-Elm.

Asked what she thinks of the tactic of the North Harvard Street residents, who tried to prevent demolition of their neighborhood for urban renewal by threatening the assessors with shotguns, a Brookline-Elm homeowner says, "I doubt if we'd be that savage. You have to go along with the government."

A poverty-stricken father of seven, asked if he thinks the government is right in wanting to put the road through, causing him to move from his low-rent apartment, cannot bring himself to criticize the government, even in words: "Who am I to say about the government? In my estimation I think that— no, I wouldn't answer that." "Why not?" "I'd be favoring families like me." "Say it anyway," the interviewers coax him. "The government is the government. It's hard to say anything about it. No, I can't say."

Indeed, one wonders if, in their attitudes of political defeatism, many Brookline-Elm people secretly—maybe so secretly they do not acknowledge it to themselves—feel they have it coming. In a society that defines their life accomplishments as not particularly notable, forced relocation might be experienced as simply another defeat. As oppressed and persecuted populations everywhere have demonstrated for millenia, the capacity of people to absorb defeat is extraordinary, even if unnecessary.

FEAR OF BEING "UNRESPECTABLE"

Most Americans are taught that it is "not respectable," "not polite," to force their will upon someone else in public, whether in interpersonal relations or in the political arena. Brookline-Elm residents anticipate that by engaging in public protest—which is considered "impolite" or even disgusting—they may lose their self-respect and the respect of others.

A middle-aged homeowner who attended the city-sponsored rally at the State House in October 1966 says such demonstrations are all right "if they're orderly, as ours was." She disapproves of a demonstration that took place about a month later, outside MIT on the day its new president was inaugurated. "That day of ceremony—I think it was improper. Also the one sitting in the office. . . . I don't go along on that, sitting on the floor, eating your lunch, bringing kids. . . . I think that's going too far."

Federal Highway Administrator Lowell Bridwell visited Cambridge in late 1967. At an SOC meeting just before his visit a woman suggests draping Brookline Street in black and hanging 500 to 600 toy rifles from windows, with signs saying "The next ones will be real." A man in the audience objects, saying he is against violence. The woman tries to protest that she is not advocating violence, but is hushed up by the meeting, and her idea is never mentioned by anyone again.

A middle-aged homeowner says, "Oftentimes I thought if I could get these people who are trying to put the road through, bring them down here, show them what they're breaking up. What I've often thought of doing is kicking mud in their face— but I wouldn't do it." She laughs with embarrassment. "I've often thought of it."

FEAR THAT POWERLESSNESS IS ONE'S OWN FAULT

In a highly competitive and highly individualistic society such as ours, most people assume that if one "makes it," it is because one is bright and clever enough to do so and if one "doesn't make it," it is because one is not bright and clever enough to do so. "Failure," in education, work or whereever, is seldom interpreted as a collective experience in which the odds have been stacked against the group (class, race, sex, etc.) to which one belongs. And in a similar way, "success" is more often attributed to hard work, talent and "luck" than to the good fortune of belonging to a group (class, race, sex, etc.) whose members have the odds stacked in their favor.[3] The classic American belief in the capacity to "lift yourself up by your bootstraps" means that if you fail, it's your own fault. As we suggested earlier, we suspect that many Brookline-Elm people believe that their political inefficacy, like their marginal economic position and some other aspects of their lives, reflects their own personal failures to make it in a system that tells them if they were good enough they would indeed have made the grade. This belief is part of an ideology that masks classism. Or to put it another way, the ideological denial of classism in our society is strong enough to blind most people to the realities of the structures and dynamics of social class.

The Paradox Resolved—Identification with Authority

People like Brookline-Elm residents might affect the system in their own behalf, if they would only act on their cynical belief that the government is influenced by power, not by justice—that is, if they attempted to form themselves into a counterpower.* But they are afraid to try. They are the victims of a vicious circle of powerlessness; by not daring to act in their own interests, these potentially powerful people allow themselves to remain powerless victims.

---

* Such action can speak to a specific issue, like the Inner Belt. It can also confront the structure and nature of society as a whole—i.e., through rebellion or revolution. Although some Brookline-Elm people may feel oppressed in more general or diffuse ways, few if any of them identify specific institutions as sources of their problems; and they surely do not identify an establishment or set of institutions in such a role, and therefore do not put themselves against the government or the establishment. Whether or not they are objectively entitled to do so, or are likely to do so in the future, is beyond the scope of this book.

And they dare not act, we suggest, because while their situation is unpleasant, they do not find it unbearable. It would be far too frightening to face the unknown and potentially disastrous consequences of opposing institutions that one has obeyed and respected all one's life.

One way in which people who feel personally powerless maintain their sense of self-respect is by identifying with a powerful person or institution, and gaining pleasure through vicarious participation in the victories of the superior.[4] An obvious example of this is the vicarious thrill that the average American gets from the exploits performed in the name of the nation, such as winning a battle or war, or placing a man on the moon. "I feel good," says the man in the street, "because *we* landed on the moon."

Among the Brookline-Elm residents we have observed various examples of great emotional involvement with political celebrities:

A 45-year-old woman who had written President Johnson about the road received an inappropriate reply about highway beautification. She tells the interviewer: "It's from Mrs. Johnson. It's a very short letter. I didn't expect anything out of this world—to *me*. He's sick, maybe that's why she did the correspondence—or her social secretary." (The letter is actually signed by Lady Bird's social secretary, on her employer's behalf.)

In April 1968, shortly after President Johnson announced that he would not seek reelection, a number of Brookline-Elm residents active with SOC, asked why they thought he had made such a decision, suggested personal reasons, and expressed great personal identification with Johnson. "I think his wife had a lot to do with it. . . . It's not his fault, it's the Congress. They're so old they don't care about the war. His two sons-in-law are going in, so he cares. . . . I thought he did it probably partly because of his health, but he didn't want to come out and say it. His age. I felt a little sad, even though I wasn't going to vote for him. He's been taking a lot. . . . I think he's fed up with all the criticism he's been getting. I don't blame him—it's not an easy job. I'd have done it long ago."

In other words, people can reconcile themselves to living under a seemingly omnipotent authority by identifying with it.

We suggest, then, that unquestioning respect for and faith in the authority of powerful institutions of American society—particularly the government—enables many Brookline-Elm residents and Middle Americans in general to maintain their feelings of security and self-worth.

The matter cannot better be illustrated than by the particular case of the Inner Belt, where, although many residents believe that the government is not acting fairly, it is still more important—for their emotional stability—for them to maintain the image of the government as omnipotent and infallible, than for them to despair over their situation altogether. They have little power in their personal lives; if they doubt the legitimacy of others' power, if they see as unjust the entire system which they have accepted all their lives, what will these people have left? Unless they discover their own potential effectiveness and how to use it, they will have nothing.

Therefore, many Brookline-Elm residents are likely to accept what they perceive as an injustice (perhaps casting the blame on individual "corrupt politicians" and businessmen, or on "fate") and silently suffer the consequences of forced dislocation, rather than question the legitimacy of the government and confront it on their own behalf.

THE ROLE OF THE LOCAL PROTEST LEADER

Others understand better than we do. [Who?] These big people who can talk for us, like the priests.
                                                        —*old woman*

It stands to reason—higher education plus wealth— naturally they're going to win. Not the underdog—not the poor people. That's why we have representatives—the city—

fighting for us. Because they have the education, they know
the law.
—45-year-old woman

[Do you think demonstrations like the one at MIT are
helpful?]
This I can't answer, because I really don't know. These
people [SOC leaders] are in with it, talking to all the big
shots. I'm a nobody, just go to meetings.
—40-year-old woman

As we noted, the anti-Belt protest movement had a variety of leaders: volunteer planners, neighborhood residents
and priests, a few particularly active local politicians. Unsure of themselves, and highly deferential to authority,
many Brookline-Elm protestors waited for their leaders to
tell them how to fight the Belt. The leaders generally *discouraged* political activity on the part of their followers.
True, they continually urged letter-writing, but as we have
said, this could not be called effective action. If members of
the audience at an SOC meeting or rally suggested some
other plan—such as contacting radio talk shows or ethnic
clubs—they were usually praised, and told to work on that
project if they liked. Rarely were formal actions approved
and deadlines set for completion; rarely were committees
assigned to work on a project, or once set up, regularly
asked how their tasks were coming along.*

Most important, the leaders did not use their role to
educate the others into whatever facts about power or the
structural aspect of politics they already knew or had
learned in dealing with politicians, professionals and institutions with regard to the highway problem. As we noted
earlier, the organization-class planners of UPA attempted
to remold the Belt fight into a technical battle in which the

---

* At the simplest level, this reveals the SOC leaders' lack of organizational ability and experience.

planners felt competent and comfortable, but did not attempt to educate the people about structural facts of political decision-making or to organize the residents of Brookline-Elm. In a similar vein, the neighborhood leaders, priests and local politicians rarely provided residents with new knowledge or perspectives that might provide a coherent basis for more effective citizen action against the Belt.

The leaders continually suppressed conflict, and rarely spoke in power terms. Almost none of them publicly acknowledged or improved upon the residents' unsophisticated perception that an elite consisting of "corrupt politicians" and representatives of powerful institutions runs society through decisions made in private. While there were mumbled references during many meetings that "politics" (i.e., behind-the-scenes power plays) were involved in this or that Belt decision by a public authority, few residents expressed such allegations explicitly or questioned their leaders about the implications for SOC strategy of these assumed manipulations by the powerful. On the few occasions that such issues were publicly pressed, SOC leaders typically ignored the cynical interpretation and advised faith in the elected political authorities, repeating once again the socially acceptable doctrine that deferential pleading by citizens before authorities would "beat the Belt." For example:

> A state politician complains at an SOC meeting that state senators from Western Massachusetts voted down the community highway veto power because highway construction means jobs. "You can't fight power," he declares. "How do you fight power?" "Man the barricades!" a local woman in the audience shouts. "I don't know about manning the barricades," the politician rejoins. "We lost the veto. . . . They don't care!" And he goes on lamenting the "hypocrisy" of certain nameless politicians.

> A priest active in SOC says in private that he does not trust then-Governor Volpe at all, but fears that if SOC criticized

Volpe, lines of communication with him would be closed. He also believes that the DPW are outright "tricksters" and that the Mayor's Advisory Committee is taken in by the DPW; but he won't relay this to SOC. He explains, "We're taught not to say anything detrimental about people. If you can't say anything good about a person, forget it."

A state politician accuses "the powers that be" of wanting to divide Cambridge by building the Inner Belt. "You're not supposed to bring politics into it, they say. This thing has been permeated with politics since its inception!" He accuses MIT (but not by name—he refers to it as "an institution out there") of caring more about the increased traffic nearby than about 1,500 families. But he never explains *how* politics is involved, or who is getting what. Nor does he ever suggest political actions SOC might take.

An SOC neighborhood leader is talking about MIT's expressed interest in building housing for lower- and middle-income people. A man in the audience angrily cries out that MIT wants the Belt because the noise of the highway traffic will drive adjacent residents away, and then students, being "night people," can move in. The SOC leader promptly puts this down with, "We have no proof of that," and continues talking about MIT's housing development plans. (This incident is especially striking in view of the fact that one week before, this same leader angrily reported that at a meeting with MIT Corporation Chairman Killian, SOC representatives were told that the only way in which MIT would involve itself with the Brookline-Elm residents would be through helping them relocate if the Belt were built.)

A variety of reasons may explain the protest leaders' tendency to avoid confronting or questioning the behavior of authorities and of the system. We might include all the factors discussed previously: fear of losing the battle with authorities, fear of "the power of the self," fear of losing self-respect by engaging in disreputable action, belief that "little people" are somehow failures, need to identify with authorities and fear of losing faith in the system altogether if one questions too deeply.

To these can be added a problem characteristic of anyone in a leadership role. Leaders of any protest group receive a certain degree of status and recognition from other authorities. If they were to encourage questioning or confrontation of those authorities, they might lose respect and status.

There is also an important tradition in our society that the proper role of the leader is to be a conciliator rather than a troublemaker, to cover over rather than open up conflict. SOC leaders carried out this role by continually dissociating themselves from anything "political."

> SOC leaders explain that the purpose of the upcoming October 1966 rally is to oppose "all highways in the metropolitan area," because "people are more important than automobiles." They stress that the rally is "not for or against Volpe. It's not political. It's to get publicity and save our homes."

> Before a SOC meeting begins officially, a woman in the audience comments aloud that people should vote in the coming election for city councilmen who oppose the Belt. During the meeting someone makes a horrified reference to the fact that earlier that day, right on Brookline Street, people were shaking hands with ex-DPW head Sargent, who is now Volpe's running mate. But no SOC leaders ever come out with the specific recommendations that, for example, people should vote against Volpe or for candidates who oppose the Belt.

> At a meeting just a few days before the November 1966 election, a SOC leader reads—with no comment or interpretation whatsoever—a clipping reporting that Volpe's Democratic opponent, Edward McCormack, "opposes current Inner Belt plans."

Particularly in the case of Governor Volpe, a powerful and outspoken advocate of the road, it is possible that SOC leaders avoided giving political advice because they feared Volpe would win (as he did), and it would not be wise to antagonize him.* However, it is also possible that they

---

* Not antagonizing Volpe, it should be pointed out, had all along gained neither Volpe's support nor his sympathy for the SOC cause.

avoided opposing him or supporting other candidates simply because, as SOC neighborhood leaders and priests frequently said, "Our group shouldn't get involved in politics." To admit that one is involved in a political controversy opens up the whole frightening world of power and powerlessness, of confrontation and examination of a system much too dangerous to question.

So while the UPA planners were off designing alternate routes and negotiating with the DPW, and while various city, state and federal politicians were pulling strings as best they could to obtain still another delay on the final Belt decision, the indigenous SOC leaders appeared to act as little more than cheerleaders whose purpose was to report on the latest plays in the game, to elicit appropriate emotional responses from the audience, and to give occasional pep talks to keep up the audience's morale. But they never explained politics or invited the audience to participate directly. And, by and large, the majority of SOC members also acted as if they were spectators at a sports event. They cheered when the leaders reported some encouraging news for their side, calmed down when the leaders asked for quiet, and rarely questioned the actions or decisions of anyone in the field.

WORKING-CLASS AUTHORITARIANISM

> The moratorium [against the Vietnamese War, October-November 1969] was a stab in the back to our boys on the firing lines. Our families don't have long-haired brats—they'd tear the hair off them. Our boys don't smoke pot or raise hell or seek deferments. Our people are too busy making a living and trying to be good Americans.
> —*a spokesman for the "silent majority"*[5]

A person who feels powerless and confused and identifies with a leader or authority can become extremely punitive toward others—toward scapegoats, as it were—who disagree with this authority. To identify with authority, then, means to use it against others as irrationally as one believes it is used against him. In their personal lives, some Brookline-Elm residents stress their identification with prevailing norms of middle-class respectability and make a point of trying to keep in line the few people over whom they have power—particularly their own children—when they violate the generally accepted norms.

> A 58-year-old man says that if his kids came home looking like "kooks" [i.e., hippies], "I'd break their heads in."

> A 47-year-old woman says, "If I had a boy and he wore his hair like that [long] and didn't take a bath, he'd wake up one morning and he'd be bald. I'd cut all the hair off of him." She goes on to say that when her 17-year-old daughter talks about not obeying her, the respondent tells her, "If you don't want to do what I want, I'll call the police to take you. They have places for girls like you [i.e., reform schools]."

We feel that this scapegoating phenomenon is common among many Middle Americans. Their response to poverty, war and university protests is to condemn the protestors and dissenters, rather than question the institutions against which the protestors are dissenting. "We may find out some day that what we're doing in Vietnam is wrong," says one of *Time's* Middle Americans, whose son was killed by a misdirected American shell, "but until then, it's my country right or wrong."[6]*

---

* During one period of our fieldwork (Fall, 1967), several Cambridge groups, mainly student based, were sponsoring anti-Vietnam War campaigns. In contrast, many Brookline-Elm residents stressed their own patriotism and their support of the government's activities in Asia and expressed great hostility toward antiwar activists who dared to question government military action.

For example, a middle-aged man said, "I have every confidence in our government to know that if they disclosed everything, we'd be with them 100 per-

This mechanism of allaying feelings of powerlessness and confusion by submitting to and identifying with a powerful authority and scapegoating those who oppose it, is called *authoritarianism* by many social scientists. Political sociologist Seymour Martin Lipset has written of its manifestations in the working class. He argues that the allegedly restricted, punitive and insecure upbringing of working-class people makes them intolerant, antidemocratic and open to totalitarian movements.[7] As Lipset puts it:

> Many . . . studies suggest that the lower-class way of life [in his view, the working class is part of the lower class] produces individuals with rigid and intolerant approaches to politics. . . . Acceptance of the norms of democracy requires a high level of sophistication and ego security. The less sophisticated and stable an individual, the more likely he is to favor a simplified view of politics, to fail to understand the rationale underlying tolerance of those with whom he disagrees, and to find difficulty in grasping or tolerating a gradualist image of political change.[8]

---

cent. . . . Those kids in college today that are objecting to the President's actions, I'm ashamed to consider them citizens. . . . I don't think much of their intelligence."

Another man, after answering questions about his stand in the current local election, told the interviewer, "As long as you're not against the war in Vietnam. If someone came around to my house with a petition [against the war] I'd throw them out." He pauses a minute. "Of course I know it [the war] is wrong, but there's some things you have to put up with."

That November, a referendum on whether or not to withdraw troops from Vietnam was put up to the Cambridge voters. In the two wards through which the Brookline-Elm route would travel, residents voted 35 percent and 36 percent for withdrawal of troops. (It can probably be assumed that many people who voted in favor of withdrawal were students, other university-affiliated people and other professionals.) Voting *against* withdrawal, a stand taken by almost two-thirds of area voters, was seen by most residents not necessarily as favoring the war, but as expressing support for the government in general, and for "our boys" in particular. (Many residents, like most working-class Americans, had friends and relatives in Vietnam.)

Lipset is making an important point: the life experiences of working-class people often encourage antidemocratic attitudes and behavior. But we would modify and expand Lipset's point in several respects.

First, working-class people, like most other poor and Middle Americans, face nondemocratic or authoritarian experiences every day. In most institutionalized areas of their lives they are the passive objects of the authoritarianism of higher-class people. We suggest that if Middle Americans tend to be significantly intolerant and punitive, it is their constant political experience—as ignored, manipulated members of this society—that is largely responsible for conditioning that tendency in them. And this political experience is reinforced in other areas of their lives.

If most of the people we are talking about engage in boring, repetitive work over whose conditions they have little control, that too must be a powerful contributing force to feelings of being manipulated and feelings that one's best interests are ignored.* A limited income that seems to shrink as prices and taxes continually rise contributes to such feelings, as does public school education, which for both poor and Middle Americans is characteristically

---

* *Newsweek* quotes several poignant statements by Middle Americans on the nature of their work life. A middle-aged machine worker from Milwaukee speaks bitterly: "I've been in the shops since I was 16. I worked like a damn fool. . . . But they don't care. We're just peons. And if you don't like it, there's always somebody waiting for your job. Day after day, year after year, climbing those same steps, punching that time card. Standing in that same goddam spot grinding those same goddam holes" ("The Troubled Americans," p. 57). Two young white-collar workers in an insurance company express quiet frustration. Says one, "It's a womb-to-tomb life. . . . It becomes frustrating. You go home wondering, 'What the hell did I do today. . . .' You're such a small cog in such a big wheel that it all gets lost in the whole mishmash." The other adds, "Sure, I wish I was a little different, but what the hell, I made this bed, I made the choice, so I have to live with it. I'm just an average slob. They wind us up in the morning and we go all day" [*ibid.,* p. 59].

restricted and punitive.* Military service, an experience strange to most organization-class youth, but extremely familiar to poor and Middle-American young men is another contributing factor. A draftee is moved from his home and familiar surroundings, probably against his will, for reasons which neither benefit nor make sense to him and by means of a decision in which he played no part and from which there is little recourse. This is a powerful authoritarian experience.

Second, neither the Middle-American nor the organization class has a monopoly on authoritarian *or* democratic attitudes and behavior. S.M. Miller and Frank Riessman speak to this issue. The authors agree with Lipset that poverty, insecurity and ignorance lead to authoritarianism. But they suggest that

> conditions of working-class existence, such as removal from competitiveness and status concern, the concentration in work places [and] extended family structures . . . produce many cooperative democratic trends. Poverty and insecurity do not necessarily and inevitably produce less "decent" values. Under certain conditions they can lead to the development of solidaristic, warm feelings. Similarly, wealth, security, and knowledge can lead to tolerant and democratic values under some conditions. Under other conditions, as we know, they may lead to smugness, elitism, intellectualism, and coldness. Many other variables in addition to wealth, education, and security are decisive in the formation of liberal and democratic values.[9]

> Neither class [the authors continue] . . . is psychologically authoritarian, but both classes have values which could be turned in the direction of political authoritarianism under certain conditions.[10]

---

* The rigidity and absence of imagination in typical Middle-American schools are documented by Peter Binzen, who discusses a large number of Middle-American urban school systems in *Whitetown, USA,* (New York, Random House, 1970), pp. 36-78.

Prodemocratic values of Middle Americans include anti-elitist, outspoken, cooperative, underdog and informality orientations. On the authoritarian side are desires for strong leadership and definite structure, anti-intellectualism and punitive attitudes toward violation of the law. Authoritarian attitudes of the organization class include conventionalism, competitiveness, status concern, fear of authority, overintellectualism and snobbery.[11] And democratic values of organization-class people focus on beliefs in equality of opportunity, equal treatment under the law and the ideals of representative government.

IMPLICATIONS

THE DECEPTION OF MIDDLE AMERICA: POLITICAL REALTY VERSUS THE PUBLIC IDEOLOGY

When belief about a society clashes with reality, a population ordinarily makes excuses and rationalizations for the reality rather than attempting to change either the belief or the reality. The classes that control society are in charge of that process of constructing rationalizations, and are able to promote their points of view through educational systems, mass media, churches, political rhetoric and other agencies of a society's mythology about itself.

Middle America believes the popular ideology about equal opportunity, democracy, etc., in America. While these circumstances do, of course, more or less result for some parts of the population, Middle Americans and poor-and-powerless Americans are very often excluded from realizing them. Even so, most Middle Americans do claim that this country is one in which the individual counts, success is up to the individual, and the government represents the people because it is elected by them every two or four years.

We are convinced, by contrast, that Middle America does not perceive the connection between its own problems and the basic structure of this society's economic and political institutions. The political powerlessness we have described is partly due, then, to a confusion between what is and what is said to be. We feel that only when Middle

America sees the reality that is now obscured by the public ideology can it possibly gain the understanding with which to change that reality. Only then will classic American ideals become possibilities for all.

The Inner Belt protest illuminates several inconsistencies between political reality and the traditional ideology of American democracy. Four crucial assumptions of the ideology are these:

1. *All citizens are equal politically.* All citizens are equally capable of looking out for their own interests.

2. *Voting is the definitive political act.* The only political act required of good citizens is to vote regularly. Voting makes them feel they have done "the right thing." After that, government should be left to elected representatives and appointed officials, who may be reached on specific issues through petitions, letters and subsequent votes. (As one of *Time's* "Middle Americans"—a librarian in Massachusetts—says, "Dissent is disgusting. If you have a complaint, write your Congressman."[1])

3. *America is a successful pluralist society.* Any group can compete on an equal basis with any other group in the political marketplace. Each has an equal chance to make its position known to government, and to be judged fairly.

4. *Government is neutral.* Government is a neutral, impartial body trying to make the fairest judgements among competing interests for the good of the society as a whole.

Examination of the SOC protest movement reveals that its members accepted these assumptions. They tried to organize for political effect. They assumed that government would respond favorably if it could be reached properly. They believed themselves neglected and discriminated against in the politics of the Belt issue, but never generalized to social-class interpretations of power and structure. They dutifully limited their political behavior to polite, deferential protest. (And most residents, whether in or out of the protest, claimed to vote regularly.) Ironically, as we have also seen, the SOC protest was unenthusiastically received by the majority of residents, and without organization-class allies and support it would have been essentially ineffective.

We can only conclude that in the Brookline-Elm case, the accepted set of beliefs about democracy did not provide a useful map of the labyrinth of political reality. Rather than guide the Brookline-Elm people into an effective way of defending their interests, the beliefs served to defuse and weaken their protest. Each of the four belief-assumptions crucial to the traditional democratic ideology is contradicted by the facts of our investigation.

THE BELIEF IN POLITICAL EQUALITY OF ALL CITIZENS

The assumption of political equality implies that all citizens feel equal and in fact *are* equal participants in the political process. The Inner Belt case demonstrates that most Middle-American Brookline-Elm residents feel so politically powerless that acceptance or avoidance of the issue seems less painful than worry over a losing battle. Inactivity generates and reinforces a vicious circle: the less the citizens protest, the greater the likelihood that the government will pursue its unpopular course of action, leading to even stronger feelings of alienation and impotence among the population.

This self-reinforcing cycle of alienation is not unique to the Inner Belt situation. It has been noted in several studies of urban displacement among poor and working-class citizens. J. Clarence Davies observes that, in New York City, "even if he is inclined to be antagonistic to the [renewal] proposal, the citizen may feel that opposition is useless."[2] Ernest Norton Tooby writes:

> The overwhelming power of the agencies causing displacement and the inability of most displacees to prevent the displacements, even when they organize, engenders a feeling of helplessness. This is especially true of lower-class displacees [and working-class; Tooby does not seem to distinguish between the two] whose lives are characterized by a general inability to control their environments. This feeling of helplessness is counterproductive, because it diminishes motivation to attempt to change the environment by instilling the conviction that any effort is futile. . . . "The relocation process increases social and civic tension by confirming feelings of the persons adversely affected that they have little or no control over their own lives, and that they are being shoved aside for others whom they feel society values more highly."[3]

The pattern of alienation leading to inactivity leading to greater alienation also appeared during the protest over urban renewal in the North Harvard Street area of Boston:

> Many of the people who moved (as opposed to those who stayed and fought the renewal plans) expressed great feelings of political impotence and alienation throughout their interviews. One woman expressed . . . her thoughts as follows: "It doesn't do us any good to vote anyway. I used to vote every year since I was 21, but I'm not going to vote this year. I lost all interest in voting as a result of that conflict with the [renewal agency]. . . ."[4]

Most North Harvard Street respondents did not seem surprised that the elected officials were not much help and even supported the renewal project that would have turned their neighborhood into a luxury high-rise development.

> [One woman] expressed the feelings of those who moved away. "How can little people fight big people? I still think the ones left down there are going to lose. . . . They [i.e., the powerful] are a bunch of bums—people who don't give a darn for the little people. They don't care if we live in pup tents. If you

have money, they pay attention to you. . . . What could we do?
It was not a rich neighborhood. If it was a neighborhood where
there were doctors and lawyers, they wouldn't have had to
move, they'd still be there. You've got to have money." Most
of the people who moved felt that there was nothing much that
could be done once the [renewal agency] had decided to take
the land. They were surprised that a protest movement was
even formed [and that it had some success].

These feelings of alienation and impotence might have
been caused by the renewal experience itself in some cases,
but a number of respondents reported holding these attitudes prior to the events described. The foregone conclusion
that "You can't fight City Hall" surely led many of the
residents to give up, to participate minimally or not at all
in the protest, and sooner or later to move out.[5]

The other side of the coin is the greater political sophistication of organization-class and rich-and-powerful class
individuals and groups. As a recent federal report on urban
problems points out, "Almost invariably, the more well-to-
do families are both more articulate and more influential
in opposing plans for highways through their residential
areas."[6]

Feelings of political powerlessness may take forms other
than apathetic withdrawal from politics. In studies which
consider defeats of various local referenda, a proposal for
metropolitan government and fluoridation referenda, author after author finds that people who vote "No" tend to
be people who feel especially helpless and distant from the
political system.[7] It is suggested in one study that such
negative votes

> may serve as institutional outlets for protest, that voting
> against local issues may be an expression of political protest
> on the part of the powerless and ordinarily apathetic members
> of the community. . . . Evidence suggests that voting down local
> issues does not represent an organized, class-conscious opposi-
> tion, but a type of mass protest, a convergence of the assess-
> ments of the powerless who have projected onto available

symbols the fears and suspicions growing out of their alienated existence.[8]

VOTING AS THE DEFINITIVE POLITICAL ACT

Americans take for granted both that voting is morally right—by definition, a good citizen must vote—and that voting every few years is sufficient to assure that the government serves the people's interests. Aside from the polite classical forms of appeal, such as writing letters and signing petitions,* any other form of political action is considered unnecessary, if not morally suspect. The government is considered to have the right to prevent citizens from engaging in direct actions such as demonstrations.

The Inner Belt case shows that voting and the classic citizen appeal methods were not sufficient in opposing the Belt. But the active residents were reluctant to attempt other actions (and the majority were perhaps discouraged from taking any part in the protest at all), not only because they are inexperienced in these matters but because they are discouraged from doing so by the popular ideology.

Our traditional democratic ideology, insofar as it discourages citizens from acting politically in any way *but* voting, encourages people to rely on leaders' images and promises at election time, and to believe that they have nothing active or critical to do with the political system at other times. Furthermore, by encouraging apathy and authoritarian attitudes in the public ("Just vote—then leave everything up to your representatives"), the traditional ideology increases the likelihood that leaders will respond to their own interests, rather than the interests of those they theoretically serve.

---

* Officials probably take letters and petitions seriously when there are enough of them to suggest possible defeat by a discontented constituency in the next election.

For example, the definition of voting as the significant political act encourages leaders to court the public, not by satisfying its real wants, but by doing anything at all that will produce votes. Prospective candidates can take advantage of the fact that the majority of every society has always lent itself to manipulation by leaders working either in their own interests or in the interests of the minority rich-and-powerful class. The terms of the manipulation are simple: anger is generated by discontent, and the critical spirit is stimulated by anger; but the critical spirit rarely leads to a coherent understanding of the conditions that gave rise to the anger. The emotion, rather than the analysis, is the central experience in the consciousness of the oppressed.

Clever demagogues, recognizing the discontent and the anger, can gain widespread support by pretending to work in their followers' interests through various devices. Two classic and currently employed ruses include confusing the cause of discontent with the symbols of it, and confusing affirmation of followers' life style with programs to improve their life conditions.

Through the first device, today's demagogue is able to design a false analysis, as simple as possible, and to encourage the majority to accept it. In this sense, Middle America is convinced to attach its fury to "commies," or hippies, or blacks, or students, or professors, or some other group which is not at all responsible for the conditions of discontent. The critics of society are deftly identified as the causes of society's troubles. Then an appealing though incorrect deduction becomes possible: silencing the critics will end the discomfort of which they speak.

Unfortunately, it is far easier and less threatening to blame one's problems on leftists or hippies or even crooked officials than to face the possibility that this may actually be a society in which the government, although responsive to powerful pressure groups, will not readily respond to ordinary citizen protest, no matter *who* is in office.

President Nixon's hominess—his fondness for meat loaf, his short hair and quiet, admiring wife, prayers in the White House and friendship with Billy Graham, his passion for football and his lack of interest in "high culture"—these are all qualities and behavior that probably describe the man genuinely, and that also endear him to Middle America. But the Middle Americans who applaud the Nixon government may have been taken in by a second ruse. They appear to confuse the President's affirmation of their life style with the likelihood that his policies will improve their life conditions. The comfortable feeling of oneness with this plain man who appears so sincere in his beliefs and style easily obscures the discrepancy between the style and the accompanying behavior that works against the interests of Middle America—high unemployment rates, regressive taxation, transportation policies that stress automobile travel over mass transit, the endless deaths in Vietnam.

In addition, the ideology's stress on periodic voting as the only acceptable or necessary form of political participation legitimates the tendency of elected and appointed politicians and bureaucrats to discourage involvement in public affairs. How responsive government officials should be to citizen political activity other than voting is an issue of much concern and debate. We suggest now that most officials probably find all forms of public petitioning a nuisance at best and conceive of their roles as decision-makers responding to "purely technical" issues and to the pressures of long-established interest groups.

How do leaders avoid being watchdogged at every step by the public? We suspect a careful analysis would reveal that they respond minimally when citizens try to make their influence felt, and respond that way consistently enough so that the discontented public eventually gives up and cynically "adapts" to a situation they appear unable to control. To use an example related to our case study, at one time in the

Inner Belt controversy, a person sympathetic to the DPW point of view told me that the DPW had at least six communities on its back demanding changes in highway designs. If it "capitulates" (not, "responds understandingly") to any one of them, he said, it would open itself up to having to deal with the others. In slightly more formal terms, elites appear to believe that their activities would be unnecessarily complicated if the public's needs were taken into account, and they must take care not to respond very much, lest still more demands be made upon them by those in whose interests they presumably work.

Most analysts of American society feel that too many citizens are unable to participate in determining their own destinies. Because "participation" is supposed to be good, planning and other public agencies endorse it on principle and claim to encourage it in fact. But nodding approval to such a principle is not the same as its implementation.

It may appear that we have come a long way from the late 1940s and 1950s, when Robert Moses chaired the Slum Clearance Committee in New York City. Moses was notorious for lacking all respect for neighborhood groups that attempted to influence the government planning bureaucracy. One student of that period reports that Moses' "philosophy of dealing with the site residents was most succinctly summed up [as] 'Neighborhood groups are crap.'"[9]

More recently, many people in leadership positions have been speaking the participation line, because it is "in" at the moment, and it is expedient for them to do so. But it is important to look at what commonly happens when government officials attempt to promote "citizen participation." For example, recent federal legislation has directed that there must be local citizen participation in federally funded urban renewal programs. In response, most cities appointed prominent businessmen and other local leaders to an urban renewal advisory committee. The low-income

citizens who would be directly affected by renewal programs were not invited to join those committees.[10] Even
such a prominent agency as the Boston Redevelopment
Authority claimed as its motto "Planning with People,"
when the people it planned with were almost always hand-
picked ministers and businessmen, the upwardly mobile
upper fringes of the low-income communities to be affected
by their plans. Able to rub elbows with important people
and perhaps to advance their own mobility interests, these
"representatives" often act less in the interests of the communities they come from than those they hope to move into.

AMERICA AS A SUCCESSFUL PLURALIST SOCIETY

Traditional popular wisdom about organized political
competition in American society holds that any citizens
with a political interest to pursue can organize themselves
into a group and effectively reach decision-makers with
their case.

The Brookline-Elm people tried to make their feelings
known through letter-writing and group meetings. The advocate planners tried to add a technically feasible plan to
those sentiments but discovered soon enough that emotion
and logic get a movement nowhere, unless power is added to
them. In others words, the Brookline-Elm people on their
own cannot really be expected to compete successfully with
established interests running counter to theirs. Such
interests operate overtly through the political system, and
also covertly.

The characteristic of power that its students most often
ignore is the limits it implicitly sets on actors' behavior.
When officials know they cannot pursue certain paths of
action because to do so would offend and antagonize certain important interests, then those interests are success-

fully exerting an exceedingly important kind of power. Peter Bachrach and Morton S. Baratz, in a provocative essay on this subject, ask rhetorically whether the student of power can "safely ignore the possibility . . . that an individual or group in a community participates more vigorously in the nondecision-making process than in participating in actual decisions within the process?"[11] That is, some people are so powerful that they can prevent various ideas and proposals from serious consideration by the body politic; indeed the threat of disapproval and counteractions are surely often adequate enough to prevent many kinds of innovations and complaints from ever surfacing at all.

The Lobby Problem in a "Pluralist" Society

Two government-sponsored reports, one issued in 1941 and the other in 1950, warn that large business interests—whether automobile producers, food-processors, drug manufacturers or whatever—often influence public policy and allocation of public resources for their own private benefit and *against* the public welfare.

The 1941 study, *Investigation of Concentration of Economic Power,* points to indirect effects of business on legislation.

> While the business community may, on occasion, elect "its man" to Congress or to the Presidency, or secure his appointment to a governmental office or to the courts, its indirect influence is of far greater importance. Pressure groups generally find it more satisfactory to influence the votes of legislators in their behalf than to try to elect their own representatives to office. Furthermore, a large number of legislators are lawyers, and the bar is on most questions sympathetic to the views of the business community. As a result of both conviction and training, lawyers adhere to a business philosophy to nearly as great a degree as businessmen themselves. Farmers, laborers, distributors, and consumers, as such, have never appeared in legislative bodies in anything like the number of lawyers.[12]

The report concludes that some pressure groups are far more able to exert power than are others:

> Theoretically, pressure groups compete with each other on equal terms, have equal bargaining power, with none enjoying an advantage over another. This assumes that the right of petition guaranteed by the Constitution is exercised by "free and equal" men. The most it assumes, under a broader interpretation, is that citizens, when they have grievances against their government, lend weight to their pleas by mobilizing their strength and directing it by organization to Congress. But it is assumed that such organization is temporary, and furthermore that the group wields no more economic power than that growing out of the aggregate resources of the individuals composing it.

> [But] the membership organization, employing the lobbyist, directed by paid executives, exerts a degree of strength, cohesion, and mobility differing essentially from the fluctuating pressures of an earlier day. As for business, the corporations whose right as persons to petition the government is exercised by lawyer-lobbyists have behind them so much wealth, such concentrated control, and such a degree of impersonality as to challenge their right to function, under democratic theory, as individuals.[13]

The authors of the report reason that the advantage of business organizations in lobbying depends on four characteristics:

1. *Continuity.* Since it persists over many years, the organization gathers experience, techniques and familiarity with problems its opponents probably lack.
2. *Cohesion.* The mutual support of members of a lobbying organization established for additional purposes is probably especially strong. By implication, responsibilities and obligations among the members have worked out in other contexts in ways that support the lobby effort.
3. *Visibility.* An organization may find it advantageous

to testify before Congressional committees behind
closed doors, but it may also have the advantage of
legitimacy in the public eye. (General Motors is better
known than Save Our Cities.)
4. *Resources*. Money for propaganda, law suits, etc., is
already available to the business organization.[14]

Calling the Chamber of Commerce of the United States
"chief among the organized groups representing business"
(in 1941) and the National Association of Manufacturers
"the outstanding employers' group,"[15] the report names the
former as "a constant factor in political opinion-form-
ing . . . probably not surpassed by any other group . . . as a
pipeline for steady, relentless, and timely opinion dissemin-
ination. . . ."[16]

Nine years later, the Buchanan Committee of the House
of Representatives investigated lobbying. It discovered that
the National Association of Manufacturers reported it
spent in one year just about $85,000 on lobbying yet also
claimed a budget of $4.3 million for "legislative activities."
It denied that its $2 million public relations program was
connected with legislation, but admitted that in 1946 it
spent $395,000, "largely on advertising" in a campaign to
abolish the Office of Price Administration.[17]

The committee reports that lobbies' goals at one time
were simply to be left alone.

> However, the developing pattern in lobbying has been one of
> cooperation, combination, and massing of effort. In its simplest
> and oldest form, this process is demonstrated by the swift
> growth of trade associations since the First World War. These
> organizations have assumed central authority for pressing the
> particular industry's case before Congress and the public.[18]

The authors of the report suggest that powerful lobby
groups have in striking ways replaced political parties in
the American political system. The responsibility may be
as much that of the parties as of the lobbies that supplant

them, but the effect is policy by lobby rather than by political organization, or to put it another way, the economic organization *becomes* the political organization.

> The conditions in which a highly developed system of pressure politics could flourish were provided by two other unique features of our governmental arrangements. First, our political parties have grown progressively more loosely controlled and undisciplined. Pressure groups thrive on the inability or unwillingness of political parties to exercise the powers of government which they have lawfully gained at the polls. The advantages of this situation to the lobby group are obvious: lack of cohesion in the parties enables well-organized private interests to secure some of the advantages of political power without having to submit to the democratic electoral process by which this power is usually attained.[19]

Four hundred ninety-five groups filed lobby reports over a three-and-a-half year period, to comply with the Lobbying Act of 1946, but the committee discounts such official reports. The committee estimates the number of permanent national lobbies at three to eight times the official figure and suggests that to accept those organizations' reported figures as true pictures of lobby expenses would be like saying "that no money is gambled on horse races other than that paid through the pari-mutuel windows. . . ." Add up letter and telegram campaigns, books, institutional advertising, salaries of executives, lawyers, and publicists, and the committee estimates a billion-dollar-a-year lobbying industry in 1950.[20]

Specifically cited is General Motors. It spent almost $5 million in the years 1947-1949, among 375 national, state and local groups, in contributions either made to tax-exempt groups or deducted by GM from gross income before taxes as business expenses or as charitable and similar deductions. These monies were paid to groups which prepare or distribute literature on public issues. Of $4,867,051 spent, GM gave $2,843,745 to the Automobile Manufacturers Association, $229,610 to the National Association of Manufacturers, $35,000 to the Foundation for Economic Education, $30,000 to the American Economic Foundation, and $346,200 to various chambers of commerce. It also spent over $1 million to print and distribute over 20,000,000 copies of 45 publications.[21]

The Buchanan committee concludes with a startling simile:

> So far as reported expenditures for lobbying are concerned, organized business far outspends other interests. . . .We believe lobbying to be every man's right. But some men are more able to make their rights meaningful than others. In practical terms, this has meant that those interests with the most to spend for protection have proclaimed "lobbying for all men" as an almost sacred article of faith. It is not unlike the elephant shouting "Everyone for himself," as he stomps up and down among the chickens.[22]

The point is that "the people" are no match for the rich and powerful class—the large stockholders and highest paid officials of giant banks, investment houses and corporations, and technicians and government officials who are from that class or serve its interests, or both. General Motors, the Chamber of Commerce of the United States, the National Association of Manufacturers, the Automobile Manufacturers Association and similar organizations represent the interests of this class. To suggest that people in neighborhoods like Brookline-Elm are free in this democracy to pursue their interests against those of the highway lobby *et al.*, with equal likelihood of affecting "the system" is to mock those people and the theory of democracy under which they live.

The Highway Lobby—A Case Study

We noted that highway controversies have both a local and a national level. We shift our attention here to the latter.

A recent interchange on the floor of the House of Representatives in Washington reveals the manner in which the economic interests of the auto and highway people conflict with noneconomic interests of unorganized constituencies. On September 4, 1969, the House debated a provision in air pollution legislation proposed by Democratic Congressman Leonard Farbstein of New York. Farbstein wanted to prohibit by law the sale and manufacture of cars powered by internal combustion engines after January 1, 1978 (owing to their prime role in air pollution and attendant health problems), in hopes that this would encourage automobile companies to devote some of their earnings to perfecting engines emitting less pollutant material.

Congressman James Harvey (R. Michigan), who describes himself as "one who represents a district in which the automobile industry is very important," opposed Farbstein's proposal:

> in this nation of ours one out of every seven workers' jobs is traceable to the auto industry. . . . The net sales of autos last year came to over \$19 billion and . . . out of our balance of payments more than \$1 billion came from the sales of autos alone. So I say to you that the industry has significance. You can knock it all you want to and say that it is not doing a good enough job in getting rid of air pollution. But this industry means an awful lot to an awful lot of people in America, and I would consider that very carefully before we tamper with writing standards that would affect it. . . .[23]

In response, Congressman George E. Brown, Jr., (D. California), who was one of the few supporters of the Farbstein proposal remarked:

> the argument that we should not tamper with the automobile industry because one person out of every six [sic] in this country is engaged in the business just does not appeal to me. What if one person in every six were engaged in the sale of heroin in this country? . . . There is no question whatsoever but

what the automobile industry and the petroleum industry and the poisons which they are emitting into the atmosphere are having a far worse effect upon the health of this country than heroin is. And that will continue to be the result of these emissions as they continue to concentrate in the atmosphere, because we refuse to control an $80-billion-per-year industry in this country.[24]

Farbstein's legislation lost by a vote of 99 to 22.[25] The obscuring of health problems by appealing to economic output as the only important consideration suggests an awesomely effective auto and highway lobby.

HIGHWAY-RELATED INDUSTRIES

The national "highway lobby"[26] is a combination of automobile and highway interests considered by many observers to be second in national influence only to the military-industrial-space lobby that for several years has controlled about half the federal budget.* An article written around 1935 pointed out:

the auto industry is a key center of American industry. It forms a vitally important link connecting such basic industries as steel, coal and rubber with the consuming market, which cannot be broken without throwing the whole of American industry out of gear. . . . About one-eighth of the gainfully employed get their living directly or indirectly out of the automobile business. . . . Directly or indirectly, the rate of its operations affect every branch of our economic life from the construction of roads and the sale of oil products to the number of police.

---

* The *New Republic* claims that the power of the highway lobby actually exceeds that of the military-industrial complex ("Highway Juggernaut," *New Republic,* July 6, 1968, p. 12). The petroleum lobby alone—one of the main constituents of the highway lobby—is seen by some as so powerful that U.S. Senator Thomas J. McIntyre (D. N.H.) refers to it as "The Secret Government of Oil" (*Boston Sunday Globe,* Nov. 22, 1969, pp. 32-44).

The influence of the auto companies is by no means confined to the United States. The limbs of these industrial giants stretch throughout the world. Raw materials for auto manufacture are imported from every corner of the globe, and the demands of the American industry are a decisive factor in the economy of many countries. The commercial and industrial activities of the auto companies are equally international in extent. The big auto companies have sales agents, manufacturing assembly plants, as well as financial and political connections in almost every important nation.[27]

With the exception of the proportion of Americans employed in auto-related industries (current estimates put it at one-seventh to one-sixth of the work force), everything in this statement is true today. The place of automobile and highway-related interests in the American economy is staggering.

1. *Industrial Significance.* In the United States, eight out of the nation's 12 richest and most productive industrial corporations are connected with the automobile industry; they are General Motors (the world's largest corporation), Standard Oil of New Jersey (now Exxon), Ford, Chrysler, Mobil Oil, Texaco, Gulf Oil and U.S. Steel (a key supplier to the auto industry). Of the 100 largest corporations, at least one-third are in auto manufacturing, oil, iron and steel, rubber and other auto-related fields.[28]

2. *Sales.* In 1969, $36.5 billion was spent on new and used car purchases.[29] Between 1962 and 1969, auto sales amounted to about 4 percent of the gross national product—or in other words, accounted for $4 out of every $100.[30]

3. *Financing.* In the same year, 1969, 53 percent of those autos were purchased on installment credit and other borrowing, with $19.3 billion borrowed for this purpose.[31] Since payments on cars typically spread over two or three years, we are probably dealing here with an industry involving around $40 bil-

lion, plus interest, in purchase financing at any given time.

4. *Insurance.* The automobile insurance industry wrote $11.693 billion worth of insurance (including auto liability, bodily injury, property damage, fire, theft, collision and comprehensive) in 1968, more than twice the amount written in 1955 ($4.464 billion), and almost five times the amount written in 1950 ($2.625 billion).[32]

5. *Raw Materials.* In 1963, 22.4 percent of all steel used in the United States went into automobiles. Of malleable iron, 56.6 percent produced goes into cars; of aluminum, 13.5 percent; copper, 12.8 percent; nickel, 14 percent; natural rubber, 64.5 percent; reclaimed rubber, 58.8 percent; synthetic rubber, 60.1 percent; and zinc, 35 percent.[33] The cement industry, asphalt, gravel, etc., are others with a major stake in road-building.

6. *Oil.* The more miles travelled, the more fuel consumed. Motor fuel used by cars, buses and trucks rose from 40.28 billion gallons in 1950 to 82.938 billion gallons in 1968. The average mileage per gallon of fuel has declined slightly but steadily. In 1940, for example, cars averaged 15.29 miles driven per gallon. In 1950 the average was down to 14.95, in 1960 to 14.28, and in 1968, to 13.91 miles per gallon.[34] The lower the mileage per gallon the more the fuel consumed.

7. **Highway Construction Industry.** In 1947, $917 million worth of contracts for construction of highways was awarded. By 1955, the figure was $2.619 billion; in 1969, it had risen to $6.657 billion, or about one-tenth of the amount awarded for all forms of construction in 1969.[35] At the end of 1968 the Interstate Highway System was 68 percent completed, with about 28,000 miles of highway in use. The 42,500

that will comprise the entire system is expected to be finished by 1974, and to cost at least $56.5 billion.[36] It has been estimated that each dollar invested in highway construction yields another dollar in land speculation, and still another in highway maintenance.[37] Some contractors make money by using cheaper materials than those specified by federal standards[38] and then, one would guess, make more money still by repairing what they have inadequately built.

8. *Engineering Profession.* Thousands of city, state and federal highway engineers and planners make up the membership of influential groups such as the Institute for Traffic Engineers and the American Association of State Highway Officials.[39]

9. *Labor.* The automobile industry, including manufacturing, service and repair, wholesale trade in vehicles and equipment like tires, and retail trade in cars, equipment and accessories (including miscellaneous aircraft and marine dealers) employed 2,882,100 people in 1969 and paid out about $16.7 billion in wages and salaries.[40] Highway construction in 1967 employed 410,500 people.[41]

10. *Trucking Industry.* In 1969, almost two million trucks and buses were sold.[42] In 1960, over two million people worked as truck drivers.[43]

11. *Real Estate.* To these considerable interests we must add real estate. Not only is money frequently made by selling land for highway construction; as much or more money is made from land adjacent to the highway. In rural areas, land becomes valuable for filling stations, restaurants, motels and suburban housing. In cities, low-income neighborhoods next to highways become transformed to commercial, industrial, and middle- and high-income high-rise housing.[44] The hundreds of millions made off such land deals

and the subsequent building and commercial efforts are, to our knowledge, not yet calculated by anyone. A related source of wealth is the occasional inflation of land values on the highway right-of-way.*

12. *Downtown Parking.* Parking lots and garages proliferate as urban highways increase.

13. *Local Business.* On the local and state levels, there are economic interests like downtown merchants, chambers of commerce, industrialists and civic associations who believe that urban highways will "revitalize" downtowns and that suburban highways will lead to suburban growth. There are also state and local governments that make much tax money off automobiles. There are states that find gas taxes providing up to one-quarter of their incomes.[45]

14. *The "Accident" Industry.* An appalling but significant spinoff of the automobile industry is what we might label the auto accident industry. Ralph Nader points out that the relative inattention to safety in auto design generates a proliferation of economic outputs the cost of which runs into billions of dollars. He lists medical, police, administrative, legal, insurance, automotive repairs and funeral services.[46] One can of course add florists, greeting card makers and sellers, construction firms that build insurance company offices, orthopedic appliance manufacturers and retailers, etc., to those who profit from auto accidents.

15. *Miscellaneous.* A comprehensive survey of the economics of automobile-related industries would also

---

* Rumors of such corruption were alarming enough that in 1960 the Federal Bureau of Public Roads froze land acquisition funds for highways in Massachusetts. An investigation led to the conviction of several men on conspiracy to overcharge the government (*Congressional Quarterly Almanac*, Washington, D.C., *Congressional Quarterly News Features*, 1962, Vol. 18, p. 453).

include items like scrappage (an estimated 5,200,000 cars and 700,000 trucks and buses were scrapped in 1963, compared with 4,598,000 cars and 636,000 trucks and buses in 1950)[47]; car radios (14,505,000 sold in 1957 and 18,281,000 in 1963)[48]; new plants and equipment for vehicle and parts manufacturing ($1.46 billion in 1965)[49]; and automobile advertising (approximately $592 million was spent on automotive advertising in 1969).[50]

Thus the automobile is the center of a gigantic segment of the American economy. More roads built means more cars using them, and consequently all branches of the economy that depend on the manufacture and use of cars also depend on the construction and use of highways.

THE LOBBYING ORGANIZATIONS

The highway lobby consists of three main groups, two formal—the National Highway Users Conference (NHUC) and the American Road Builders Association(ARBA)—and what is sometimes called the "Road Gang," an informal grouping of "about 190 business consultants, trade association officials, public relations men and lobbyists connected with highway transportation. . . ."[51]

NHUC was organized in 1932 for "the advancement of highway transportation in the public interests." It lists as a "vital concern . . . resisting efforts to choke off urban automobility by excessive taxation and controls, and encouraging sound methods to cope with increased traffic." A decade ago, the organization had Washington offices staffed by 55 people, and an annual budget of about $750,000. Two thousand organizations belong to NHUC or one of the 50 affiliated state highway users conferences.[52]

Among the members of NHUC, some of which maintain separate lobby operations apart from that group, are the American Automobile Association, American Farm Bureau Federation, American National Cattlemen's Association, American Petroleum Institute (representing 59 oil companies), American Retail Federation, American Trucking Associations, Inc., Automobile Manufacturers Association (representing General Motors, Ford, Chrysler and American Motors), National Association of Motor Bus Operators, National Automobile Dealers Association, National Council of Private Motor Truck Owners, Inc., National Grange, National League of Wholesale Fresh Fruit and Vegetable Distributors, Rubber Manufacturers Association, National Sand and Gravel Association, the Truck Trailer Manufacturers Association, associations of bakers, bottlers, hotel and motel owners and many, many others.[53]

ARBA numbers among its members 2,300 contractors and 1,500 federal, state, county and city highway officials (including, in 1962, the Federal Highway Administrator), and 2,500 equipment manufacturers, materials suppliers, consulting engineers, professors of highway engineering and others. The association employs about 20 people and operates on a yearly budget of over $400,000.[54] A key segment of ARBA is the American Association of State Highway Officials (AASHO), which represents "political muscle" in all 50 states. According to Denison and Tomlinson in the *Readers' Digest:*

> When road legislation is considered in Congress, AASHO's Washington headquarters summons key state officials to help lobby. These same officials then return home to administer the federal dollars that they helped secure. Working closely with the U.S. Bureau of Public Roads (equally pro-highway), they supervise freeway construction, largely determining where the new roads are routed. Rep. James C. Wright, Jr. (D. Texas), says, "Among those groups coming to Congress on highway matters, AASHO is probably the most respected and influential."[55]

To these two giant combines of auto- and highway-related interests can be added the two most important business lobby groups: the Chamber of Commerce of the United States, representing 3,400 local and state chambers of commerce,[56] and the National Association of Manufacturers, whose membership includes some 20,300 business firms.[57]

The members of the "highway lobby" have promoted their interests in three ways: through encouraging the general public to accept what we call the "national ideology of the private automobile," through influencing federal and local governments to spend enormous amounts of public revenue on subsidizing highways and private driving, and through discouraging public expenditures for research and implementation of mass transit alternatives.

Influencing Public Opinion: The National Ideology Of The Private Automobile

In 1939, the National Highway Users Conference published an anti-toll road pamphlet, entitled "Highway Transportation Re-Makes America." An elegantly bordered page of the pamphlet, headed "Highway Transportation," lists 15 points. The most stunning is the first: "1. Freedom of the highways is a basic human right." This is followed by a specified form of ownership: "2. Every free American should be secure in his right to transport himself, his family, his friends and his own goods in his own vehicle."[58] On the cover of the publication a brunette lady bountiful stands, in the midst of a landscape of fields, factories and electrical transmission wires. Towering high over the scene, light radiating all about her, she holds forth in her arms, beneath a warm and open smile, a gigantic four-door convertible sedan. Later in the pamphlet, another lady bountiful, blonde and like her brunette sister a hundred times human size, nestles in her arm a giant cornucopia. Mountains lie behind her, and soft clouds rise above, broken only by lines of light shining from her body. Dozens of people cheer, their arms upraised, as from the horn of plenty flow houses and, in larger scale, automobiles and trucks. The automobile is treated, in this NHUC publication, with a quasi-religious reverence, and the importance of driving is argued—almost ludicrously—to the point of trying to make "freedom of the highways" comparable to freedom of speech or freedom of the press.

In fact, the auto in some industry publications becomes more important than human beings. Reports written for the Automobile Manufacturers Association in 1966 assert that "American cities can increasingly adapt to the motor vehicle"[59] and that "the nation's urban centers are striving for a new equilibrium attuned to the motor vehicle—an adaptation essential for their continued prosperity and dominance. . . ."[60] The implication, astounding though it may appear, is that Americans must dedicate themselves to making life comfortable for cars, or to put it more bluntly, that the welfare of the auto-highway industry is more important than the welfare of the people it affects.

Add to such specific attempts the millions of dollars spent on countless advertisements, through magazine, radio, billboard and television, that suffuse automobile ownership with images of beauty, status advancement, erotic splendor, security and autonomy. This massive campaign has reinforced the credo held by millions of Americans that the freedom to own and drive a car is a major realization of the right to "life, liberty and the pursuit of happiness," and the acqusition of a driver's license and a car is an important rise in social status, comparable to starting and ending school, marriage or parenthood. The building of more and more highways on which to drive these cars is of course demanded by this credo.

Influencing Government Decisions

The most significant impact of the highway lobby is its direct influence over federal legislation. For years the high-

way lobby has worked to persuade our legislators to allo-
cate ever more money for road building and to make it
ever easier and more alluring for states to engage in highway construction. It has opposed restrictions on road building aimed at preserving historical landmarks or natural
areas and has fought significant expenditures for mass
transit.

Lobbyists for the highway interests, like any other interest, work through personal contacts, monetary relationships and campaign contributions. Lobbying also includes
providing congressmen with technical reports, gifts, free
transportation, parties and so forth, and organizing people
back in the home district to urge their congressmen to support legislation the lobby wants.

Since 1946, lobbyists have been required by law to register with Congress and to list amounts of income and expense in their lobbying activities. But many corporations do
not register annually—some not at all—and it is not uncommon to see expenses of $50 a year listed by a major
corporation. Some report salaries but not other expenses;
some vice versa; some list only Washington expenses. For
most years, the three major automobile manufacturers, the
powerful Automobile Manufacturers Association, NHUC
and ARBA do not register as lobbies with Congress.

The Highway Trust Fund, established in 1956 to pay the
federal 90 percent share of the cost of the Interstate Highway System, is the crowning accomplishment of the power
of the highway lobby. Fueled by federal taxes also imposed
by the 1956 legislation on auto purchases, accessories, tires
and gasoline, the fund is an ever-growing golden egg that
not only does not require annual congressional approval
(making it startlingly unlike almost any other federally
funded program), but can *only* be used for highway construction. As one author points out:

> The real genius of the Trust Fund is that the more roads are
> built, the more they are used and the more money becomes

available for further road building. This increasing spiral plus increases in the actual tax rates (gasoline taxes have increased from 1¢ to 4¢ per gallon since 1957) has meant a tremendous revenue fund to draw upon. Limited to highway construction as the fund is, it means that the more the fund grows, the greater grows the power of the highway building interests.[61]

Denison calls the Interstate Highway System "the most mouth-watering pork-barrel device ever conceived," adding that "nearly all members of Congress—liberals and conservatives, Republicans and Democrats alike—unite on one issue: the absolute need for heavy highway spending."[62] Mary Perot Nichols adds that state governors use federal highway funds as "patronage for the construction . . . trades and unions."[63]

In addition to pushing for massive federal funding of highway programs, another significant activity of highway lobby members is to see that as little money as possible goes to public transportation alternatives to private automobiles and their roads. For example, in 1962, the National Association of Manufacturers (NAM) and the Chamber of Commerce of the United States, both of which consistently support road legislation, were successful in opposing the creation of an urban affairs department of the federal government and the federal funding of urban mass transit (as well as medicare, federal aid to education and other measures).[64] In 1963, NAM and the Chamber of Commerce again successfully opposed mass transit legislation. This legislation would have authorized $500 million over four years for constructing new mass transit facilities and improving old ones, research and development in mass transit, and relocation payments for families moved by transit efforts.[65]

Most striking is the continually accumulating evidence that the highway lobby has literally "bought" many legislators who are in key decision-making positions on highway funding and other road laws. Many thousands of dollars have been contributed to the political campaigns of 13 members of the House Public Works Committee (the committee in charge of highway legislation) by the Truck Operators Non-Partisan Committee, whose head fund raiser says, "We do what we can for those who might help us." When Representative George Fallon (D. Maryland), the chairman of the House Public Works Committee, faced severe opposition while running for reelection in 1968, the American Road Builders Association helped him by holding a $50-a-plate dinner that netted $13,000. The Associated General Contractors also helped raise money for Fallon in contributions, including $1,000 each from two contractors in Pennsylvania, $500 from a cement lobbyist in California and $850 from road builders in South Dakota; these contributions enabled Fallon to mount a campaign that returned him to office.[66]

Denison also notes that House and Senate subcommittees that wrote highway legislation in 1968 included seven members whose law firms (with whom they retained connections while in Congress) number auto, truck, bus, oil and road construction companies among their clients. This is clearly a case of conflict of interest.[67]

The highway industry also "helps" its friends in state governments. Denison describes how a lobbyist for an oil company spends up to $2,000 a month on entertaining California legislators. A California state senator considered the "father of California freeways" benefited in 1966 from a fund-raising dinner, at $100 a plate, the program for which displayed nearly $17,000 worth of advertising by the Motor Car Dealers Association of Northern and Southern California, the California Trailer Coach Association, nine construction firms, etc. Former California Governor Edmund G. Brown complains, "The lobby has blocked good urban transit in this state."[68]

A startling example of the highway lobby's power appears in its role in shaping the 1968 Federal Highway legislation. In spring 1968, when conservation and beautification provisions to preserve parkland, historic sites and wildlife areas were being considered by Congress as part of the latest highway legislation, the NHUC, which was meeting in Washington, D.C., at the time, labeled conservation advocates "beautniks" and "nuts."[69] As a result of pressure from NHUC and other highway lobby groups, the final version of the 1968 Federal-Aid Highway Act, according to the *New York Times,*

> wiped out vital safeguards against routing highways through parks, historic sites and wildlife areas . . . emasculated Federal powers to impose standards on billboard placement, leaving to the states controls states rarely impose . . . [and] demanded that the District of Columbia complete a freeway system through the capital that has been opposed by local conservationists, citizens groups, and residents of poor neighborhoods. . . .[70]

President Johnson called several provisions of the final bill "unfortunate, ill-considered and a setback to the cause of conservation," and signed it with serious reservations. Johnson's strongest objections were to the provisions forcing construction of an unwanted freeway system in Washington, D.C.[71]

Yule Fisher, director of NHUC, said, however, that the 1968 Act was "'highly desirable' and that the 25 organizations his group represents are gratified it was signed. A veto would have been 'a catastrophe and a severe rebuff to the highway program,' Mr. Fisher said."[72]

Fortunately, there have been changes. By 1972 even transportation Secretary Volpe had shown increased interest in mass transit and has taken the widely publicized daring step of suggesting legislative changes to allow the Highway Trust Fund to be used partly for mass transit development. This sounds like a great victory for the citizens groups opposing further highway development. But even such a nonradical publication as *Forbes* business magazine suggests that Volpe's celebrated move may be a "disguised victory for the highway lobby." Volpe's plan would extend the Highway Trust Fund until 1980. The Urban Mass Transportation Act of 1970 is heavily funded and is intended to provide only for mass transit development. Volpe's plan is to phase out the Urban Mass Transportation Administration (UMTA) established by the 1970 Act and to provide mass transit funds only from the Highway Trust Fund, in such a way that mass transit would have less money to spend than if the UMTA were continued. As *Forbes* suggests, "Clearly construction man Volpe, who was the first Federal Highway Administrator in 1956, hasn't forgotten his friends."[73]

The Cambridge Inner Belt conflict at a superficial level appears as a controversy between the ad hoc citizens group, and a local university and the state highway department. Considering the role of the national highway lobby in making construction of roads like the Inner Belt so attractive and almost inevitable, we suggest now that the reason the neighborhood people were so ineffective on their own was because in essence, *the people of Brookline-Elm are no match for the highway lobby* and for the organization-class planners, officials and engineers whose work promotes the interests of the highway lobby over those of Middle Americans like the Brookline-Elm population.

GOVERNMENT AS NEUTRAL

Democratic government supposedly decides and acts in the name of the "general good." It is further assumed that government decision-makers listen to all arguments and make decisions as fairly as they can based on the evidence and arguments presented to them by the contending parties.

From the Inner Belt experience, we learn that in reality the "general good" is often confused with the interests and values of the organization class or the rich-and-powerful class. (Recall General Motors' President Charles Wilson's declaration, that what was "good for the country was good for General Motors, and vice versa.") There appear to be two reasons for this phenomenon. Most obviously, organized, powerful interests are more successful politically than ad hoc groups like SOC in having their views heeded. Less obviously, government decision-makers in general are themselves either organization-class or rich-and-powerful-class members, whose actions are shaped, perhaps sometimes unwittingly, by their own social-class interests and values, frequently to the detriment of people in other social classes.

For these two reasons, we suggest that much government policy systematically (but not necessarily consciously) discriminates against citizens in the poor-and-powerless class, and in Middle America. As we have implied and will now document further, the uprooting and relocation involved in government highway and urban renewal programs clearly exemplifies this discrimination. Further examples are the draft, which until recently offered exemptions to college students or those able to obtain special legal or medical assistance (all options more likely to apply to sons of the organization class and the rich); and the tax structure, which extracts proportionately more from low- and middle-income citizens than anyone else. The choice of the Brookline-Elm neighborhood for a highway location is just one of many specific instances of social-class discrimination in public policy.

Social Class Discrimination in Public Construction Programs: A Case Study

In 1968, the National Commission on Urban Problems, headed by a former senator, Paul H. Douglas, issued a

significant report entitled *Building the American City*.
Mainly concerned with housing needs, it studied the nature
and effects of federal construction programs, primarily
urban renewal and highway projects, that required the dislocation of large numbers of citizens. The estimated total
number of dwelling units demolished by all federal programs, starting in the 1940s and ending with 1967, is approximately 1,054,000,[74] or about three to four million
people displaced. Dislocations for highways contributed
about one-third of the total, about 30,000 "families and
individuals" displaced each year since the Interstate program began in 1956, or a total of about 330,000 "families
and individuals"[75]—about one million people.

Who are these people, the report asks, and what happened to them? Its conclusions are shocking. "It has been
primarily the poor, the near poor, and lower-middle class
whose houses have been demolished."[76] But

> urban renewal . . . has failed to help the poor and near-poor
> who make up most of those who have been displaced. They
> have not been rehoused on the urban renewal sites, nor has the
> total volume of public housing been adequate to meet the needs
> created by demolitions, deterioration, and population growth.
> Relocation efforts have brought mixed results. But urban re-
> newal has in the past gone on its way relatively oblivious to
> the housing needs of the poor, although it has not been as in-
> different as the highway program, which in the past has de-
> molished several hundred thousand homes without showing
> until recent years the least tangible interest in what happened to
> the occupants.[77]

Of 400,000 primarily low-rental dwelling units demolished
for urban renewal, only 41,580 low- and middle-income
units had been replaced under this program by 1966. Highway construction programs had replaced *no* units.[78]

Large-scale disruption has always brought with it a
wide variety of problems. As Chester Hartman suggests:

> Large-scale relocation of families and individuals, such as
> that occasioned by highway construction and urban renewal,

necessarily raises basic questions of social welfare and public policy . . . how relocation affects the family's ability to meet the society's minimum standards for quality and quantity of living space; the extent to which the family can fulfill its needs and desires in terms of housing and neighborhood characteristics and convenience to employment, community facilities, family, and friends; the costs—financial, social, and emotional—involved in experiencing forced change, and the unintended consequences of such changes; the differential incidence of benefits and costs on various groups within the relocation population; the effect of population redistribution on the city's ecological patterns, particularly with respect to racial segregation, and how these more general effects influence the individual family's housing experience.[79]

In a study of urban renewal in New York City, J. Clarence Davies, III, points out:

Neighborhoods within a city differ widely with respect to the social contacts the individuals in the neighborhoods maintain with each other and with neighborhood institutions. We may speak of some neighborhoods as having an on-going social system, a system that ties the individuals in the area to each other. To the degree that their friendships and contacts are within the neighborhood, individuals will have an important stake in maintaining the *status quo.* People may lose economically or politically by having their environment altered, and they may also lose socially.[80]

Further costs of relocation are discussed by William Key in a Kansas study which contrasts effects of relocation from a highway project and an urban renewal project. As a result of the move, both sets of displacees had to travel farther to facilities they used.[81] Older displacees and children had special problems:

Older people suffer more, objectively and subjectively, from both forced and voluntary moving. While some may welcome the opportunity to acquire housing more suited to their needs, the problem of providing satisfactory and adequate housing for older people is particularly difficult. Subjectively, one cannot replace memories and years of involvement with places and people. Objectively, the elderly have few remaining years in which to adapt and to replace the sights, sounds, and people from which they are separated by a move. In addition, if they are isolated from their friends and relatives, they frequently lack the means of transportation for re-establishing the contacts. . . .[82]

Children suffered a great deal because they were dependent upon the neighborhood, and it was difficult for them to replace the uses of the neighborhood. They had little involvement in the moving process and no counselling to assist them in sorting out their feelings or planning for the move.[83]

The author also notes that some small businessmen in the old neighborhood provided functions not easily replaced. One drugstore owner, for example, "performed the role of landlord, guardian, counselor, banker, job placement expert, and moral supervisor."[84]

In all displacement programs, the majority of people who are forced to move are working-class and poor people, both black and white. As many studies show, such groups can least afford dislocation, for emotional, social and financial reasons. For example, Ernest Norton Tooby, a lawyer writing about the social, psychological and financial effects of displacement, speaks of the importance of feelings of familiarity with a home and neighborhood, feelings of belonging and security, and the myriad of exchanges of minor services among people and households that characterize many long-settled working-class and lower-class areas.[85]

Marc Fried's well-known study of the effect of forced displacement on working-class residents of Boston's old West End dramatically reports yet another facet of the emotional and social costs to many displacees. He describes the feelings caused by loss of home and neighborhood as remarkably similar to feelings of grief for a deceased relative or friend.[86] As these and other studies show, the costs of neighborhood disruption, loss of home, social life and familiar surroundings are inflicted upon millions of Americans who can ill afford them.

The Douglas report suggests, however, that the particular problems of poor and Middle-American displacees are rarely taken into account in highway and urban renewal programs. The evidence is striking that many displacees are actually worse off after being moved from their low-rent (not necessarily slum) apartments, in terms both of overcrowding and increased rents.[87]

More important, figures from the Douglas report suggest that hundreds of poor and near-poor families displaced from highway and urban renewal sites were made to sacrifice for the benefit of more well-to-do elements of society. In the case of urban renewal, many low-income residential sites were replaced by commercial, educational or civic facilities[88] which are not of particular benefit to the original low-income residents but are highly profitable to the developers and users. Even when new housing was built on these sites, "the rents for most of the new housing sites were so high that the vast majority of the original occupants could not afford to return."[89]

The same with highway construction: the Douglas report notes that "the various freeways into and through our major cities more often than not avoid the areas where the well-to-do and affluent live and tend to cut through areas inhabited by families with comparatively low incomes." Three reasons for this phenomenon are suggested: land in poor areas is cheaper to purchase for highway right-of-way; wealthier families are better able to oppose plans for highways through their areas; and some planners actually use highway location as a "slum clearance" device.*[90] The

---

*   The Douglas Report adds a relevant and ominous footnote: ". . . over most of the country . . . housing assistance [programs] to low-income families, despite all the brave talk, are still developing at a relatively slow rate, while the rates of urban demolition because of urban renewal and highway construction are being speeded up. Families are therefore

frequent social-class discrimination that characterizes the
selection of highway sites was noted by former United
States Secretary of Transportation Alan Boyd, who stated:

> We should not just tear up the homes of poor people and
> Negroes. . . . We are going to have to find a better way to
> [build roads] than say we're going to take the property of poor
> people and leave everybody else alone.[91]

The latest 1968 Federal-Aid Highway act is an attempt to
ease the relocation costs of those who are displaced. Re-
locatees cannot be moved until they are guaranteed the
availability of replacement housing meeting certain minimum standards. Payment to displaced homeowners can
exceed market value of their dwelling by up to $5,000, and
for the first time, tenants can receive up to $1,500 to help
them pay for relocation housing.[92] It is too early to know
how satisfactory this law will be in practice.

Causes of Discriminatory Government Actions

"RATIONALITY," "OBJECTIVITY" AND HIDDEN BIASES IN PLANNING

We have suggested that the desires of economically and
politically powerful interests are usually paramount in the
government planning process. In addition to the obvious
effects of lobbying, the desires and interests of the rich and
powerful are honored by planners in a subtler manner. Most
planners think they are, or at least try to be, as objective
and rational as possible when they plan the renewal of an
area or the design of a highway. We suggest, however, that
what is considered "objectivity" or "rationality" in govern-

---

being displaced on a large scale, and this cannot be overlooked as among
the main contributing causes of urban unrest " (p. 86).

ment planning often entails unrecognized identification with the interests and viewpoints of established authorities, influential institutions and private interests.[93]

One branch of highway research is now devoted to developing methods for determining and scaling community values in order to help plan highway design and location. For example, a paper entitled "A Rational Decision-Making Technique for Transportation Planning" (one of many of this type) attempts to quantify social costs of various kinds.[94] The authors want to consider time saved by drivers due to availability of new highways. Figuring that 6,000 rush-hour commuters would save five minutes each way of their commuting trip, they decide to calculate the *money worth* of that time. They assign $1.50 per hour as the value of the time saved, and multiplying by number of trips and number of travel days per year come up with an impressive figure of $375,000 annual savings by this five-minute time advantage on the decongested highways. The point we make is not whether there is any truly "rational" basis to deciding that time saved by drivers can be assessed at $1.50 an hour (though we do find this an intriguing methodological issue), but rather the seductiveness and frequent absurdity of "objective" economic measures.

In another study, the author considers attitude surveys "probably the best way we have to determine values." He reports that attitude surveys have been used in the past only to evaluate existing attitudes and not to measure reactions to various transportation plans, and recommends the attitude survey because it can be used, he claims, "to quantify the relative weights of such things as the cost of the transportation system, user benefits, impact on taxable revenue, relocational problems, consistency with development goals, and aesthetic considerations."[95]

Not only are the methods of investigation purely quantitative, the choice of problems is limited to that narrow range that can be studied by such methods. In neither of these examples can the methods of investigation begin to grapple with the sorts of political, social and psychological issues we have examined throughout our study and analysis. Indeed the methods themselves are ways to avoid (whether deliberately or not is beside the point) such issues almost altogether.

Converting any and every conceivable variable into an "objective" measure only obscures the sociological and political issues under consideration. For example, although many current highway research studies deal with topics such as "Indirect and Sociological Effects of Highway Location and Improvement," and "Community Values and Socioeconomic Impacts,"[96] these studies usually restrict "social impact" to quantitative considerations such as whether land values rise, or whether there is an increase in commercial activity following highway construction. Usually, though not always, "social implications" turns out to mean economic consequences, aesthetic appeal to the driver or narrow immediate residential changes. And careful attention must be paid to optimistic-sounding conclusions such as "there has been an increase in land values since highway construction" or "the living conditions of those displaced by the highway have been upgraded." As economist Floyd I. Thiel asks, "What comfort can we take from the fact that residents relocated from highway-right-of-way typically improve their living conditions if this upgrading results because the relocated resident cannot find housing in the price range of his former home?"[97] And what comfort can relocated residents take from the fact that the highway built through their former homes or businesses brought wealth to real estate speculators, industrial plant and service station owners, and restaurant and motel-complex franchisers building on adjacent land? Property values may have gone up for the new owners, but at the expense of former residents moved out to make way for the highway that brought wealth to others.

Such quantitative enterprises are, however, generally considered by professionals as the only appropriate way to determine the "objectively" best plans. In this book, we have continually implied that people's *feelings* are crucial variables in the evaluation of a road plan. In professional circles we have opened ourselves to charges that we have "lost our objectivity." It is generally taken for granted that concern with people's use of money, motion and time are considered "rational" and "objective," while attention to people's *feelings* is interesting but narrow, not especially relevant to the problem, sentimental rather than hardheaded, or of only secondary importance to technical and economic issues. In other words, we are said to be objective if we ignore feelings, and subjective or sentimental if we include them as crucial data in an investigation.

But it is only the feelings of the victims of planning that are thus discounted. Planning itself is ordered and managed by people who are not neutral or objective but who also have interests of various kinds. The very definition of a road plan as an unalterable given, for example, sidesteps the all-important issue of whether in *some* cases the question might properly be not where to locate a highway but whether to build it at all, or how to look for alternate transportation systems. It can even be argued that the planner who decides not to think planning issues out to these kinds of ramifications is responding too much to feelings—the feelings of higher authorities that grand visions of elaborate highway networks must not be altered too much; the feelings of rich-and-powerful class interests—of automobile and concrete companies, construction and oil companies, of elected and appointed officials—that money, profit and power take priority over the desires of threatened citizens to remain in their homes and neighborhoods. In other words, the critical issue is not whether planners consider feelings when developing highways, it is *whose* feelings they actually consider.

Since planners almost automatically take into account the values and feelings of people who support and build highways, it is fully logical and rational also to expect them to take into account the values and feelings of any people whom the highway would affect. If the planners do not automatically respond to the feelings of such people, then the potential displacees themselves must speak out. But as we have seen, here is where poor and Middle Americans are at a distinct disadvantage.

SOCIAL-CLASS DIFFERENCES: LIFE STYLE

Organization-class professionals who staff government agencies at decision-making levels are most familiar with the socially and geographically mobile way of life characteristic of their own class. As we discussed earlier, many such people are unaware of the different life styles and values of other social groups, or else tend to disparage them.[98]

One common response of planners to the problem of whether poorer people ought to be moved is, "I myself would not mind it." In the course of this research, I spoke to a government official who pointed out that his family had moved to Washington not long before and not only did not suffer the move but enjoyed the new part of the country and the new life they found there. I pointed out that his family's move was voluntary (there is an enormous difference between moving of one's own initiative and being forced against one's will); it was connected with a move upward in income and prestige (rarely the case for poor and Middle-American urban displacees); the move was probably to a better house and neighborhood (also seldom true for those forced out by highway construction and urban renewal), and probably to a better job (another highly unlikely chance for a displacee). For organization-class people whose moves are connected with career and status aspirations moving may be a positive experience. People displaced by highway or urban renewal projects rarely share those possibilities.

We have previously referred to another related issue— government planners mistakenly tend to assume that if there is only a little overt neighborhood protest about plans for dislocation, the residents do not care whether or not they move.

The class values of government bureaucrats color their understanding of public issues, and their work and class positions lead them to favor the interests of the rich-and-powerful class. The consequence is plans and policies that discriminate against members of the Middle-American and poor-and-powerless classes.

THE DECEPTION OF MIDDLE AMERICA

Middle America is deceived; it fails to see that its many problems—high taxes, military sacrifice, unemployment, neighborhood disruption, etc.—are not chance misfortunes or caused by "outside agitators," but are an integral part of the way American institutions function.

The traditional ideology of American democracy not only obscures the fact that members of two social classes are at a disadvantage in promoting their own interests; even more significantly, the ideology tends to encourage a situation in which members of those classes remain apathetic and uninvolved, while turning all authority and power over to the "leaders"—members of the organization class and the rich-and-powerful class—who are then free to run the system in their own minority interests.

8

THE DECEPTION OF THE ORGANIZATION CLASS

Time suggests that the upper-middle class, or what we call here the organization class, "the nation's intellectuals, its liberals, its professors, its surgeons," do not belong to the "Middle Americans."[1] We have suggested that this class, albeit often unwittingly, systematically violates the interests of Middle America. At the same time the organization class is confused about its own power and interests.

ORGANIZATION-CLASS AUTHORITARIANISM

The standards by which Seymour Martin Lipset[2] and other organization-class observers judge "authoritarian" or "democratic" tendencies reflect their own class experiences in such a way as to portray working-class or other Middle Americans as more authoritarian than organization-class people. If, however, Middle Americans may be judged antidemocratic from an organization-class perspective, organization-class people may also be judged antidemocratic from a Middle-American perspective.

Organization-class members do not see themselves as authoritarian for several reasons. First, they are misled by the traditional American belief that social classes do not exist, or if they do, that they do not play any significant role in determining a person's life experience and chances. Second, most people usually reside, attend school, work and associate with others of the same social level. Organization-class people are rarely well acquainted with Middle Americans, except insofar as Middle Americans offer themselves as employees and as consumers of objects, services, entertainment and politics. These two conditions encourage the more affluent, optimistic, politically involved and potent organization-class members either to ignore or to disparage the life style, outlook and concerns of classes "below" their own.

In its relations with Middle America, the organization class asserts its superiority. Assuming superiority and acting against the interests of others is no more reasonable than assuming inferiority and identifying with the class-opposed interests of one's "superiors." In other words, the other side of Middle America's irrational identification with authority is the organization class's irrational exercise of it.

Examples of such assertions of superiority abound. Many liberal or radical organization-class adults and students who are proud of their own involvement in civil libertarian, civil rights, poverty, welfare and peace movements, often speak disdainfully about the "hard hats" and "straights" and other angry Middle Americans who appear to support the war, oppose welfare, and follow racist or reactionary politicians.* But the liberals and activists often seem to be strangely insensitive to specific problems of Middle-American life. Stewart Alsop comments on this insensitivity:

---

* We understand that the organization class includes many conservatives, as well as liberals and radicals. We focus on the liberals and radicals here because, unlike the conservatives, they believe they are enlightened about ways of life other than their own, and claim to be dedicated to "raising" the classes "below" them.

... what makes Wallace so immensely effective a demagogue is that there is a lot of truth in what he says. What he says, again and again, is that "the pseudo-intellectuals" and "the guide-line writers" and "the ivory-tower editorialists," who are for integrated schools and open housing and restrictions on the police power and so on, are forcing the working man to pay the real price of their liberalism. . . . And in the very truth, there is something a bit contemptible about the affluent liberal who lives in the safe suburbs, and reserves all his sympathy for the Negro militants and the radical young, with none at all left over for the hard-pressed, hard-working Wallace man.[3]

As if to illustrate exactly this point, *Time* quotes a "Middle American" on the building of low-income housing in lower-middle-income suburbs:

I'm angry because I keep getting kicked around. I'm getting squeezed by the Urban Coalition, these bankers, everybody who thinks they are doing these poor people a favor by moving them into somebody else's backyard—as long as it isn't *their* backyard.[4]

This is a cycle of organization-class insensitivity feeding Middle-American resentment and backlash. What makes the cycle especially complex is the fact that organization-class people are usually in positions of power and influence: *they* staff the government planning offices; *they* write in our newspapers and magazines; *they* speak on our radio and television programs; *they* write our books, devise theories to explain our behavior and teach in our colleges; *they* organize or at least sympathize with protests that antagonize Middle America. Consequently, not only are the reasons for Middle-America class anger not recognized, they are frequently aggravated by the same group that then self-righteously condemns the bitter expressions of this anger.

Government

Herbert Gans devotes part of his study of Boston's West End to a discussion of the discrepancy between organiztion-class and Middle-American outlooks. He notes that working-class West Enders tended to view local government as unresponsive, exploitative and partial to "higher" status people, and explains why this view is valid in terms of working-class experience, as well as why such an outlook is difficult for the organization class to comprehend:

> Such a conception of the governmental process [as exploitative and discriminatory] . . . may seem irrational to the middle-class person who learns early in life to understand bureaucratic organization and behavior. And, as I have already noted, it also may appear paranoid. . . . But given the West Enders' status in the larger society . . . the West Enders' explanation of governmental behavior may be distorted, [but] it fits the phenomena they observe more often than not.

> There are several reasons for the "fit" of the West Enders' theory. In the first place, most of them have had little direct experience with bureaucratic organizations. . . . And, since bureaucracies do not generally explain the reasons for their actions to clients, there is little opportunity to learn how they work.

> In addition, many of the actions of the government do tend, whether intentionally or not, to hurt them and to benefit the more well-to-do citizens. The clearest case in point is the redevelopment of the West End itself, which took their homes to construct apartments for the wealthy few. In earlier years, West Enders could see that the city tore down part of the North End [another working-class area] in order to build an expressway that aided the suburban residents who drove downtown to work or shop. They also saw that the quality of municipal services on Beacon Hill [an adjacent upper-class area] was much better than in the West End. . . . [Third, West Enders are frequently aware of government corruption.] Middle-class peo-

ple have a much different type of contact with their city governments. . . . Most of the time, they see only the performance of
civic progress and democracy that the government puts on for
their benefit. . . . Not only do they have little direct contact
with corruption, but most important, their contact is limited to
those times when they are the beneficiaries.

The West Enders more often are found behind the scenes,
either as employees, or as friends and relatives of employees.
They are hired or turned down for patronage jobs, and many
work on city construction projects. Thus, when bribes are
passed, illegal influence employed, and shoddy materials used
in construction, they are closer to the evidence than the middle-
class person. They confront corruption every day, and see
others gain by it, without reaping any benefit from it themselves.

Consequently, the West Ender's theory of government is frequently supported because they are closer to the seamy side of
city operations.[5]

Media

The role of organization-class-controlled media rein-
forcing the cycle of organization-class insensitivity and
Middle-American class resentment is particularly important. Gans describes the stand of the Boston newspapers
with regard to the proposed West End renewal:

Newspapers, at least in Boston, seem to be written on the
assumption that poor people, like the West Enders, do not read
them. They either present the news from a middle-class perspective or leave out the kinds of information that would be of
most interest to the West Enders. For example, the Boston
press not only favored the redevelopment of the West End in
repeated and enthusiastic editorials, but also covered the news
only from the point of view of the Redevelopment Authority.
Press releases or interviews with the officials about the West
End were never complemented by the West Enders' version of
the matter. Features, moreover, depicted the West End as a
vice-ridden set of hovels in which respectable human beings

could not be expected to live, insulting the West Enders and making them feel like outcasts.*[6]

A classic example of such media insensitivity occurred during the Boston mayoral campaign of 1967. A leading candidate was Mrs. Louise Day Hicks, a "law-and-order" candidate who had the support of large sections of Boston's white working-class population. *Newsweek* magazine decided that Mrs. Hicks was the typical "white backlash" spokesman, and described a reception attended by her supporters as follows:

> They looked like characters right out of Moon Mullins. . . . Sloshing beer at the long tables . . . a comic-strip gallery of tipplers and brawlers and their tinseled, overdressed dolls . . . .[7]

It apparently never occurred to the writers that this snide example of class-biased journalism would be read by other than its intended audience. But in an ironic footnote, Mrs. Hicks promptly published a full-page advertisement in the Boston papers, headlined "A Reply to *Newsweek* Magazine's Insult to Boston and its Citizens," in which the above quotation and several similar excerpts were reprinted, along with the candidate's heated response to *Newsweek's* "insult" that she was "proud to be a Bostonian."†[8]

Academia

The organization class controls most schools, either directly through administration or indirectly through the pro-

---

* As we pointed out in Chapter 3 these same papers played a similar role with regard to construction of the Inner Belt through Cambridge.

† Barbara Brandt learned of this incident while giving out campaign literature next to a Boston public housing project. Several local residents, who probably never read *Newsweek* magazine, had seen Mrs. Hicks' advertisement, and were furious about the magazine's reference to them as "Moon Mullins."

duction and sale of teaching materials. In this way, even in a public school system run by Middle Americans—the Boston system is a good example of this—curriculum ideas, books, and innovations of all kinds are "sold" to school authorities by education schools and educational research firms whose policies and programs reflect the needs, interests and world-view of the organization class.

It is noteworthy that the fact of social class is rarely taught before college, and seldom taught critically, if at all, in college. Potential sensitivity to class issues is thus muted through 12 or more years of schooling that ignore them. And when social class does arise in the academy, it appears in a particular way that rarely confronts the student with the role of the organization class in sustaining class inequalities and injustice.

For example, the work in sociology of Seymour Martin Lipset asserts that the uncertain, restricted, and punitive life experience and upbringing of working-class people fosters "authoritarianism." But instead of focusing on the institutions responsible for working-class life experiences, his tone and content imply that working-class people themselves are responsible for their condition. This comes through, for instance, in the derogatory emphasis he places on working-class child-rearing styles. His bias also comes through in the language he uses to describe the working-class outlook.

> As the sociologist C.C. North has put it, isolation from heterogeneous environments, characteristic of low status, operates to "limit the source of information, to retard the development of efficiency in judgment and reasoning abilities, and to confine the attention to more trivial interests in life."[9]

In an elegant way, Lipset, by way of North, is saying that working-class people are ignorant, intolerant brutes.*

---

* Such judgments abound in the professional literature. As another example, James Q. Wilson makes a similar class-biased point, seemingly

The standards by which organization-class intellectuals like Lipset judge "authoritarianism" and "democratic tendencies" should also be called into question. Lipset, for example, notes that people subjected to economic insecurity tend to support totalitarian movements, and explains this by saying that economic insecurity makes people search for a villain whom they can view as responsible for their plight. Unlike gradualist liberal parties, totalitarian parties, in Lipset's view, offer a view of society that provides a villain.*[10] It apparently does not occur to Lipset that economic insecurity for working-class people is a consequence of organization-class political and economic theories and political and economic policies that unilaterally, in an authoritarian manner, neglect the interests and viewpoints of Middle Americans directly affected by them. A federal decision to maintain a certain level of unemployment and call it "normal," for example, serves the interests of the economy's large investors and managers more than it does the families of people who wind up unemployed. So, too, with numerous tax, housing, school, war, and other policies. As another example, the belief of many political scientists and political sociologists that all Americans can organize to defend their interests in a politically plural decision-making marketplace works to the advantage of those interests

---

in an objective way, in comparing the viewpoints of "higher" and "lower classes," on planning matters: "Upper- and upper-middle class people are more likely to think in terms of general plans, and the neighborhood or community as a whole, and long-term benefits (even when they might involve immediate costs to themselves); lower- and lower-middle class persons are more likely to see such matters in terms of specific threats and short run costs" (from James Q. Wilson, "Planning and Politics: Citizen Participation in Urban Renewal," in James Q. Wilson [ed.], *Urban Renewal: The Record and the Controversy,* [Cambridge, Mass.: MIT Press, 1966], p. 414).

* Although the anticommunism of "gradualist liberal" ideologies involves designation of a villain, Lipset avoids that label, despite the fact that it is difficult to discover any other interpretation.

which are already organized and against all interests which have yet to develop an organization.

It is logical that the Middle American objects of such policies are attracted to a political party offering economic security. In many countries, liberal parties, as spokesmen for more affluent elements, do not speak to working-class interests as clearly as do parties (such as the communist party, which Lipset cites as a typical totalitarian party) that make economic well-being of the working class a key issue. By denying that workers' political behavior is rational, Lipset—a typical class-biased organization-class thinker—fails to accept many kinds of working-class problems as valid.

Lipset is one of America's most influential social scientists. His view of the working class is widely taught in university sociology and political science courses. Thus his biases often become part of the established reality taught to the children of the organization class, and those who aspire to membership in that class.

One can find other examples in academia of the contempt in which organization-class people hold Middle America. In Chapter 7 we attempted to show how the traditional American democratic ideology seems to perpetuate the exploitation of an apathetic majority by a rich and powerful minority. It is astonishing to learn that many leading contemporary political theorists justify this state of affairs.[11] The truism that organization demands leadership, for example, is shifted by what we might call "establishment political theory"* to a proposition that leaders must make decisions and cannot be bothered at every point with what their followers think.

---

* There are, of course, differences among the leading political theorists we have cited. But distinctions will be sacrificed for the advantage of portraying an "ideal type" of what we might call "establishment political theory"; and none of the leading theorists we mention diverges significantly from this model.

If elites are to be powerful and make authoritative decisions, then the involvement, activity, and the influence of the ordinary man must be limited. The ordinary citizen must turn power over to elites and let them rule.[12]

The "establishment theorists" sympathize with the democratic problem of the citizen making his needs known to elites, but accept what we might call the "elitist imperative" as democratic and necessary. V.O. Key claims that

the critical element for the health of a democratic order consists in the beliefs, standards, and competence of those who constitute the influentials, the opinion-leaders, the political activists in the order.[13]

With regard to the majority, their *belief* that they are participating seems to the theorists to be more important than their *actual* participation, and mechanisms of elite responsiveness (except for periodic elections) seem not to be a serious issue. There is implicit, then, a conviction that there is no way to organize a society intelligently other than by enlightened leaders supported, but not nagged too much, by relatively apathetic, uninvolved citizens. It appears further to be assumed that somehow or other the leaders will work in the public's interests.

Some establishment theorists even define apathy and low-level participation as normal and functional for the smooth operating of the system. Bernard Berelson welcomes apathy as a " 'cushion' to absorb the intense action of highly motivated partisans."[14] Apathy "helps the democratic system to function smoothly by facilitating change and reducing the impact of fanaticism, thus guarding against the danger of total politics."[15] Talcott Parsons calls apathy the "indifference reaction," which is the "element of flexibility necessary to allow sufficient shift of votes to permit a two-party system to function effectively without introducing unduly disruptive elements within the system."[16]

These authors are saying, in effect, "If many people make demands upon the system, it cannot continue to function smoothly." That it might then become something else satisfying more people (and find a *new* equilibrium) is a possibility never seriously entertained. All these authors apparently assume that "apathy" is a more or less rational decision not to bother with politics and to place time and energy into other things that an individual may find more important. Apathy as a reaction to frustration, impatience and despair does not appear in their conceptual schemes, as far as we can tell. Even if it did, they would probably explain that stability has to be purchased at some price, and that apathy is not a bad price (from the theorists' point of view) to pay. But apathy can also be conceived of as alienation—feelings of estrangement and objectively real estrangement from the political system. We suggest that there *are* people whose vote really does make no difference and that no other political act of theirs makes a difference; that there *are* decision-makers who are unresponsive to the "average citizen"; that there *are* people who are defenseless before political processes that victimize and manipulate them.

Political and Civic Activity

The limited empathy organization-class people show for Middle America is dramatically evident in antiwar and other protests carried out by organization-class adults and increasingly often by their alienated activist and/or hippie youth. Ironically, organization-class critics, young and old, often engage in their own class equivalents of exactly the processes they complain are directed at them by Middle America and its spokesmen (like Nixon, Agnew, Wallace and Hicks): indifference to the feelings, values and interests of other classes.

ANTIWAR PROTEST

It is completely understandable, for example, that Middle Americans resent organization-class antiwar protests. The end of the war can mean the end of work for millions of workers in war industries. Antiwar plans that do not take conversion to a peacetime economy fully into account clearly run counter to the employment interests of Middle America. Draft resistance and demands for amnesty for draft evaders can be interpreted as an insult to the patriotism of Middle Americans, whose sons, brothers, fathers and neighbors have been killed in Vietnam. They may also seem to be an indirect assault on the life style of its members, who unlike the children of the organization class, were not socialized into norms that permit numerous ways of evading the draft, and who could not afford lawyers to pursue the legal avenue to draft exemption.

WELFARE AND POVERTY PROTEST

The organization class denigrates Middle Americans for their scorn for the poor. In doing so, organization-class people in yet another way reveal their ignorance of the interests and fears of Middle America. Middle America believes welfare protest and poverty programs are promoting sloth and social irresponsibility. It does not understand the nature and complexity of the lives of the poor and powerless (any more than its own lives are understood by members of the organization class). Members of the organization class seem somehow in league with the poor and powerless to take money away from Middle Americans and give it to the poor. (There is, of course, some truth in that charge; its investigation lies outside the scope of this book.) Middle America understands neither the sociology of poverty nor the likelihood that most of the poor would leave that state if they could. And Middle Americans, unlike organization-class people, know that they could fall into the poor-and-powerless class if things went wrong for them.

BLACK PROTEST

Blacks' victories, such as increasing admissions to prestige universities and colleges, special training and hiring programs in many businesses, special funds from churches and other organizations, are supported by organization-class liberals and radicals. These gains clearly anger large numbers of whites in Middle America who are in similar economic and educational straits but have as yet no base for organization to pursue economic, educational and other interests in ways similar to those increasingly used by blacks.

STUDENTS VERSUS POLICE

The young antagonists of authority—whom we suspect often act out the prejudices of their parents, even if seemingly at odds with them—take out their anger at the injustices and follies of institutions like the military, the courts and the schools by scapegoating the visible representatives of these institutions—judges, teachers, military officers, corporation executives—and above all the literal enforcers of the law, policemen. Policemen, unlike most such representatives, make few policy decisions. Why do some of the young scream "pig" at them, even more than at organization-class professionals who keep the institutions going? Because, we speculate, the young critics of our society are as prone to scapegoating as are anyone else and are not sensitized to the real class structure and dynamics of our society. Romantically fascinated by the "working class," they in fact know little about its members and find their different life styles "square," tradition-bound and stuffy (a perfect complement to the working-class tendency to find the "counterculture" youth immoral, anarchic and irreverent).

Consider this social-class interpretation of the well-known mutual hostility between politically active college students and policemen. The police, who are usually from a working-class or other Middle American background, stand for organized, legal authority. The students, often from a liberal, expressive organization-class background, are hostile to the rigid and punitive order the police represent. At the same time, the policemen resent the apparent disregard of organization-class youths for their own educational privileges and opportunities,* just as they resent the scorn of many activists for the whole complex of Middle-American-class life style and values. Further, the hostility to policemen offends Middle Americans' attachment to a symbol of authority and order that is an essential part of their culture and also insults people they personally know and love. In some parts of Middle America, becoming a policeman is a step upward in the social order, and an eminently respectable position. To mock the policeman is to mock norms of upward mobility and of "law and order" and, we suspect, to allow the mocker to displace hidden scorn for "the masses" onto their most visible and powerful representative. Policemen, like the "hard hats" who are symbolically similar, come to stand for old ways and old authorities, even though they have no control over the decision-making structures and processes that perpetuate the old ways and authorities.

---

* A middle-aged maintenance man from Dallas, quoted in *Newsweek,* gives the typical Middle-American attitude toward student demonstrators: "I get mad when I see these rich kids tearing up the schools and throwing away that opportunity. I had to work, I would have liked to go to college so I could have a job where I could sit up there all day and be clean" ("The Troubled American," p. 49).

LIMITS OF POWER OF THE
ORGANIZATION CLASS

The organization class tends to operate in such a way as to maintain the interests of the rich-and-powerful class.* The "managerial revolution" notwithstanding, the organization class does not act in ways that would jeopardize the eminence of the people in ultimate power. It is not likely, for example, to recommend to banks and majority stockholders that a static gross national product might be better for our society than a growing one, that automobile production and use might be discouraged in favor of bicycle production and use and expanded mass transit systems, that the insurance industry as currently organized is an enormous waste of resources, or that in general where private profit and human welfare collide, the latter need not so often give way to the former.

As another example, if the liberal intellectual seems to be an apologist for the rich and powerful businessman and politician, it is because each lives well in our society and needs the other to continue doing so. The politicians and businessmen need the intellectuals to praise and justify, and, increasingly, to perform their work. The intellectuals need the politicians and businessmen to legitimize and to finance their work. Economic and ideological support are then complementary, and the majority is really left out.

Their own high standard of living, general esteem and participation in high-level decision-making processes combine not only to make organization-class people more likely to identify their interests with those above them, but also

---

* That many organization-class adults protest against war, racist and other policies of the establishment of which they are part does not weaken our central argument. Because the protests are always against specific policies and not against class-biased structures, the protestors altogether avoid the structural issue we raise throughout this book.

mistakenly to underestimate the limits on life chances of those below them.

Our nation has the highest average standard of living in the world; the class structure itself is relatively open, so that some members of lower groups do move into higher groups; and the two characteristic sets of freedoms of this society—the classical democratic freedom of speech, religion, assembly and press, and the freedoms to better oneself economically and socially—are available to many. But even these benefits have different meanings for the different social classes. The classical civil liberties, for example, mainly benefit the organization classes, particularly the intellectuals and academics whose stock in trade is expression of ideas. Several studies show that most respondents, when confronted with the Bill of Rights minus its title, believe it is communist material. We might add that the right to express one's opinion that, for example, a particular highway should not be built, is of no real benefit when the affected people lack the power to convert that opinion into political action. Similarly, for poor and Middle American-class people, the right to choose one's own occupation, and try to advance oneself economically and socially, is of little benefit when the actual choices are limited by the constraints of poor public education systems, family poverty and social-class discrimination by employers (such as requiring college degrees for work where higher education is irrelevant).

Rich and organization-class people may well be democratic toward their peers. There is some real democratic give-and-take among upper levels of bureaucrats, politicians, businessmen and professionals; in fact they probably enjoy and value that interplay so much that they delude themselves into thinking that everyone else in the society can easily be involved in the same activity. But the real freedoms of this society, the freedoms to make money at others' expense and the freedom to enjoy classical democratic civil liberties, are freedoms theoretically for everyone but actually for the minority.

We have asserted that the organization class, whose members exercise and enjoy these freedoms, is also a part of the "deceived majority." Except for those few individuals in positions of actual control and influence in business, finance, government, law, medicine, and academia, the political viability of the organization classes also is relatively low.* The glaring crises of urban education, housing deterioration, garbage collection and so on, are bypassed by moves to exclusive suburbs or residence in elite sections of cities where services are adequate and good schools are available. But what of the effects on the whole society of deteriorating cities, and of an aggressive foreign policy, environmental pollution, welfare law, taxation and even highways? We suspect that typical organization-class citizens feel little more influential than poor or Middle-American class citizens on all but immediate local matters, but that their feelings fall short of despondency, cynicism and total apathy for three sets of reasons. First, pleasure in material comforts is great and can come to substitute for control over nonmaterial aspects of a person's life. Second, by believing themselves to be "better" than people of other classes, organization-class people gain a sense of superiority that substitutes for genuine self-esteem and inhibits

---

* Here is an example of the inability of organization-class people to alter a highway design. One of the arterial roads that would connect with the Inner Belt is the Route 2 Extension, which would enter Cambridge from the northwest, through areas including the largely organization-class suburb of Lexington. Its route was to travel through a small parcel of land in the Peacock Farms area of Lexington, an undeveloped piece that state naturalists prized as important in its natural condition. The Peacock Farm area people, wanting to preserve land for ecological and practical purposes (the highway would border, if not travel across, a recreational site), hired an engineer to design an alternative way of handling one small part of the road. The DPW turned down the professional's suggestion.

clear perceptions of the common interests of all people in a society, for maximizing conditions that allow control of all, over their own lives. Third, in contrast to the experience of people "below" them socioeconomically, the work of organization-class people often provides genuine feelings of pleasure, autonomy and fulfillment.

Thus, in a number of significant ways, organization-class people are more fortunate than those in the poor and Middle-American classes; but in terms of feeling adult strength and meaning in political participation, and human identification with people outside their class, they are not much better off. And the advantages they do have disguise the crucial areas in which their interests and those of other classes are the same.

To stretch the point, we might even add that the rich-and-powerful class, the small fraction of the population that exerts the greatest degree of political control and reaps the bulk of the power, financial, consumption and status harvest, also suffers from processes of deception. To the extent that people's positions in society and their exploitation of others separate them from fellow-feeling with all mankind, their own humanity is diminished. Ultimately, that is to say, the rich-and-powerful class is deceived by complex social-historical processes into believing that its deepest interests are opposed to those of the majority of the population. Thus, it could be argued technically that all Americans belong to a "deceived totality." But those in the highest positions of control and decision-making have the power to make changes that would benefit everyone, including themselves. That they have this power but do not use it distinguishes them crucially from those who do not have the power but mistakenly believe they do.

Our assumption that most institutions of our society, including the political ones, work in the interests of those at the very top of the socioeconomic power structures, is not a suggestion of conspiracy against or even neglect of the interests of those beneath. Indeed, human motives are usually mixed, and it is perfectly conceivable that people in high positions promote some of the interests of the poor and Middle-American classes for at least two reasons: to keep those people from rising up against them, and honestly to improve their condition in life. But the people on top, and their agents in the organization class, surely do not want to share all wealth, esteem and decision-making prerogatives with the entire society. The ideology of democracy has traditionally been accepted by those in power as a nice idea that also helps them stay in power.

9

TOWARD NEW FORMS
OF PARTICIPATION

THE MYTH OF DEMOCRATIC PARTICIPATION

Hannah Arendt claims that two illusions beset demo-
cratically ruled countries: the illusion that the majority of
citizens are either active in government or at least sympathetic with one of the major parties (we observe that political scientists and political sociologists who poll people
to see which party they prefer omit the option of "neither"),
and the illusion that the masses are somehow neutral and
do not really matter. She argues that the success of totalitarian movements among the masses during the 1930s
showed that "the politically neutral and indifferent masses
could easily be the majority . . . that therefore a democracy
could function according to rules recognized by only a
minority," and that "democratic government had rested as
much on silent approbation and tolerance of the indifferent and inarticulate sections of the people as on the articulate and visible institutions and organizations of the country."[1]

Arendt's implication is enormous. She would have us believe that democratic societies pretend to include all citizens in their politics but actually *use* the myth of participation (for example, the voting ritual) to conceal an absence
of actual participation by the majority. On the rare occa-

sion that the majority senses that it is being had, it might then rise up in anger and strike down the agents of deception, that is, the minority that has used them for its purposes. If such a mass is totalitarian-prone, it would appear to be so for several reasons. It never was part of the democratic system anyway, except in the most passive, ritualistic way. And its anger on learning of its duping is likely to be formidable. (We suggested earlier that one reason an oppressed mass is so slow to realize its condition is because the action implications of the realization are potentially overwhelming.) Further, the promise of a new order, any new order, would at least in appearance serve admirably to assuage the anger. Speaking of Germany in the 1930s, Reinhard Bendix says,

> The impetus to radicalization among the German masses arose in the first instance among those who were just entering political life. It is probably characteristic of many non-voters to regard political participation as "useless," to believe that politics will only benefit the crooks anyway, and to profess a lack of concern with public affairs. Such people are likely to vote only under extreme provocation, and they are likely to support a party which proposes to clean the Augean stables and to establish an entirely new order.[2]

We have attempted to show that the condition of democracy in the United States today resembles in a number of ways the situation of which Arendt speaks: beyond voting, most citizens do not participate in the political process (almost half do not vote even in presidential elections); and although many interests are ignored, nearly everyone pays lip service to the belief that there is nothing the matter with our democratic institutions.

The facts, of course, are that the social classes in America who make up the majority Arendt refers to are consistently at a disadvantage in fighting for their interests. Middle Americans are brought up to feel politically powerless, and are encouraged to remain apathetic or to express discontent by complaining and scapegoating, rather than by taking action that affects the causes of their discontent. Even when Middle Americans organize to fight for their interests, they are at a double disadvantage: long-established interests representing the rich-and-powerful class are much more effective than they; and the government, rather than being a neutral arbiter, is consistently likely to set policies and make decisions that favor the rich-and-powerful class and, to some extent, the organization class.

We caution that there are at least four ways in which Middle Americans attempting to gain true power over their lives may be fooled into thinking they have such power when they actually do not (organization-class observers can also be subject to these deceptions):

1. Being misled by political figures who blame scapegoats such as blacks, hippies, students, "commies," outside agitators, etc., for Middle-America's problems, and who encourage repression of dissidents by (or in the name of) the "silent majority," or Middle America, as the solution.
2. Being encouraged to confuse increased consumption of goods, and choices among remarkably similar brands, with having power over one's own life.
3. Believing that participating in the pluralist arena as a voting bloc is sufficient.
4. Believing that because government officials speak about "citizen participation" in government programs, there will actually be such participation.

MIDDLE AMERICA ORGANIZES

Ever since the late sixties, when "Middle America" and the "silent majority" became catchwords and the group they represent started to evolve into a self-conscious entity, many politicians have attempted to appeal to this group specifically, sometimes with notable success. One thinks immediately of the recent rash of "law and order" candidates—from Richard Nixon and Spiro Agnew to Senator James Buckley of New York and the Democratic mayor of Philadelphia, Frank Rizzo.

Yet it is not imperative that a spokesman for the "silent majority" (Middle America) be pro-establishment, anti-long-hair, and implicitly or explicitly racist. Occasionally politicians have had the gift of being able to build coalitions that unite white Middle Americans with more vocal dissenters such as blacks, students and organization-class liberals. The best known recent example of such a figure was the late Robert Kennedy. Recently, some segments of Middle America have themselves begun to think in terms of forming similar coalitions. Recognizing the identity of their interests with other more vocal dissenting groups, some representatives of Middle America have begun a movement to ally with, rather than to scapegoat, these groups.

In June 1970, the Urban Task Force of the United States Catholic Conference called a Workshop on Ethnic Community Development at Catholic University in Washington, D.C. Attending were priests, politicians and community workers familiar with the lives and problems of the white working class in America. Over and over, the predominant theme seemed to be that white Middle America is a victim of the rich-and-powerful philosophy of "divide and conquer." In the words of Cleveland City Councilman Anthony Garofoli, "The enemy is not the black man. It is the power structure that plays off one group against another."[*]

---

[*] *New York Times,* June 17, 1970. In this context, "ethnic Americans" or "white ethnics" refers mainly to the millions of predominantly working-class whites of Southern European or Eastern European heritage—the Italian-Americans, Polish-Americans and others.

The Rev. Paul Asciolla, who edits an Italian-American newspaper in Chicago, continued the theme:

> What we have to do is get ourselves together for something positive. If we don't, the right-wing reactionaries like George Wallace are going to take us over. Nobody has done anything for ethnics since Social Security. Yet here . . . are they are [sic] being blamed for White racism. But they're not the people in the executive suites who would not hire a single Jew or Negro for so long. The ethnics are just the people whose own jobs are threatened. That's why they are all reacting so spastically.[3]

Perhaps the most eloquent speaker at this conference was Barbara Mikulski, a community organizer with the Southeast Community Organization in Baltimore. She read a stinging statement that said in part:

> The ethnic American is sick of being stereotyped as a racist and dullard by phony white liberals, pseudo black militants and patronizing bureaucrats. . . . He pays the bills for every major government program and gets nothing or little in the way of return. He himself is a victim of class prejudice.[4]

Following the lead of the Black Power-Black Pride movement, which stresses pride in one's unassimilated ethnic identity, some white ethnics are beginning to press for similar recognition from the establishment. Cleveland groups are seeking representation on boards and commissions in that city and are particularly interested in ethnic identity appearing favorably in school history books. The Pan-Slavic Alliance in Pittsburgh is working toward government-sponsored research centers on ethnic issues.[5]

Another new phenomenon is the growing attention that organization-class liberals are paying to the legitimate concerns of Middle America. For example, in his campaign for attorney general of New York State, former Robert Kennedy aide Adam Walinsky made a major campaign issue of industrial safety, and pointed out to many groups of workers (often speaking to them on construction sites) that the present administration was lax in prosecuting offending employers.[6] (The incumbent remained in office, nevertheless.)

Also in 1970, in Cambridge, Massachusetts, in an effort to bring workers and academics together, Victor Reuther and Leonard Woodcock of the United Auto Workers and Harold Gibbons of the Teamsters met with Nobel Laureates George Wald and Salvador Luria, political activist Professor Howard Zinn of Boston University, and Harvard Junior Fellow Joseph Rhodes of the Nixon Commission on Student Unrest. They began to plan a coalition of labor, student and faculty groups on the issues of race, defense spending and poverty.[7]

In December 1970, 150 working-class organizations in Northwest Indiana formed the Calumet Community Congress. Its platform indicates action interest in fighting "pollution, political corruption, and tax law inequities." Seven religious organizations and two organizers trained by Saul Alinsky helped get the CCC under way; Ralph Nader has agreed to work with it, and Senator Edward Kennedy has endorsed it.[8]

CONSUMPTION AS A SUBSTITUTE FOR POLITICS

The majority has traditionally been seduced into abandoning the search for control over their own lives and for some sense of community, by being encouraged to focus on its "freedom" to buy and consume. America differs from most other societies, not so much in its class structure as in its ability to blur class distinctions and antagonisms by means of the remarkable behavior and ideology of consumption. It is not voting that marks the true citizen of this republic, but rather buying and consuming. "The good life" is defined as gaining higher and higher "status" by making more and more money, and by spending it, mainly on consumer items. The ultimate political act in this society is not voting, but buying. Buying signifies participation in the economy, and that means contributing to its stability. Because the stability of the society and the stability of the economy are at this point hard to distinguish from each other, the object purchased becomes practically the central symbol of citizenship.

More than one critic of American institutions has observed that we tend to confuse, or equate, economic "progress" with human well-being. As John Kenneth Galbraith puts it, in his accustomed caustic way:

> The rate of increase in income and output in National Income and Gross National Product, together with the amount of unemployment, remains the all but exclusive measure of social achievement. This is the modern morality. St. Peter is assumed to ask applicants only what they have done to increase the GNP.[9]

One need not attribute the national obsession with economic output to mean motives. For people who try to run a society and judge how well they are doing, objective indices of anything are easier to deal with, and in all ways, or almost all ways, less threatening than any other kind. To borrow Galbraith's phrasing again:

> There is a further advantage in economic goals. The quality of life is subjective and disputable. Cultural and aesthetic progress cannot be easily measured. Who can say for sure what arrangements best allow for the development of individual personality? Who can be certain what advances the total of human happiness? Who can guess how much clean air or uncluttered highways are enjoyed? Gross National Product and the level of unemployment, on the other hand, are objective and measurable. To many it will always seem better to have measurable progress toward the wrong goals than unmeasurable and hence uncertain progress toward the right ones. . . .[10]

The ideology of our economy tries to make people believe, usually with success, that owning and operating a car is a major achievement of human existence, and that consuming more and more things is essential for the good life, even as the proliferation of things is increasingly absurd (electric shoe polishers, fake antiques, special makeup and powders and perfumes for nearly every part of the body and so on). Our economic institutions deceive people into believing that human fulfillment lies not in love, spontaneity, honesty of emotions, good relationships with other people, creativity and exploration of as much of life as possible, but in obsessive worrying about the appearance and odors of one's body and a mindlessly escalating consumption of material objects. It follows that, since the only purpose of work is to earn money with which to buy, the work itself may be totally mindless and boring, to be endured, not enjoyed. Further, the institutions have gone so far as to avoid problems of minimum material subsistence for the poor, in favor of loading up the relatively well-off with more and more and more. Our economic institutions have plundered the nation's own poor and those of other nations to pursue that central American madness: an ever-expanding-at-any-price gross national product.

Thus, the ideology of our economic system prevents members of most classes from seeing the real limits on their political behavior, their personal growth, and the ways our institutions operate systematically against the majority's interests.

INHERENT LIMITS OF PLURALISM

The pluralist image is of an arena, with teams all roughly of the same size and strength. Marginal differences in the political arena, as in the athletic one, make all the difference, of course, and are really the essence of the contest. (It is interesting, peripherally, that many theorists refer to politics as a "game," with rules and players. That games are usually played by parties roughly equal who return to equal status after the game, and that the politics game has no end in real life and thus no reinstatement of equality, apparently eludes these thinkers.)

Pluralism thus implies Social Darwinism on an institutional scale; somehow in the pluralist arena, the best or fittest institution or group of people will survive. In the ideology of capitalism, to take a comparable and integrally related case, it is said that other things being equal, the most efficient competitor wins (the use of government favoritism, market manipulations and other chicanery are omitted from the ideology). This becomes the ideology of the pluralist political system: let all those groups battle it out with the DPW and somehow the best solution will appear, like lilting April after a hard, cruel March. The fallacy in Social Darwinism, and the fallacy in pluralism, is the obliviousness to the fact that many people find the odds against living their lives as they wish to stacked against them in ways for which they have no responsibility and over which they have little or no control.

Feelings of political powerlessness are reinforced by an assumption in American democratic theory that failure lies with the individual and never with the structure of the system itself. Because, according to pluralist democratic theory, the individual is allowed to act on the basis of his own interests, we are led to believe (and indeed are taught) that problems in the smooth functioning of institutions directly reflect the weaknesses of their leaders and staff, not by any stretch of possibility, weaknesses in the structure of the institutions themselves. That "throw the rascals out" and "corruption" become the battle cries of reformers implies a theory that when institutions work poorly the matter is with their personnel, not their design.

The belief that the incumbent of an office is the difficulty, not the nature of the office itself, leads to an obverse effect, namely, the participant in a democracy must feel somehow that if he is ineffective it is his own fault. He is a failure in life, perhaps; had he moved higher in his work and social station then he would have influence. Or he is not clever, or smart, or articulate, or whatever. The Horatio Alger mythology in our society dovetails neatly with pluralist ideology in that both rely ultimately on the Social Darwinian metaphysic: ultimately, those who do not make it deserve not to make it, and that is that.

The Social Darwinist and the pluralist must eventually fall back upon the crude, twisted version of Darwinism that states that the toughest (not those best adapted to the environment) survive. In other words, ultimately it is brutality in the marketplace and the political arena or the planning office that wins. The implication is that might makes right. The theorists of pluralism seldom admit that some people are not as able to organize into groups as others, and that some groups may operate from an impossible disadvantage vis-à-vis others. As we said, SOC was on its own no match for the highway lobby. We return to the Buchanan report's vivid image of an elephant declaring, "Every man for himself" as he stomps up and down among the chickens.

But the weakness in the pluralist ideology is not just the inequality of institutions. It is the assumption that all significant sides of problems in a society will, if they are worth solving, have adequate institutional representation. It would follow from pluralist theory that a rapid-transit lobby and a bicycle lobby would be competing fiercely with the auto-highway lobby. But this is not the case. Consumers who would benefit from wider availability of rapid transit services and bicycle paths have no natural base of organization, and many may not realize the advantages of non-auto travel until they see them. Further, once a self-sustaining juggernaut like the Highway Trust Fund is in operation, all competing interests operate at a huge disadvantage.

The reader may object at this point, observing that the Inner Belt (at least the Cambridge segment of it) *has* been cancelled, that urban highway plans are in trouble all over the country, and that mass transit is gaining an increasingly favorable hearing at all levels of government. These developments do speak of course to some adequacy and life in the democratic institutions we criticize here, and to that extent, we surely are not condemning those institutions. But we must observe at the same time that the fortuitous rise of the pollution issue has lent weight to arguments against highway programs and that all the actions cited have been promoted and organized primarily by organization-class people. In other words, only when urban traffic congestion and pollution affect the organization class do its members move into action. To put it another way, Middle America's interests are supported by organization-class people when they coincide with their own, but not very often or systematically otherwise. Housing, inner-city education, taxes, work conditions and the like are problems the organization class has yet to attend to seriously.

There is a third critique of pluralism. Even where power confronts power, pluralist ideology too often calls for ignoring the substance of issues in favor of "compromise." Both power and compromise methods of resolving conflicts ignore the legitimacy, on political or moral grounds, of either (or any) party to a dispute. The political strength of the forces that want urban highways are still strong enough that they can offer compromises like high-rise housing over the highway or forms of "joint development." But what of the political rights of people like those of Brookline-Elm to live their lives unthreatened by public works planners? Even if the Brookline-Elm people, through organization-class support, become represented in the political arena as nearly equal in strength to the highway lobby, the issue remains, Which is marginally stronger? not, Is injustice about to be done? The compromise notion is essentially mathematical when it seeks to give the aggressor at least half of what he wants rather than, say, seeking to minimize damage to all parties concerned or to establish the legitimacy of a proposed action.

Compromise works to the advantage of the stronger party. The claim of the stronger party on the weaker, or of the weaker on the stronger, is resolved by the margin of strength, ordinarily, not by the merits of the claim. It is conceivable that an aroused Middle America can build itself into a power bloc sufficiently strong to counter already established interests. We have seen that some Middle Americans are beginning to lose their fear of speaking out, even against established authority if necessary. Particularly significant is the emergence of groups and spokesmen able to see beyond the traditional scapegoating and divisiveness.

But as we have pointed out, this movement will fail to gain power to promote the interests of Middle America if it does not go beyond the formation of voting blocs to put its candidates—or coalition candidates—into office. Stress on voting in elections as the only form of political expression tends to result in apathy on the part of the people and self-service on the part of elected officials. While poor and Middle Americans can try to organize to pursue their interests effectively, we believe it is possible—and desirable—for the political system to move in the direction of taking their interests into account by encouraging their expression in a variety of ways beyond merely voting.

EXPERIMENTAL FORMS OF PARTICIPATION

By now the federal government agrees that "participation" is good. We must distinguish at this point between the appearance of participation and control and the fact or actuality of it. Co-opting a leader from a low-income neigh-borhood and making him one of the organization-class crowd is not participation of the poor or increased control. Tokenism is not participation. Nor is bringing several indigenous low-income people to a board and allowing them a minority vote the same as full participation and control. Planners and politicians are usually clever enough to figure out any number of ways of making it look to the federal government and the local newspapers *as if* there is full participation, without it being so. But appearance must be derogated in favor of actually involving people so that, through effective community organization and local leadership, they can shape their own future.

The goal of a reinvigorated democracy must be to extend the competence of as many people as possible into politics, that is, the management of public events. This statement by Lane Davis of the "immediate objective of classical democracy" is a good beginning of an ideology of maximum participation and broadest possible control:

> The immediate objective of classical democracy has always been to extend the opportunity for individuals to take an equal and effective part in the management of public affairs. Through this opportunity, it was believed the horizons of the participating individual would be widened, his knowledge extended, his sympathies made less parochial, his practical intelligence developed. Participation in the management of public affairs would serve as a vital means of intellectual, emotional, and moral education leading toward the full development of the capacities of individual human beings. Participation in politics would provide [people] with opportunities to take part in making significant decisions and to transcend the narrow bounds of their private affairs. It would build and consolidate a sense of genuine community that would serve as a solid foundation for government. It would provide a strenuous and rewarding field of endeavor by extending opportunities for free activity and self-government beyond the control, or the hope of control, of ordinary men.[11]

It should be made clear that we do not assume that all people enjoy political activity or that they necessarily should. The *polis* is not all there is to life. But people who prefer to do other things can be made free to use politics as a means of assuring the freedom to do the other things they want, including being left alone when they want.

Believing that experiments in new forms of participation are important, we offer here several of our own suggestions for possible new forms.

First, neighborhood associations could be encouraged (not simply grudgingly recognized when necessary) as essential units in the democratic political process. Meryl Ruoss suggests that neighborhood associations may be replacing political machines.[12] And James Q. Wilson agrees that such organizations could curtail neighborhood people's alienation from the political process.[13] Wilson cautions, though, that such groups are concerned usually about their own situation and not with city-wide problems, as "the member's attachment is often at most only to his immediate family and neighborhood, not to the community as a whole."[14] There is a curious implication in that warning. It is that somehow planners' concerns with the city as a whole are "better" or healthier, even though the planners usually care little and know little about local residents' concerns. (In Chapter 7, we suggested that often government planners' alleged concern with the city as a whole in reality reflects the interests of some classes over others.) At the very least, a proliferation of local associations would serve to counterbalance the planners' tendencies to minimize the interests of poor and Middle-American neighborhoods. At the most, neighborhood associations might become a new means through which the previously powerless would be able to promote their interests.

Second, neighborhood associations could be elected, as they often are at present, but they might be structured in other ways. What if citizens were chosen by lot to serve on councils dealing with specific problems or even with the welfare of the local area in general? While at first glance random appointments of people to such boards seems absurd, we offer the following thoughts in support of it:

We select people not by political interest or professional training but by random choice, to serve on juries that determine matters as grave as whether or not a certain human being may continue to live. If citizens can be chosen at random for such service (the challenges and various forms of exemption built into the jury system could be adapted here), why not for planning and other political matters too? And the age-old problems of "leaders" rarely representing all groups in the community would finally be short-circuited. By random choice, many parts of the community would suddenly be represented directly in ways they never were before. Instant constituencies would be created. One might even think of employing cable television for purposes of broadcasting proceedings of many kinds of such groups, so that maximum following of their deliberations would be possible. Survey, field study and phone techniques could be employed to maximize participation. (It ought to be noted that poor and Middle-American class people seem fully comfortable with using radio "talk shows" to ask questions and offer opinions on public affairs. Rather than denigrating such events as circuses, organization-class people might well imagine, as we do, using such programs to discuss issues of immediate substantive importance to all citizens.)

Third, granting funds to neighborhood groups to hire advocates of one kind or other would enable them to have useful access to technical and political skills they might want in order to analyze and defend their position. Some of the dangers of this form of advocacy have been mentioned; the potential for its becoming a process into which neighborhood clients are developed as fully educated and active participants must be stressed. Funding for such activities could come from private sources or from government agencies, or both.

Fourth, agencies planning projects such as the Inner Belt can make genuine attempts to learn the needs and wishes of the people whose lives they would disrupt. In learning about stability and duration of living patterns and integrity of life styles as we did along Brookline-Elm, they may decide to place highways elsewhere, or work on alternative transportation systems to solve travel problems. Such genuine inquiry into the way potential displacees live and feel, and planning according to the findings, would be an indirect but honest and powerful way of including would-be displacees in the planning process. That is to say that neighborhood councils could be augmented by other ways of bringing people into participation in planning decisions. Extensive use of sociologically and anthropologically trained observers, rather than hurried and superficial surveys, could be conducive toward the desired end.[15]

The difficulties in working with any of these plans are several. Let us not delude ourselves into thinking that political, business and most other leaders want real participation on as broad a base as possible. Private gain and elitist convictions are too strongly embedded in our system for many spokesmen to take their own participation rhetoric seriously. To really want to see others grow in their capacity to control their lives and explore and express their capabilities means living by an ethic not so much of altruism as of recognition of a species-wide stake in the empathetic involvement of all with the creation of conditions permitting, encouraging and treasuring full dignity of all human beings. It means seeing the true growth of self linked with nonoppressive relationships with all other people. It means taking great pleasure in seeing others govern their own lives. Some parents, teachers, therapists, social workers and clergymen know this attitude. What Erik Erikson calls "the caring professions" are for some of their members built upon it.

It is, further, unclear what directions such experiments as we suggest might take and therefore difficult to convince authorities to risk the chance of failed efforts. Even if such experiments worked, privileged interests could suffer. They might be willing to sacrifice privilege for the greater welfare, but this is unlikely.* Either new forms of resistance to their objections would be developed, or they would overwhelm any efforts at real change.

How likely is it that the kinds of reform we have suggested will generate genuine participation, or fundamental changes in the structures we have criticized throughout this book? We have our reservations, our doubts; yet the dramatic alternative of revolution, so casually bandied about during the late 1960s and early 1970s, strikes us as hardly the answer either. Even revolutions that raise standards of living too often substitute one form of political tyranny for another, or substitute political totalitarianism for economic exploitation. While such substitutions may be necessary and appropriate for societies in early stages of industrialization, they seem unnecessary and undesirable for our society, in its advanced stage of industrialization. In America, we have a mighty productive machine. Our problem is not production but distribution. To whom shall we distribute the outflow of our industrial cornucopia? More to the rich-and-powerful and organization classes than to the others, as is our tradition? Less to the first two than is customary and more to the others? More to the rest of the peoples of the world, so many of whom we exploit mercilessly for the gain of our own standard of living? Is it not insane, indeed evil, to pay farmers for not growing food, when people in

---

* For a brief period, it appeared as if VISTA workers might be able to aid in neighborhood organizing. But such efforts were apparently successful enough to be seen as a threat by people in power, who then undermined them increasingly. VISTA now seems near its demise.

.

other nations starve? And to pay very low wages to workers in other countries and take out of those countries handsome profits for our own investors? If the reasons we do these things are tied to the nature of our economic system, then does it not make greater sense to change that economic system rather than to watch people die of starvation or live on miserably low wages so that our economic system and those who profit most from it remain forever privileged?

In other words, what would the goals of a revolutionary America be?

We need to turn to the primary problem we have raised throughout our discussion, that of structure. As long as our economy is structured to insure that monetary profit takes precedence over human well-being, and as long as our political system supports that peculiar priority, then the objectionable limits on the personal well-being of the majority will remain. It is time for our society to think of major ways to restructure economic and other institutions so as to maximize all people's satisfaction in their lives.

Consider what is possible if we subordinate efficiency for the sake of profit to peoples' satisfaction in their work. We could restructure work usually considered boring so that each worker does a great variety of tasks instead of a few or just one task; bring all people at a work place into the processes of making policy and operational decisions there instead of delegating the tasks to a chosen elevated few; and insist that highly trained people do some unpleasant work and that no one spends much time doing it. We would then have begun to restructure the work part of our economic institutions.

And what of ownership? Can we conceive of a society without ownership by a powerful few, the profits enjoyed largely by them and secondarily by their aides in the organization class? What would genuinely shared ownership be?

What would an economy look like if it abandoned its purpose of maximizing profits by creating artificial needs and exploiting fears and doubts about potency, attractiveness and well-being? Can we orient our economy toward making products that last as long as possible rather than ones that wear out as soon as possible? And cease talking people into buying silly things they do not need? Can we even, those of us who live fairly comfortably, find ways to reduce our standards of living, our levels of consumption, in the interest of sharing our talents and selves and wealth with all of humanity and feeling at one with them?*

Our society appears to be moving toward revision of its institutions, or toward developing new institutions to cope with the full industrialization and potentially fully shared affluence of a degree that no other society has created. We suspect that this process will involve searching and groping and stumbling and searching and groping some more, testing out now this form of organization and association and now that.

There is evidence that this is beginning to happen already. From "straight culture" and "counterculture,"

---

* And what of America's relationship with the rest of the world? For just as there is a class structure in this society, so there is one in the world. America is the "rich and powerful" nation, and the advanced industrial nations of the West together with tiny elites in the Third World, serve as a sort of organization class helping America maintain its world hegemony. The two higher classes live well off the rest of the noncommunist world. Russia appears to be attempting to duplicate America's efforts, with Eastern European elites providing organization-class support. Russia's trade with Third World countries appears to be as exploitative as America's; both countries have ideologies that should prevent that from being the case, but Russia seems to be as capable of subordinating ideology to short-term economic gain as is America.

Japan is surely entering the ranks of the rich and powerful, and China aspires to that position. There is a question whether some societies will dominate others (American tradition and balance-of-power political theory assume this as a natural state of affairs) or whether all nations can be brought into a world system where no people dominate others, economically, politically or otherwise.

there are now experiments involving workers in as varied a work life as possible, hippie communes, "community development corporations" for encouraging neighborhood-based businesses run by and for residents, "maximum feasible participation" on some poverty program and Model Cities boards, neighborhood law offices and free medical clinics in low-income areas, VISTA, the Black Panthers' breakfast program, urban collectives, free child care centers, full retirement pensions and so on.

And there are movements underway to decentralize control and operations of schools, and to create "free" schools with no ties to establishment school administrators. In many cities, food cooperatives have arisen which share the tasks of buying and distributing produce to members at prices far below those of the supermarkets. There are profound critiques available now of such "sophisticated" professions as architecture and planning and suggestions for how to deprofessionalize them in the direction of far greater lay involvement and creativity.[16]

Much experimenting on many levels with goals, forms of relationships, roles, norms and rituals and other shared experiences is likely to generate some forms of behavior and association that "take." A mature society at this point would, we believe, applaud and encourage innovative efforts, from ways to move people around in cities to ways of crystallizing real involvement of all people in decisions that affect their lives. It is more change and not less that we need at this point in our history—the establishment of a new social equilibrium based on institutions that permit full human development, not "law and order" to ensure that nothing of substance that threatens established powers is ever changed.

We believe, frankly, that as yet no analysis of our society leads with any confidence to predictions of how major changes are likely to come about, or should, and we are not able to offer a comprehensive analysis of our own. What happens over the longer range could be determined in part by short-range innovations such as those we have mentioned. And of course all concerned parties should continue working toward a greater analytic, theoretical understanding of these matters and possible changes, than any of us now have.

Our society has operated, from the start, more in, by and for the interests and well-being of the rich-and-powerful class and the organization class than of what we now call Middle America and of the poor-and-powerless class. These latter two, especially Middle America, appear to be increasingly discontented with things as they are, although not clear about possible ways to change them. Liberalism has tried to make changes. The New Deal, the Fair Deal, the New Frontier and the Great Society all tried to bring more and more Americans into the middle levels of consumer status but they have neither succeeded nor intended critically to confront the fundamental nature of our institutions and their relationship to the degree and quality of control of the majority over all aspects of their lives. Liberals have conscientiously wanted to improve the lot of all their fellow citizens, but with no disruption or re-examination of the liberals' privileges and "superior" positions.

The developing welfare state to which this position has led seems now to be near the end of its tether. Public housing has not worked, and we have found no ways to produce adequate housing for all, within the framework of the welfare state ideology. The Model Cities program has been a near-disaster. Efforts to create new towns within old cities have failed.[17] Medical care programs are riddled with graft and confusion, and community development efforts seem similarly beleaguered. Indeed, everywhere that funds are intended to benefit the poor-and-powerless classes and Middle America, much of the money seems to wind up, as usual, in the pockets of the rich-and-powerful and the members of the organization class. A few members of the Middle-American and poor-and-powerless classes manage to get in on the hustle, with the effect that their own mobility aspirations are enhanced, but most of their class brothers and sisters benefit minimally or not at all.

The liberals' ideas seem almost bankrupt by now, and the conservatives' ideas remain those of increasing the wealth of the few, with the expectation that some of it will trickle down the class ladder. Some does, sometimes, but with the effect of increasing consuming power at most, not of bringing more people into fully political citizenship. Even conservatives tend to increase centralization of funds and thereby, intentionally or not, centralization of control. And the New Left has been far more helpful in criticizing the war machine and related structural problems than in formulating new institutional structures and processes.

It is possible that further New Deals can bring our present crises under control, and that more efficient ways will be found of distributing tax burdens more equitably and shoring up the faltering welfare programs, but we are convinced that issues of freedom, growth and political efficacy will remain problems.

We need, then, further experimentation, greater efforts to understand structural constraints and changes, and continuing discussion to bring to the consciousness of Middle Americans and all others the nature of the unnecessary constrictions on freedom and growth to which we are subject.

Politically, Middle America seems at this writing to be "up for grabs." It can be manipulated unscrupulously, not for the first time, by "leaders" who deflect the energy and anger of Middle America from its real concerns to jingoistic wars, racism, sexism, the never-ending escalation of consumerism and the squashing of change implicit in activist political and countercultural movements among the young. Or the anger and energy of Middle America can be recognized in its fullness and its true roots by leaders who abandon the tradition of governing primarily in the interests of the rich-and-powerful and organization classes, and seek ways to make America the first fully industrialized society to bring its entire citizenship into the freedoms of inquiry, expression and growth theoretically available to all but in reality restricted, for the most part, to members of the two "more privileged" classes.

Indeed, it seems to us that our system need not quarrel with other systems on terms of economic organization— "we" and "they" have much to learn from each other— "they" can learn from "us" about technological efficiency, initiative and innovation, and "we" can learn from "them" about sharing and humanizing work and distributing the wealth more nearly equitably.

The unique strengths of our political system, in the liberties guaranteed to all and the possibilities of universal participation—were we genuinely to extend them to all, to make into reality that potential universal participation— would provide a model of political freedom that we tout rhetorically to other nations but do not honor as conscientiously as we might, even on our own soil.

As long as democracy remains confused with economic structures that allow us to subordinate human growth and freedom to private profits, we are bound to live with constrictions of the sort we have examined. While the conservatives and liberals fear we would diminish that democracy by making basic changes in economic and other institutions, we believe it more likely that our society can discover changes that can move us in exactly the other direction, toward, as it says in a supremely inspired phrase in our tradition, liberty and justice for all.

It is our discovery, then, that trying to understand as limited a social phenomenon as a small protest movement leads through a labyrinth of planning, social structural, political, economic and ethical issues to fundamental questions concerning the goals and directions of our society and the relationships of these to our major institutions. Greater attention to humanitarian issues can inform the planning process even as things are now, and this we strongly urge; but we doubt that the specific planning questions raised can ultimately be disentangled from the broader ones.

Strange though it may seem to some, to look deeply into any single problem in a society means to discover its relationship with numerous other problems. The Inner Belt protest movement in Cambridge, like school discrimination, the Vietnam war, air pollution, urban decay or any other pressing issue becomes a keyhole through which we all find, perhaps to our surprise, much more than we bargained for. We can snap our eyelids shut and declare we didn't see a thing, or we can begin to ruminate on how things fit together and how late twentieth-century people capable of such remarkable "progress" and innovations in economy and technology, might turn their minds to creating a social order that encourages political participation and individual growth in all parts of their society.

NOTES

Introduction

1. See articles by Gouldner, Mannheim, Seeley and others in Maurice Stein and Arthur Vidich (eds.), *Sociology on Trial* (Englewood Cliffs, N.J., Prentice Hall, 1963), for a representative sampling of statements of this view. An extended treatment of this issue is in Alvin Gouldner, *The Coming Crisis of Western Sociology* (New York, Basic Books, 1970).

2. For a more elaborate explanation of this method and its rationale in this piece of research, see Gordon Fellman, "Sociological Field Work Is Essential in Evaluating Community Values," *Highway Research Record*, No. 305, pp. 123-131.

3. See Gordon Fellman, "Neighborhood Protest of an Urban Highway," *Journal of the American Institute of Planners*, March 1969; Gordon Fellman, Barbara Brandt, and Roger Rosenblatt, "Dagger in the Heart of Town," *trans*action, September 1970; Gordon Fellman and Barbara Brandt, "A Neighborhood a Highway Would Destroy," *Environment and Behavior*, December 1970; Gordon Fellman and Barbara Brandt, "Working-Class Protest Against an Urban Highway: Some Meanings, Limits, Problems," *Environment and Behavior*, March 1971; and Gordon Fellman, "Implications for Planning Policy of Neighborhood Resistance to Urban Renewal and Highway Proposals," 1970, National Technical Information Center, Sprinfield, Virginia 22157, Accession Number 193151.

Chapter 1: Social Class Discrimination in American Society

1. Studies of this group include: C. Wright Mills, *The Power Elite* (New York, Oxford University Press, 1956); Gabriel M. Kolko, *Wealth and Power in America* (New York, Praeger, 1964); G. W. Domhoff,

Who Rules America? (Englewood Cliffs, N.J., Prentice-Hall, 1967); Ferdinand Lundberg, *The Rich and the Super Rich,* (New York, Lyle Stuart, 1968); G. W. Domhoff, *The Higher Circles* (New York, Vintage Books, 1971).

2. Good recent studies of America's poor include: Michael Harrington, *The Other America* (New York, Macmillan, 1964); Oscar Lewis, *La Vida* (New York, Random House, 1966); Elliot Liebow, *Tally's Corner* (Boston, Little Brown, 1967); and S. M. Miller and Pamela Roby, *The Future of Inequality* (New York, Basic Books, 1970).

3. "The Troubled American: A Special Report on the White Majority," *Newsweek,* October 6, 1969 (the whole issue); and "Man and Woman of the Year: the Middle Americans," *Time,* January 5, 1970, pp. 10-17. *Newsweek* focuses on white Americans, but we believe that a significant number of black Americans would also be considered, or consider themselves, in "Middle America." (Popular journalism of the newsweekly variety often yields interesting and timely data; we rely on these two issues of major magazines for anecdotal and mood information which we find accurate in terms of our four-year study of a largely Middle-American population.)

4. "The Troubled American," p. 29.

5. "The Middle Americans," p. 11.

6. "The Troubled American," pp. 48-49.

7. "The Middle Americans," p. 10.

8. "The Troubled American," p. 35.

Chapter 2: Middle-American Life Styles: The Meaning of Neighborhood

1. Herbert J. Gans, *The Urban Villagers: Group and Class in the Life of Italian-Americans* (Glencoe, Ill., The Free Press, 1962), pp. 308-317.

2. Gans, *The Urban Villagers.* See also Marc Fried, "Grieving for a Lost Home," in Leonard J. Duhl (ed.), *The Urban Condition* (New York, Basic Books, 1963), pp. 151-171; Marc Fried and Peggy Gleicher, "Some Sources of Residential Satisfaction in an Urban 'Slum,'" *Journal of the American Institute of Planners,* Vol. 82, No. 4, November 1961, pp. 305-315; Marc Fried, "Transitional Functions of Working-Class Communities: Implications for Forced Relocation," Chapter Six in Mildred Cantor (ed.), *Mobility and Mental Health* (Springfield, Ill., Charles C Thomas, 1965), pp. 123-165.

3. U. S. Bureau of the Census, *Current Population Reports,* Series P-60, No. 59, "Income in 1967 of Families in the United States" (Washington, D.C., U. S. Government Printing Office, 1969), p. 28.

4. *Ibid.*, p. 28.

5. Cf. U. S. Bureau of the Census, *1960 Census of the Population,* Vol. I, *Characteristics of the Population,* Part 23, Massachusetts, Table 43, "Year Moved Into Present House," P. 128.

6. *Ibid.*, Table 64, "Means of Transportation to Work," p. 144.

7. Cf. Will Herberg, *Protestant, Catholic, Jew* (New York, Doubleday, 1956), p. 62.

8. Gans, *The Urban Villagers,* pp. 244-245.

9. Lee Rainwater, Richard P. Coleman, and Gerald Handel, *Workingman's Wife* (New York, Oceana Publications, 1959), p. 103.

10. Robert J. Havighurst and Kenneth Feigenbaum, "Leisure and Life Style," *American Journal of Sociology,* January 1959, Vol. 64, pp. 396-404, p. 400.

11. Estimate for 1967-1968 by the Cambridge Redevelopment Authority.

12. Cf. Fried, "Grieving for a Lost Home."

Chapter 3: The Inner Belt Controversy

1. *Cambridge Chronicle and Sun,* January 18, 1962, pp. 1-2.

2. See p. 72, n.

3. *Study of the Belt Expressway through Cambridge* (Boston, Bruce Campbell & Associates; Cambridge, Mass., Planning and Renewal Associates, for the Cambridge Planning Board, November 1, 1957).

4. *Interstate Route 695* (Cambridge, Mass., Cambridge Planning Board, May 10, 1960).

5. Statement by Edward B. Hanify on behalf of MIT at a hearing before the Cambridge City Council on February 20, 1966, in the Harrington School, Cambridge, Massachusetts; Office of Public Information, MIT.

6. *Location Restudy* (Boston, H. W. Lochner, Inc., for the Commissioner of the Massachusetts Department of Public Works, May 1967), pp. 43 ff.

7. *Boston Globe,* May 13, 1967.

8. *Boston Herald-Traveler,* May 24, 1967.

9. *Boston Globe,* May 27, 1967.

10. Kenneth R. Geiser, Jr., *Urban Transportation Decision Making* (Cambridge, Mass., Urban Systems Laboratory, MIT, 1970), p. 291.

11. *Interstate Rt. 695 (Inner Belt) Relocation Study, Cambridge, Mass.*, by Commissioner of Massachusetts Department of Public Works, Right-of-Way Bureau, September 1, 1967.

Chapter 4: Middle-American Political Behavior: Alienation and the Meaning of Protest

1. James Q. Wilson, "Planning and Politics: Citizen Participation in Urban Renewal," in Hans B. C. Spiegel (ed.), *Citizen Participation in Urban Development,* Vol. I (Washington, D. C., NTL Institute, 1969), p. 51. See also Chapter 8 for a discussion of working-class cynicism and suspicion of politics and government.

2. See Chapter 5 for a fuller discussion of "big people."

3. Many studies of populations in various sections of the country show that lower income and education are associated with low membership and activity in political, community or other formal organizations. See, for example, Morris Axelrod, "Urban Structure and Social Participation," *American Sociological Review,* Vol. 21, February 1956, p. 13; Wendell Bell and Maryanne T. Force, "Urban Neighborhood Types and Participation in Formal Associations," *American Sociological Review,* Vol. 21, February 1956, p. 25; Charles R. Wright and Herbert H. Hyman, "Voluntary Association Memberships of American Adults: Evidence From National Sample Surveys," in Roland L. Warren (ed.), *Perspectives on the American Community* (Chicago, Rand McNally, 1966), p. 448; Julian L. Woodward and Elmo Roper, "Political Activity of American Citizens," in Heinz Eulau (ed.), *Political Behavior* (Glencoe, Ill., The Free Press, 1956), p. 133; and Gabriel A. Almond and Sidney Verba, *The Civic Culture* (Princeton, N. J., Princeton University Press, 1963), pp. 248-249.

4. Leonard Reissman, "Class, Leisure, and Social Participation," *American Sociological Review,* Feburary 1954, Vol. 19, p. 76.

5. Frances Fox Piven, "Participation of Residents in Neighborhood Community Action Programs," in Hans B.C. Spiegel (ed.), *Citizen Participation in Urban Development,* p. 117.

6. Arthur Vidich and Joseph Bensman, *Small Town in Mass Society: Class, Power and Religion in a Rural Community* (Princeton, N. J., Princeton University Press, 1958), pp. 297-320.

7. Frances F. Barker, David Greenwald, and Robert Sherman, with Nancy T. Whit, "The North Harvard Street Protest Against a Luxury High-Rise Urban Renewal Plan," in Gordon Fellman (ed.), *Implications for Planning Policy of Neighborhood Resistance to Urban Renewal and Highway Proposals* (Springfield, Va., Department of Housing and Urban Development, 1970), p. 249.

Chapter 5: Political Misperceptions and Realities

1. Lincoln Steffens, *The Autobiography of Lincoln Steffens,* (New York: Harcourt, Brace, 1931), p. 638.

2. Two articles describing the work of advocate planners in more detail are Paul Davidoff, "Advocacy and Pluralism in Planning," *Journal of the American Institute of Planners,* v. 31 (Nov. 1965); and Lisa Peattie, "Reflections on Advocacy Planning," in Hans B.C. Spiegel, ed., *Citizen Participation in Urban Development,* Vol. 2, NTL Institute for Applied Behavioral Science, (Washington, D.C., 1969), pp. 237-250.

Chapter 6: The Problem of Authority

1. *Boston Globe,* July 17, 1969, emphasis added.

2. See p. 139, n.

3. Cf. Eliot Liebow, *Tally's Corner;* Schoolboys of Barbiana, *Letter to a Teacher;* George Jackson, *Soledad Brother* (New York, Bantam Books, 1970); Philip Slater, *The Pursuit of Loneliness* (Boston, Beacon Press, 1970); and classic social-class discussions such as Robert Lynd and Helen Merrell Lynd, *Middletown* (New York, Harcourt, Brace, 1929), and *Middletown in Transition* (New York, Harcourt, Brace, 1937); August Hollingshead, *Elmtown's Youth* (New York, John Wiley, 1955); John Dollard, *Caste and Class in a Southern Town* (New York, Doubleday, 1957); August Hollingshead and Fritz Redlich, *Social Class and Mental Illness* (New York, John Wiley, 1958); Arthur Vidich and Joseph Bensman, *Small Town in Mass Society* (New York, Doubleday, 1960).

4. See discussion of the concept, "identification with the aggressor," in Anna Freud, *The Ego and the Mechanisms of Defence* (New York, International Universities Press, 1946), Chapter 9.

5. Paul Deac, Executive Vice President of the National Confederation of American Ethnic Groups, quoted in "The Middle Americans," p. 10.

6. "The Middle Americans," p. 15.

7. S. M. Lipset, *Political Man* (New York, Doubleday, 1959), Chapter 4 "Working-Class Authoritarianism," pp. 97-130.

8. Lipset, *Political Man,* pp. 98 and 115.

9. S. M. Miller and Frank Riessman, "Working-Class Authoritarianism: A Critique of Lipset," *British Journal of Sociology,* Vol. 12, Sept. 1961, p. 271.

10. Miller and Riessman, "Working-Class Authoritarianism," p. 272.

11. Miller and Reissman, "Working-Class Authoritarianism," p. 272. See also Chapter 8.

Chapter 7: The Deception of Middle America: Political Reality Versus the Public Ideology

1. "The Middle Americans," p. 13.

2. J. Clarence Davies, III, *Neighborhood Groups and Urban Renewal* (New York, Columbia University Press, 1966), p. 149.

3. Ernest Norton Tooby, "The Interest in Rootedness: Family Relocation and an Approach to Full Indemnity," *Stanford Law Review,* Vol. 21, April 1969, pp. 801-870, p. 816.

4. Barker, "The North Harvard Street Protest," p. 249.

5. *Ibid.,* p. 251.

6. *Building the American City,* Report of the National Commission on Urban Problems (Washington, D. C., December 1968), p. 82.

7. See, for example, Arnold Simmel, "A Signpost on Fluoridation Conflicts: The Concept of Relative Deprivation," *Journal of Social Issues,* Vol. 17, No. 4, 1961, pp. 26-36; William A. Gamson, "The Fluoridation Dialogue: Is It an Ideological Conflict?" *Public Opinion Quarterly,* Vol. 25, Winter 1961, pp. 526-537; John E. Horton and Wayne E. Thompson, "Powerlessness and Political Negativism: A Study of Defeated Local Referendums," *American Journal of Sociology,* Vol. 68, 1962, pp. 485-493; Edward L. McDill and Jeanne Clare Ridley, "Status, Anomia, Political Alienation, and Political Participation," *American Journal of Sociology,* Vol. 68, 1962, pp. 205-213.

8. Horton and Thompson, "Powerlessness and Political Negativism," p. 485.

9. Davies, *Neighborhood Groups,* p. 14.

10. *Ibid.,* p. 17.

11. Peter Bachrach and Morton S. Baratz, "Two Faces of Power," *The American Political Science Review,* Vol. 56, 4, December 1962, pp. 946-952; in Charles A. McCoy and John Playford (eds.), *Apolitical Politics: A Critique of Behavioralism* (New York, Crowell, 1967), p. 150.

12. Donald G. Blaisdell and Jane Greverus, Temporary National Economic Committee, *Investigation of Concentration of Economic Power,* Monograph No. 26, Economic Power and Political Pressures (Washington, D.C., U.S. Government Printing Office, 1941), p. 2.

13. *Ibid.,* p. 13.

14. *Ibid.,* p. 16.

15. *Ibid.,* p. 14.

16. *Ibid.,* p. 25.

17. Interim Report, House Select Committee on Lobbying Activities, House of Representatives (Washington, D.C., Government Printing Office, 1950), p. 6 (also known as the "Buchanan Report," after the chairman of the committee).

18. *Ibid.,* p. 47.

19. *Ibid.,* p. 62.

20. *Ibid.,* pp. 7-8.

21. *Congressional Quarterly Almanac,* Vol. 6, 1950, p. 763.

22. *Buchanan Report,* pp. 8-9.

23. Quoted in the *Congressional Record,* Vol. 115, Part 18, Aug. 13, 1969-Sept. 10, 1969, p. 24368.

24. *Ibid.,* p. 24370.

25. *Ibid.,* p. 24376.

26. Data on the highway lobby can be found in many sources. Some of the more notable recent ones include: A. Q. Mowbray, *Road to Ruin* (Philadelphia, Lippincott, 1969); David Hapgood, "The Highwaymen," *Washington Monthly,* Vol. 1, No. 2, March 1969, pp. 2-11 and 73-80; Kenneth Geiser, Jr., "The Highway Construction System," (Cambridge, MIT, Urban Systems Laboratory, 1970) unpublished paper; Stephen H. Kaiser, "Influence and Decisionmaking in the Interstate Highway Program," (Cambridge, MIT, January 1970) unpublished paper; George Denison and Kenneth Y. Tomlinson, "Let's Put Brakes on the Highway Lobby," *Readers Digest,* May 1969, pp. 97-102.

27. A. J. Muste, "The Automobile Industry and Organized Labor" (Baltimore, The Christian Social Justice Fund, 1935), p. 5.

28. See "The 500 Largest Industrials," *Fortune,* May 1971, pp. 172-175.

29. U. S. Bureau of the Census, *Statistical Abstracts: 1970* (91st ed.) (Washington, D. C., U. S. Government Printing Office, 1970), p. 547.

30. *Ibid.,* p. 546.

31. *Ibid.,* p. 546.

32. *Ibid.,* p. 547.

33. Automobile Manufacturers Association, "Automobile Facts and Figures," 1965, p. 14.

34. *Statistical Abstracts: 1970,* p. 548.

35. *Ibid.,* p. 536 and p. 676.

36. *World Almanac, 1969,* p. 111.

37. Hapgood, "The Highwaymen," p. 7.

38. *Ibid.,* p. 9.

39. Geiser, "The Highway Construction System," p. 13.

40. *Statistical Abstracts: 1970,* p. 544.

41. James I. Walsh, "Federal Highway Programs and Employment," *Monthly Labor Review,* August 1968, p. 37.

42. *Statistical Abstracts: 1970,* p. 546.

43. *Statistical Abstracts: 1969,* p. 225.

44. Hapgood, "The Highwaymen," p. 6.

45. Geiser, "The Highway Construction System," p. 23.

46. Ralph Nader, *Unsafe at any Speed* (New York, Pocket Books, 1966), p. vi.

47. "Automotive Facts and Figures," p. 20.

48. *Ibid.,* p. 2.

49. *Ibid.,* p. 1.

50. *Statistical Abstracts: 1970,* pp. 757-759.

51. *Congressional Quarterly Almanac,* 1963, Vol. 19, p. 554.

52. *Ibid.*

53. *Congressional Quarterly Almanac,* 1951, Vol. 7, p. 703.

54. *Congressional Quarterly Almanac,* 1963, Vol. 19, p. 555.

55. George Denison and Kenneth Y. Tomlinson, "Let's Put Brakes on the Highway Lobby," *Readers Digest,* May 1969, p. 98.

56. *Congressional Quarterly Almanac,* 1962, Vol. 18, p. 935.

57. *Ibid.,* p. 934.

58. "Highway Transportation Re-Makes America" (Washington, D. C., National Highway Users Conference, 1939), p. 3.

59. Wilbur Smith and Associates, *Transportation for Tomorrow's Cities* (under commission from Automobile Manufacturers Association, 1966), p. iii.

60. Wilbur Smith and Associates, *Parking in the City Center* (under commission from the Automobile Manufacturers Association, 1965), p. iii.

61. Geiser, "The Highway Construction System," p. 13.

62. Denison, "Brakes on the Highway Lobby," p. 102.

63. Mary Perot Nichols, "Too Much Pork in the Highway Barrel," *Village Voice,* January 2, 1969, p. 3.

64. *Congressional Quarterly Almanac*, 1962, Vol. 18, p. 935.

65. *Congressional Quarterly Almanac*, 1963, Vol. 19, p. 556.

66. Denison, "Brakes on the Highway Lobby," pp. 98-99.

67. *Ibid.*, p. 98.

68. *Ibid.*, p. 100.

69. "Beautniks are Drag, Highway Users Say," *Washington Star*, April 14, 1968.

70. "Scars Across the Land," *New York Times* editorial, July 10, 1968.

71. "LBJ Signs Highway Bill with Protest," *Boston Globe*, August 25, 1968.

72. "Road Law Alarms Conservationists," *Christian Science Monitor*, August 31, 1968.

73. *Forbes*, April 15, 1972, p. 27.

74. *Building the American City*, p. 82.

75. *Ibid.*, p. 81.

76. *Ibid.*, p. 82.

77. *Ibid.*, p. 167.

78. *Ibid.*, p. 82.

79. Chester Hartman, "The Housing of Relocated Families," *Journal of the American Institute of Planners*, Vol. 30, 1964, pp. 266-286.

80. Davies, *Neighborhood Groups*, pp. 162-163.

81. William H. Key, *When People Are Forced to Move*, Final Report of a Study of Forced Relocation, Study supported in part by Grant No. 067 from the Welfare Administration with cooperation of the Social Security Administration, May 1967, p. 278.

82. *Ibid.*

83. *Ibid.*, p. 279.

84. *Ibid.*, p. 283.

85. Tooby, "The Interest in Rootedness," p. 814.

86. Fried, "Grieving for a Lost Home."

87. *Building the American City*, p. 167. See also Herbert J. Gans, "The Failure of Urban Renewal," *Commentary*, April 1965, pp. 29-37; and Hartman, "The Housing of Relocated Families."

88. *Building the American City*, p. 162.

89. *Ibid.*, p. 163.

90. *Ibid.*, p. 82.

91. *New York Times,* January 28, 1968.

92. Provision of the Federal-Aid Highway Act of 1968, *U. S. Code Congressional and Administrative News, Laws, 1968* (St. Paul, West Publishing Co., 1968), pp. 943-970.

93. See also Kenneth J. Geiser, Jr., *Urban Transportation Decision Making: Political Processes of Urban Freeway Controversies,* Urban Systems Laboratory, MIT, Cambridge, Mass., 1970, pp. 388-389.

94. William Jessiman, C. Roger Brussee, Alfred Tumminia, and Daniel Brand, "A Rational Decision-Making Technique for Transportation Planning" (unpublished paper prepared for presentation to the 40th Annual Meeting of the Highway Research Board, January 1967).

95. Alan M. Voorhees, "Techniques for Determining Community Values" (unpublished paper prepared for the Committee on Community Values, Department of Urban Transportation Planning, Highway Research Board, 44th Annual Meeting, Washington, D.C., January 1965). The ambiguous title implies a study in learning what they should be.

96. *Highway Research Record,* Washington, D. C., Highway Research Board of the National Research Council; see issues 75 and 96, 1965, and 277, 1969.

97. Floyd I. Thiel, "Introductory Remarks to Seminar on Sociological Effects of Highway Transportation," *Highway Research Record,* No. 75, 1965, p. 75.

98. See Chapter 2. For an expanded discussion of the class backgrounds at all levels of personnel in highway planning, see Geiser, *Urban Transportation Decision Making,* pp. 464-478.

Chapter 8: The Deception of the Organization Class

1. "The Middle Americans," p. 11.

2. See Chapter 6, footnote 14. See also section on academia in Chapter 8.

3. Stewart Alsop, "The Wallace Man," *Newsweek,* October 21, 1968, p. 116.

4. "The Middle Americans," p. 12.

5. Gans, *The Urban Villagers,* pp. 166-169. See also Chapter 7.

6. *Ibid.*, p. 172.

7. *Newsweek,* November 6, 1967, quoted in *Boston Globe,* November 6, 1967.

8. *Boston Globe,* November 6, 1967.

9. Lipset, *Political Man,* p. 120.

10. *Ibid.,* p. 100.

11. See for example, Gabriel Almond and Sidney Verba, *The Civic Culture* (Boston, Little Brown, 1965); Robert Dahl, *Who Governs?* (New Haven, Yale University Press, 1961); Robert Dahl, *Modern Political Analysis* (Englewood Cliffs, N.J., Prentice-Hall, 1964); Edward C. Banfield, *Political Influence* (New York, The Free Press, 1961); Edward Banfield and James Q. Wilson, *City Politics* (New York, Vintage Books, 1963); James Q. Wilson, *The Amateur Democrat* (Chicago, University of Chicago Press, 1962); Angus Campbell, Philip E. Converse, Warren E. Miller, and Donald E. Stokes, *The American Voter* (New York, Wiley, 1960); Seymour Martin Lipset, *The First New Nation* (New York, Basic Books, 1963); V. O. Key, *Public Opinion and American Democracy* (New York, Knopf, 1961); David B. Truman, *The Governmental Process* (New York, Knopf, 1960); Talcott Parsons, "Voting and the Equilibrium of the American Political System," in Eugene Burdick and Arthur J. Brodbeck (eds.), *American Voting Behavior* (Glencoe, The Free Press, 1959), Chapter Four.

A collection of essays critical of the "establishment theorists" named above is Charles A. McCoy and John Playford (eds.), *Apolitical Politics: A Critique of Behavioralism* (New York, Crowell, 1967).

12. Almond and Verba, *The Civic Culture,* p. 343.

13. V. O. Key, *Public Opinion,* p. 558.

14. See Berelson, "Democratic Theory and Public Opinion," *Public Opinion Quarterly,* Vol. 16, Autumn 1952, pp. 313-330, quoted in Graeme Duncan and Steven Lukes, "The New Democracy," *Political Studies,* Vol. 11, 2, 1963, pp. 156-177; reprinted in McCoy and Playford, *Apolitical Politics,* pp. 178-179.

15. Berelson, "Democratic Theory and Public Opinion," p. 179.

16. Talcott Parsons, "Voting," p. 179.

Chapter 9: Toward New Forms of Participation

1. Hannah Arendt, *The Origins of Totalitarianism* (New York, Meridian Books, 1958), p. 312.

2. Reinhard Bendix, "Social Stratification and Political Power," in Reinhard Bendix and S. M. Lipset (eds.), *Class, Status, and Power* (Glencoe, Illinois, Free Press, 1953), pp. 606-607.

3. *New York Times,* June 17, 1970.

4. *Ibid.*

5. *New York Times,* November 27, 1970.

6. *Village Voice,* October 15, 1970.

7. *Boston Phoenix,* November 3, 1970.

8. *Boston Globe,* December 6, 1970.

9. John Kenneth Galbraith, *The New Industrial State* (New York, Signet Books, 1968), p. 414.

10. *Ibid.,* p. 414.

11. Lane Davis, "The Cost of Realism: Contemporary Restatements of Democracy," in Charles A. McCoy and John Playford (eds.), *Apolitical Politics: A Critique of Behavioralism* (New York, Crowell, 1967), pp. 185-198.

12. Meryl Ruoss, "A Closer Look at Mass-Based Organizations," in Hans B. C. Spiegel (ed.), Vol. 2, *Citizen Participation in Urban Development,* (Washington, D. C., NTL Institute for Applied Behavioral Science, 1969), p. 61.

13. James Q. Wilson, "Planning and Politics: Citizen Participation in Urban Renewal," in Wilson (ed.), *Urban Renewal: The Record and the Controversy* (Cambridge, Mass., MIT Press, 1967), p. 420.

14. Wilson, "Planning and Politics," p. 420.

15. See Gordon Fellman, "Sociological Field Work Is Essential in Evaluating Community Values," *Highway Research Record,* No. 305, pp. 123-131.

16. See, e.g., Robert Goodman, *After the Planners* (New York, Simon & Schuster, 1971).

17. Martha Derthick, *New Towns In-Town* (Washington, D.C., The Urban Institute, 1972).

INDEX

257

THE AUTHORS

Gordon A. Fellman is associate professor of sociology at Brandeis University. His research on the Inner Belt protest movement has given him material for numerous articles on neighborhood protest, housing, urban planning and social-class discrimination. This is his first book. Other interests include the role of the intellectual in politics, and relations between a university and its surrounding community.

Barbara Brandt, formerly a graduate student in sociology at Brandeis University, left the academic world to become a community organizer in Somerville, Massachusetts, largely as a result of her experiences while working on this book.